MEET THE RECRUITS OF PLATOON 1036

CALVIN S. HALL

Openly defiant, he's hoping to buy a ticket back to civilian life . . .

FRANCISCO J. GUERRA

He can't do the push-ups but refuses to give up . . .

TONY GARCIA

Weight-lifting tough guy, he's a veteran who found the army too soft . . .

AL CHARNESKI

Uncoordinated in Physical Training, but then he gets a rifle in his hands . . .

AND FIFTY-TWO MORE YOUNG MEN WITH THE SAME DREAM . . . TO BE A MARINE

—

BOOT

DANIEL DA CRUZ

St. Martin's Paperbacks

BOOT

Copyright © 1987 by Daniel da Cruz

All rights reserved. No part of this book may be used or reproduced in any manner whatsoever without written permission except in the case of brief quotations embodied in critical articles or reviews. For information address St. Martin's Press, 175 Fifth Avenue, New York, N.Y. 10010.

Library of Congress Catalog Card Number: 86-29636

ISBN: 0-312-90060-0

Printed in the United States of America

St. Martin's Paperbacks edition/December 1987

10   9   8

To Leila, Lina, and Danny—
shipmates in the assault on the beachheads of life

con amore, and
Semper Fidelis

Contents

Acknowledgments

Officers and enlisted men and women of the Marine Corps contributed their time, expertise, and goodwill in volunteering information for this book. Without it, *Boot* would have been fiction instead of a narrative firmly grounded in fact. Over a six-month period the following Marines aided my research practically on a daily basis.

S/Sgt.	Thomas Dawson	Captain	Reed R. Bonadonna
	Edwyn Gladden	Gy/Sgt.	Steven C. Lyon
Sgt.	Michael E. Montgomery	Sgt.	Mark D. Raymond
Major	James L. Vance		

A veritable regiment of other Marines, both active and retired, who contributed encouragement, facts, statistics, analyses, examples, insights, criticism, sea stories, hot coffee, and welcome guidance through the bureaucratic labyrinth include:

Major-General	Stephen G. Olmstead	Lt.Col.	Charles Balchunas
Col.	Robert J. Gladwill		E. A. Benes
	Gene McDaniels		Dennis E. Clancey
	Kenneth D. Jordan		John P. Farrell
	Donald J. Myers		Harry Jensen
	David C. Townsend		Humberto W. Rodriguez
	William Winoski		Victor Russillo
	James K. Van Riper		D. F. Sortino
Capt.	James G. Shanley, USN		R. D Sortino
	James M. Heaster, USN		E. R. Stepien

T. W. Stone
John M. Shotwell
Willam J. Vankat

Major Donald L. Bailey
Drew Blice
Don Kappel
Alfred A. Cortez
Robert E. Ferris
Fred Lash
Patricia Mauck
Anthony P. Rothfork
Stuart W. Wagner

Capt. Jeff Bearor
Robert L. Beveridge
Ronald J. Breedlove
Michael C. Castagnero
Ed Cawthon
David H. Curry
Tom L. Earwood
G. Mark Ferketish
Bill Graves
P. A. Greis
Jeffrey Holmes
Tom McGowan
Jonathan B. Martin
James H. Jeffries
James C. Olsen
Robert W. Rall
Michael E. Ratliff
Raymond J. Sturm
Robert S. Trout
Denise R. van Peursom
M. D. Weltsch
Eric M. Wolf

1st Lt. Charles L. Beckwith
Richard L. Conner
Gerald N. Gaskins
David S. Greenburg
Louis Herrera
Peter D. Larison
Richard F. Maguire
Gary R. Oles
Martin W. Schramm
Keith R. Wilkes

CWO J. E. Jerrolds
Charles D. Wright

W/O Henryk A. Walczyk
G. E. Girard
James D. Langford
Sgt/Maj. A. R. Aguilar
T. J. Collins
Edgar W. Johnson
Joseph J. Johnson
Douglas L. Wildenhaus
MGy/Sgt. Jeffrey J. Cooper
Charlie E. Duncan, Jr.
Billy G. Fowler
Patricia A. Hurlburt
C. W. Johnson
James E. Jones
Jacob Sattler
1st/Sgt. Lee P. Collins
Thomas J. Crisp
Gy/Sgt. Ron D. Allender
Gerald Bechard
Dwight E. Bowman
Michael J. Branski
Angel Castro
Robert A. Conway
Eli Ditchkoff
Paul L. Forney
G. F. Jones
H. W. Jones, Jr.
Christopher E. Lindbeck
Parris Moultrie, Jr.
Carlos R. Paul
Paul R. Richardson
Charles P. Rogers
Joseph L. Shockey
Robert L. Towry
Carson W. Wynn
S/Sgt. Duwayne D. Angrimson
Anthony Coleman
Randall J. Colson
J. A. Fountain
Kurt H. Frank
Rudy Hernandez
T. H. Howard
Paul R. Mason
Derrick J. Pass
Walter Sansbury
Robert L. Schafer

	Phillip W. Scott		Alan D. Morton
	Joseph Singleton		Matthew E. Oakes
	Michael D. Tyra		Michael R. Western
Sgt.	Michael A. Bentley	Cpl.	W. J. Chisholm, Jr.
	James W. Daniels		Jeff K. Malone
	Scott W. Ellerman		William H. Paro
	Jimmy M. Evans	Mr.	Larry Crivello
	Isaiah E. Harrison	Mrs.	Susan L. Gibbs
	Leland Hatfield	Mr.	Raymond Labas
	Brian K. Henderson	Dr.	Stephen Wise
	Russel Klika		

The young men of Platoon 1036, Class of 1985, Recruit Depot, Parris Island, South Carolina, were prototypes of recruits in every age and nation; at the beginning of training, soft and diffident, fearful and awkward; and at the end, proud, tough, and confident. The survivors—and also-rans whose experiences proved instructive—include:

Gregory S. Adams	John J. Grasso
Michael L. Anderson	Francisco J. Guerra
George W. Anderson III	Calvin S. Hall
Sean X. Atkins	Clinton H. Hardison*
Dennis R. Bail	John W. Hatfield
Jeffrey M. Barker	Reid M. Hollander
Thomas P. Barr, Jr.	Darrell E. Johnson
Albin B. Charneski	Vernon L. Karopchinsky
Halsey Congreve*	John M. Kater
Dale L. Copper, Jr.	Robert G. Keane III
David W. Cowley	Dion E. Kirkland
John D. Cox	Michael E. Knight
Brian D. Cyr	Ralph J. Laureano
Donald R. Daugette	William A. Lawrence
Jarvis D. Davis	Anthony D. Lawson
David H. Douglas	Scott Lundstrom**
Mark Ferrara	Christopher Marrocco
Mark J. Fischer	Charles L. Maxfield
Maurice J. Fleury	Benjamin J. McClellan
Antonio Garcia, Jr.	John P. McGrath
Jude T. Giblin	Danny J. McPheron
Thomas C. Gillen	Kenneth Michaelson*
Nathan E. Gordon	Christopher D. Musser
Marvin B. Graham	Velezar Petrović*
Dean W. Grant	Lester W. Page

John L. Prayso, Jr.
William Richards
Dane M. Robinson
Edward A. Santiago
Cyprian Scott
Aubrey Shields*
Clarence L. Sharp, Jr.
Harris Slaney*
Michael E. Spaulding
Murray K. Stone*

Donald W. Thomas, Jr.
Andrew R. Townshend
Joseph D. Weeks
Timothy C. Wiley
Timothy A. Williams
Tony Williams
Stanley Winters*
David J. Wright
Thomas E. Young

As a writer, I acknowledge a debt of gratitude for their various contributions to this book; as an American, I count myself lucky to have such men standing between me and our nation's foes.

*nom de guerre
**a composite enlistee

THE BOY

It's eleven o'clock. One hour to go.

Through the tinted window, the pine forest along the road slowly emerges from the darkness to throw its jagged silhouette against a rising moon. He sits up to light a cigarette, then slumps back, leg hooked over the arm of the seat, and lets the smoke trickle from his nostrils. Ahead, the lights of an approaching car dim and rush past, briefly cutting through the miasma of cigarette smoke that fills the bus. The desultory monologue from the seat behind him starts up again, falters when there is no response, and finally sputters into silence. He is left alone with the sibilance of the bus tires against the pavement—and his thoughts.

For a moment, in the darkness, panic grips him. What could have possessed him to gamble the next four years of his life—the *best* years—on an undertaking about which he knew nothing, except that it sounded romantic at the time? And it wasn't as if he hadn't been warned. Any number of people had told him they would be the toughest four years he'd ever know, and might even cost him his life. But the panic quickly passes. It's true he doesn't know what lies ahead, but at least he knows what he has left behind.

And it isn't very much, when he adds it all up: the necessity of looking for a job—a job that will at best be menial, considering his lack of experience or educational qualifications; the chance to get those qualifications by working days for years so he can attend college part-time at night; a girl who says she wants to marry him—when he finally does get that good job; a mother and father who have sweated blood on every one of their 160 acres to get him through high school, and now reasonably expect him to support himself; some good friends, most of whom have scattered since graduation. But mostly he leaves behind the prospect of a sterile, plodding nine-to-five existence, devoid of adventure, that blood-brother of youth. He leaves behind the small-town blinders that limit the view of far horizons. Above all, he leaves his boyhood—not a bad one, all things considered, but a phase of life it is time to put behind him.

The hour passes. Up ahead there are lights; a widening of the road; a kiosk; and men in immaculate greens, their caps pulled squarely down over the brow, wearing sidearms.

Parris Island.

A Few Good Men

It was in his second semester as a senior at McKinley Technical High School in Washington, D.C., that Scott Lundstrom made the astonishing discovery that, despite the absence of a military draft, it's harder to get into the United States Marine Corps than it is to get out.

Slouching into the school auditorium for the semi-annual pitch of armed services recruiters—the voluntary session was preferable to study hall, since he could catch up on his sleep—he listened, dozing, as the Air Force recruiter enlarged upon the electrifying opportunities in electronics, the Navy recruiter rhapsodized about sun and sand in voyages to distant lands, and the Army recruiter promised a golden future from schooling in a rich variety of marketable skills.

Then the Marine recruiter, resplendent in undress blues with three rows of ribbon across a bulging chest, woke him up.

The Marine Corps, he said, promised nothing—nothing, that is, beyond a tough, man-eating four-to-six years of personal discomfort, rigorous physical exertion, unremitting study to master basic military skills, strict observance of military customs and courtesies, and the privilege of risking life and limb to defend the country which had given them the unparalleled advantages Americans now enjoy: health, education, security, and freedom in the pursuit of happiness.

Some sales talk! How, Scott Lundstrom asked himself, could the Marines ever hope to compete with the blandishments of the other armed forces, stressing sacrifice while its sister services offered tangible, saleable skills? And yet, he knew some Marines, former students at McKinley. They walked with a spring in their step, with a confident, even cocky air. Not one carried an ounce of fat. They were able; they were proud; they were tough. They were men.

Scott Lundstrom had to admit he was none of these. A bright student, he slid through school with the bare minimum of effort, middling grades, and a nagging awareness of his shortcomings. A gray flabbiness betrayed his fondness for fast-food and sugar-loaded soft drinks. He moved with the crowd, did the easy things, indulged his appetites without restraint, shirked responsibility. The soul of a child inhabited his man's body. He suddenly realized that maybe it was time to grow up—to *join* up.

His resolve to become a U.S. Marine came suddenly, unexpectedly, and with the rush of exhilaration that accompanies sensible decision long deferred. It was the antidote for the boredom, the drift, the lack of accomplishment that had characterized his last few years and, he felt sure, would follow him as he plodded robotlike through college.

That night at the dinner table, he mentioned casually that a friend of his was contemplating enlisting in the Marines. His mother deplored, his father—a Korean War veteran—approved, and his young sister volunteered that Marines were the coolest. The ayes had it. Scott went to the Marine recruiting station the next day, prepared to sign up and ship out.

With dawn came the awakening. The Marine Corps, it turned out, had fixed ideas about the "few good men" it was seeking. Candidates for enlistment were judged by six basic criteria: age, prior military service, number of dependents and mental, moral and physical fitness. The Corps wanted intelligent, alert high school graduates. While age limits were seventeen to twenty-nine years, seventeen-year-olds had to obtain the consent of both parents. The history of hard drug use or conviction of a felony were absolutely disqualifying. Also disqualifying were defects of vision, asthma, epilepsy, abnormal height and weight, certain childhood diseases, bedwetting as an adult, and AIDS. Prior honorable military service was an advantage: a veteran could expect a rank and MOS (Military Occupational Specialty) close to that held previously, though it wouldn't exempt him from Marine boot training. Dependents were a handicap, since the Marine private can seldom support a family either with his presence or his pay check.

About 5 percent of the young hopefuls would be rejected on physical criteria. Others would fall by the wayside as a result of ASVAB (Armed Services Vocational Aptitude Battery) tests, which measure mental and mechanical aptitudes. Other services accept ASVAB scores as low as 21; the Marine Corps will not enlist even high school graduates unless they have a minimum mark of 31. Moreover, only 37 percent of Marine enlistees fall in the 31-to-49 point category; the other two-thirds, usually including the approximately 1 percent of recruits who are college graduates, have scores exceeding 50.

The new rigor in recruiting reflects a sharp shift in Marine Corps philosophy. Formerly, the prevailing attitude was: "You enlisted, and you're going to be a Marine even if it kills you." Today the thinking is: "We're choosing only good men, and training will make them better. We don't have time and resources to waste on slackers, incompetents, and foul balls."

Vindication of increasingly selective recruiting is implicit in the sense of fulfillment most recruits feel upon becoming Marines, as evidenced by the precipitous decline in Unauthorized Absence (UA)—formerly called AOL (Absent, Overleave) or AWOL (Absent Without Leave). As recently as 1977 UAs could average two per platoon (60 men) at any given time; today the figure is closer to two per *division* (18,000 men). Part of the credit for soaring morale and tight discipline is the Marine Corps' policy of mercilessly eliminating drug users and criminals from the ranks. As a result, today's Marine Corps is virtually free of drug abuse and crime. As an example, when the Marines returned in 1984 from their year's sojourn in Lebanon, where drugs are easily obtained, official sources reported that every man in the 1,700-man detachment tested negative on urinalysis for drug use.

Scott Lundstrom had no fear of being rejected for a history of delinquency. He had never used drugs nor been arrested, except twice for speeding, and he rather looked forward to the prohibition on smoking in boot camp to break his pack-and-a-half-a-day cigarette habit.

Another habit he would break was that of expecting things to happen at once. He had walked into the recruiting office in May, only to learn that the earliest date the Marine Corps might accept him was at least six months away—next January or February.

Like the 70 percent of future Marines who enlist within two weeks of their first contact with a recruiter, after undergoing initial screening at the recruiting station Lundstrom was sent to the Military Enlistment Processing Station (MEPS) in Baltimore.

Bearing his high school diploma, he arrived at five in the afternoon (1700 in military time) on 28 June, was lodged in a local motel and given chits for his meals. The following day was filled with a comprehensive physical examination, the

ASVAB intelligence test (on which he scored 53), a succession of interviews—where he would be offered the chance to correct any misstatements of fact, failing which he would be guilty of fraudulent enlistment and face instant discharge. Interminable stretches on hard chairs gave him an insight into the common denominator of all services: hurry up—and wait.

During the day, several of his new-found MEPS acquaintances dropped out. One had confessed to having used hard drugs, another to faking parental consent to his enlistment as a minor. A third, aged twenty-six, admitted having served two prison terms for car theft. Some failed the physical, usually for orthopedic problems. Lundstrom was luckier: he not only passed all the tests, but his 50-plus score on the AFQT (Armed Forces Qualification Test) qualified him for the Quality Enlistment Program (QEP).

That result guaranteed him an occupational field of his choice. For instance, should he choose Data/Communications Maintenance (Occupational Field 28), he could look forward to assignment after boot camp to training in one of seventeen disciplines, with course work running from 3 to 35 weeks. Had he scored 65 or over, he would have been guaranteed a specific occupational specialty—for example, that of Improved Hawk Fire Control Technician, whose 42 weeks of schooling ranks highest among the thirty-odd electronics-maintenance specialties. Aviation training is particularly coveted by recruits for the wide range of specialties offered by Marine Air, which has the eighth largest jet fleet in the world.

The QEP also guarantees the choice of either San Diego or Parris Island for boot training, promotion to Private First Class (Pfc) on entering active service (worth an extra $100 a month), and promotion to corporal within eighteen months. The catch: QEP inducements are balanced by a six-year-service commitment, so that the Marine Corps can expect a fair return on the frequently very expensive (sometimes tens of thousands of dollars) courses of study involved in military specialization.

Another incentive under the new G. I. Bill is that Marines,

upon completion of their hitch, may receive from $300 to
$1,300 a month for thirty-six months. To qualify, Marines
may opt to set aside up to $100 a month of their pay, with
benefits dependent on the total accrued at the end of enlistment, as well as length of service and MOS. Even for those
not attending service schools, educational opportunities are
generous. Near each Marine installation is a college or university, where 75 percent of the costs of off-duty education
are paid by the Marine Corps.

Scott Lundstrom does not seek technical specialization; formal schooling is precisely what he's trying to get away from.
His motive in joining the Corps is to become a member of a
fighting elite, in which maximum effort and sacrifice is the
norm, and challenge the only constant. The fighting elite is
epitomized by the infantry—the grunts—and in the Marine
Corps it *is* an elite: only nine infantry regiments comprising a
maximum of 40,000 men are authorized—one out of five of
the 200,000 Marines on active duty. The grunts are the
spearhead of the Marines, the "Force in Readiness," which,
since World War II, has been called upon some 230 times to
saddle up and ship out for offensive, defensive and rescue
missions.

The grueling three-hour battery of lab tests, medical histo-
ries, x-rays, color and visual acuity exams, audiograms and
thumps with rubber hammers will eliminate 5 percent of the
applicants. Others will fall by the wayside for mental or
moral deficiencies, some of which turn up on "national security clearance" investigations to which all enlistees are subject. Still others will fail to meet standards which may not be
immediately apparent to recruits filling out nineteen forms
with their more than eleven hundred blanks and boxes.

Suddenly, it's all over. Late that June afternoon, a recruiter
assures Scott Lundstrom that, once a boot camp billet becomes available, probably next February, he will be wel-
comed into the ranks of Marine recruits. Of course, he will
first have to take a blood test for AIDS (and wait five days for
the test results), and then update and review all paperwork.

Coming in at 0630 that last morning, he will be finished by 1100. At 1500 he will take a plane from nearby Baltimore-Washington International Airport for Atlanta en route to Charleston, South Carolina. There, a Marine NCO (Non-Commissioned Officer) will greet him with a kind smile he will not see again on a sergeant's face for quite some time. At 10:30 p.m.—2230, he must remind himself—he will board a Greyhound bus for Parris Island, seventy miles away down a long, dark road.

By the time he climbs into the bus, the U.S. Marine Corps will have invested $3,200 in Scott Lundstrom. It isn't a one-way transaction: Scott Lundstrom has just committed his next four years to the Marine Corps. Whatever happens, they are very likely to be the four most memorable years of his life.

RECEIVING

Getting Their
Feet Wet

Once the Greyhound bus passes the guard kiosk at the main gate, conversations slacken. Apprehension tightens throats. Up ahead, amid the cluster of distant lights, lies eighty-eight days of labor and hardship such as the twenty-six young men on the bus have never known. Up ahead also lies hope—that they'll endure the rigors of boot camp and earn the title United States Marines.

The recruits on this draft are male. Female recruits—women constitute less than 5 percent of Marine Corps strength—are also trained at Parris Island, but the sexes are kept so strictly segregated that they will see each other but rarely, wistfully, and from afar.

The bus whispers across a flatland of tidewater marsh, over the hump of a bridge, through a ghostly tunnel of live oak dripping Spanish moss, past palmetto palms stiffly lining the road like soldiers on parade. The Greyhound glides through empty streets and pulls up before the Receiving Barracks, a white two-story World War I "temporary." The brakes sigh, the door opens.

It is nineteen minutes past midnight, Friday, February 22.

A stocky Marine, hard-muscled and erect, his face shadowed by the broad brim of his olive-green campaign hat, climbs briskly into the bus.

"On behalf of Major-General Olmstead, Commanding General of the Recruit Depot," he booms, "I welcome you to Parris Island. Now, put out all cigarettes, get rid of your gum. When I tell you to get off the bus, hit that pavement running and get your sweet little tootsies on the yellow footprints. Understand?''

"Yes, sir," comes a ragged, tentative chorus.

"Understand?"

"Yes, sir!"

"I must be getting deaf. I didn't hear anything. . . . *Understand?*"

"Yes, Sir!"

"Then *move!*"

The recruits tumble out of the bus and take their places upon ranks of yellow footprints painted on the pavement. Most are dressed in jeans, jackets and sneakers. They have heard horror stories about boot camp. They stand rigidly at what they imagine is attention, waiting for the stories to come true.

The Marine plants himself in front of them, hands on hips.

"My name is Sergeant Bentley. Now, listen up, and listen good. Article 86 of the Uniform Code of Military Justice prohibits absence without leave. Article 91 prohibits disobedience to a lawful order. Article 93 prohibits disrespect to a senior officer. Burn those articles into your brains. You're going to live by them. Understood?"

"Yes, sir!"

Sergeant Bentley cups hand to ear. "I thought I heard a wind whispering in the willows."

"Yes, *sir!*"

Sergeant Bentley shakes his head in sorrow, lines up his twenty-six charges toe-to-heel, and, at double-time, lock-steps them up the steel stairs into a long room with row upon row of wooden classroom chairs bearing writing materials. The floor is a worn brown linoleum, exuding the sharp odor of disinfectant. On the wooden beams overhead are stenciled legends engraved on every Marine's heart with exclamation points: *Semper Fidelis, Esprit de Corps, First to Fight, Gung Ho.*

"Sit down," commands Sergeant Bentley. "You are Platoon 1036. With the magic marker pen on the arm rest, write 1036 on the back of your hand. . . . Hold it!'' he says sternly, as one of the recruits puts pen to paper. "I didn't say to write on the paper. I didn't say write in your memory book. I said to write 1036 on the back of your hand. *Do it!*

"Now, pick up the ballpoint pen. Write your last name, Social Security number and platoon number—that's the number on the back of your hand, you with the IQs of 200— on the white tag. . . . Put the top on the magic marker and pass it up. Take your time. We don't want you little darlings to tire yourselves. *Hurry up!*''

Their first hour on a Marine base is spent as will probably be their last, doing paperwork.

At 0120, the recruits are summoned, five at a time, to a long steel table upon which trembling hands empty pockets of the last reminders of civilian life. Brass knuckles or drugs are sometimes discovered—one romantic even showed up with a bowie knife strapped to his thigh, but tonight the contraband is innocent: cigarettes, lighters, matches, pornographic photos, combs, keys, condoms. Sgt. Bentley flicks them to the floor. The recruits hand over for safekeeping their wedding rings, wristwatches, necklaces, wallets, and money, listed by denomination and serial number; these will be returned when they leave Parris Island.

Sgt. Bentley next reviews an inventory list of the PX gear they will be issued shortly. It consists of fifty-four separate items, some seldom associated with leathernecks, such as Q-tips (for cleaning the M16), shoe trees, fluoride mouthwash, shower shoes and deodorant, as well as socks, razor and blades, writing materials, towels and five different brushes. These will supplement the "782 gear"—canteen, war belt, poncho, field jacket, gloves, and other clothing and equipment costing the government some $900. For budgetary reasons, the jacket and all other 782 gear are recycled from the Fleet Marine Force, and are usually dilapidated and in tatters.

Inventory and issue complete, Sgt. Bentley falls out his men in the chill, moist, early morning darkness. It is 0400.

"Stand straight," he admonishes the men. "Head up, chin in, shoulders back, eyes to the front. Your knees are relaxed, not locked—stand with locked knees and you'll pass out like those Brits during the Queen's parade. Heels together, feet at a forty-five degree angle, arms at sides, elbows in, thumbs along your trouser seams, fingers curled and touching the trouser legs. That's attention. *Don't look at me!*"

He glares at the recruits as they strive to assume the correct posture. He drills them for ten minutes, correcting the angle of a head, positioning thumbs against seams, pulling shoulders back, tucking chins in.

Again he commands: "Attention!"

They bob and wobble, wriggle and writhe. Bentley sighs. He tells them to face the right and move out. At each intersection, though no cars are in sight on the darkened roads, he halts the platoon and sends out four "road guards," recruits equipped with reflective fluorescent vests, to face toward and stop any approaching traffic.

In the mess hall, Sgt. Bentley forms his men into four toe-to-heel lines. They pick up steel food trays, and hold them tight against their chests, like shields. On command, they pass in front of a steam table manned by recruits in their second phase of training, and fill their trays with the first installment of the three thousand two hundred calories they will eat, on average, daily during their twelve weeks at Parris Island. During meals they are allowed the privilege of talking among themselves. They have, by strictly enforced regulation, twenty minutes for each of the 264 meals they will consume in boot camp.

For these first four hours, the recruits have been indistinguishable from civilians. They will continue to act like civilians, in the wry opinion of their drill instructors, until graduation day, but their looks are about to change.

Back at the Receiving Barracks at 0445, the recruits form lines before three folding chairs. Three barbers armed with electric clippers appear. Half a dozen quick fore-and-aft swipes and the recruits are shorn to the skull. Each haircut takes twenty to twenty-five seconds. Having already shaved during a break in the paperwork, they are now herded to their first class in hygiene. In a room with sixty unpartitioned stalls, they shower as they will do virtually everything else these next twelve weeks: by the numbers.

"Throw your towel over the overhead bar," orders Drill Instructor/Sergeant Bentley. "Pull the ring and wet your head. Soap your head and face thoroughly. . . . Rinse. Soap your left arm, then your right arm. . . . Rinse. Soap and rinse your crotch. Don't be bashful—who'd want to look at you, anyway . . . ? Now your legs—soap and rinse. Rinse once all over. Put on your clogs and dry yourself off. Put deodorant under your arms." He says this with distaste, but orders are orders, and this one emanates from the Commanding General, Recruit Depot.

With their towels wrapped around their waists, the recruits move to an adjoining room where upon a table thirty yards long are ranged two rows of large wire baskets, separated by an elevated runaway from which a short-fused supply sergeant monitors the uniform issue. Recruits are measured, cami (camouflage) "covers" pulled down over bare skulls, and baskets filled with four sets of cami utility uniforms, six sets of skivvies and other clothing in one of three sizes—small, medium, and large. Then, as each item is called out, the recruit stuffs his issue into his seabag beneath the table. After receiving two pairs of mid-calf-length black leather boots, he dresses for the first time in a Marine uniform. The PX gear, prepackaged in another section of Supply, is added to his burden, beneath which he staggers back to the Receiving Barracks.

There each recruit deposits his seabag in a row and puts his civilian shoes in a brown paper bag, followed by his shirt, trousers and jacket, tightly rolled. The bag is sealed with masking tape, and will be held until the recruit's graduation from boot camp or, if he fails, for Entry-Level Separation (ELS), the modern Corps' euphemism for discharge. Underwear and socks, which would become intolerably ripe after three months in storage, are thrown in a garbage can.

In their home for the next three days, on the second deck of the Receiving Barracks, recruits are issued linen and blankets and shown how to make a rack the Marine Corps way, with the blankets tucked tight enough to make a quarter bounce. After traveling since the morning before, followed by a non-stop, six-hour barrage of bellowed and bewildering orders since their arrival, they are more than ready to climb right in, but this is not to be.

At 0600, Sgt. Mark Raymond, relieving Sgt. Bentley, marches Platoon 1036, now up to its full complement of sixty with the addition of earlier arrivals, to the Recruit Administration Center (RAC). There each recruit will be afforded the opportunity to sign up for Servicemen's Group Life Insurance, a term policy of $35,000, at the government-subsidized rate of $2.80 per month. These policies will continue in force at the active-service premium levels even when the policyholder retires or is discharged from the Marine Corps.

Recruits have been forewarned of the Moment of Truth. That moment now arrives. Recruits are required to swear to the accuracy of previous statements about their age, education, dependents, prior military service, medical and police records, the use of drugs, and false statements made previously. This is their last chance to set the record straight. If they fail to do so, and fraudulent statements are later discovered, they will be speedily separated from the service. The same fate awaits those who admit to conviction for a felony, or the use of drugs, or homosexuality. All the recruits in Platoon 1036 attest that the statements they have made are the truth, and nothing but the truth. The Marine Corps, however, is from Missouri: routine investigations will be made with the recruits' local police, and later in the day a definitive test for drug use will be administered.

So far, the recruits have been subjected to what is, by Marine Corps standards, gentle handling. It is true they have experienced certain inconveniences. Some find the daily bath excessive. They have been deprived of tobacco and alcoholic beverages and soft drinks; during their entire training this denial will be absolute. Cheating will be difficult: the boot is

never alone, going nowhere unless accompanied by a shipmate—even the toilet stalls lack doors. Also, it is a military
offense to give a recruit such forbidden fruit, and the cropped
head and diffident manner make it impossible not to distinguish a recruit from higher forms of life.

On the other hand, recruits are shocked to discover that
their drill instructors (D.I.s), though obviously subsisting on
a diet of rusty nails and stove lids, are never—at least hardly
ever—profane. Their speech abounds in "gol-darns," "dog-
gones," "freaking" and other circumlocutions. Gone are the
non-stop blistering four-letter word-strings of yesteryear. In
today's Marine Corps, drill instructors and officers, however
much they swear among themselves—and it is not a lost
art—are strictly prohibited from using profane, obscene, eth-
nically or racially degrading language to, or in the presence
of, a recruit. The recruit, incidentally, may be addressed only
by his last name, the billet he occupies, or as "recruit" or
"private."

Indeed, as early as the second day, the drill instructor asks
the assembled platoon:

"Since you've come aboard, has anybody verbally abused
you—called you an s.o.b., or a slimebag, or a maggot or
faggot, or addressed you in any other degrading terms? If you
were singled out, and a remark made about your race, color,
religion or national origin—that's abuse. Well?"

Silence.

"Has anybody abused you physically—hit, pushed,
shoved, slapped, kicked, beat, tripped, kneed, elbowed or
punched you?"

Silence.

"Very well. If you feel you were abused, physically or
verbally, you are to inform your Senior Drill Instructor at
once."

Allegations of abuse are handled with dispatch. The accused drill instructor is relieved of duty immediately, while
statements are obtained from principals and witnesses. D.I.s
found guilty of abuse are subject to fine, demotion, or transfer to other duty.

During this initial period of minimal stress, Platoon 1036 is administered a series of interviews, evaluations and tests. Personal interviews with non-commissioned officers verify, once again, the information sworn to at the Moment of Truth. Then each takes a battery of three exams, lasting four hours, to confirm the recruit's mechanical and mathematical aptitude and verbal facility previously tested at MEPS. The results of these exams will to a large degree determine the recruit's eligibility to pursue, after graduation, a particular MOS—Military Occupational Specialty. Other factors include the recruit's academic qualifications, physical fitness, military bearing, the terms of his pre-enlistment contract, and the instructor's judgment of his progress in fifty-seven training days at boot camp.

Additional confirmation of the accuracy of the recruit's statement at the Moment of Truth comes with a urinalysis, during which strict precautions are taken to ensure that there be no substitution of specimens. Each recruit's sample is identified by his Social Security number, which doubles as his Marine Corps Service number. If the recruit denied the use of drugs—and analysis shows that he actually used drugs within the previous two months, he will be prosecuted for fraud and separated from service after suffering a court martial's punishment.

For the second and last time the recruits inventory their personal possessions and turn them in for safekeeping until they depart Parris Island—as Marines if they survive the training, as civilians should they fail. From now on, practically the only reminders of their civilian life will be family pictures and, perhaps, a wedding band, though recruits are advised to stow rings as well, since they are easily lost in the mud during Individual Combat Training. Even the glasses that exactly one-third of Platoon 1036 now wear will be gone, replaced by government-issue glasses they will be fitted for next day.

On the evening of the second day, in the second-deck squad bay of their wooden "temporary" barracks (built during World War I), the recruits are seated on the deck between close-ranked rows of double-deck iron bunks. Men who have yet to earn their own way, they are surrounded by the reminders of others who have already earned theirs: battered foot lockers, faded canvas canteen covers, worn war belts. In these austere surroundings, D.I. Bentley gives the recruits the first of many lectures they will receive on physical and mental stress, study, achievement, pride, concentration, discipline—the mix of qualities that make Marines.

"If you've got *this* far," he concludes, "it means you have the intellectual and physical ability to go the distance. Never give up, and you'll make it."

He surveys the silent group, automatically gauging from hard-won experience who will not make it. In the two days he has had to work Platoon 1036, he can already spot candidates for failure: the belligerent, the foot-draggers, the Alibi-Ikes, those resentful of order and discipline.

"Anybody want to quit?" he asks.

One hand goes up. It belongs to a pale, thin boy with eyes which don't quite focus.

The D.I. takes the boy aside. It's obvious the kid is dead scared. Of what? The squad bay, and the other recruits, the discipline, the bellowing D.I.s, of course—*everything*. At night he has visions of cages full of writhing worms and other scary things.

Sgt. Bentley assures the boy that he is not alone. Everybody in 1036 is scared of something. They'd be fools if they weren't. "But you've got to *start* before you can quit, lad. Now, get back to your quarters, because tomorrow we start."

Despite his abrupt dismissal, the boy will be carefully watched until he shapes up or is singled out for ELS (Entry-Level Separation). Suicide attempts occasionally occur, some in earnest, some as attempts to attract sympathetic attention.

Of the former, there was the case where Standard Operating Procedure (SOP) was violated by sending a recruit unaccompanied to the next building on a brief errand. When he didn't return after a few minutes, a search was made and he was found hanging by his belt. Cardiopulmonary resuscitation was administered, and the boy was saved—but not for the Marine Corps. Like all recruits attempting suicide, he was immediately discharged, as are those found to have used drugs after signing up but before being called to active duty. Borderline drug cases include those who briefly experimented with marijuana, but any confirmed use of cocaine, heroin, amphetamines, LSD, or other drugs is grounds for unconditional release.

The recruits' remaining administrative obligation in Receiving is a medical examination, usually performed on the third day. In the depot sick bay, the recruit is first examined for allergies; if found to have none, he receives an injection of penicillin to rid him of any minor infections he may have brought aboard. Then he gets additional vaccinations for typhoid, paratyphoid, tetanus, diphtheria, yellow fever, and influenza.

The obese, the rare recruit who has had open-heart surgery, and those with sickle-cell anemia, usually blacks and natives of eastern Mediterranean countries, will be closely observed during HOT SOP, the period 15 April to 15 October, and during physical training, as they are less than normally resistant to heat and heavy exertion.

The medical history taken at the Recruiting Station is confirmed, and any defects or conditions detected are treated by a Navy physician. These include foot disabilities, such as excessive pronation (turning-in of the ankles), which are treated by staff podiatrists who prescribe and supply orthotic corrections. The recruits receive a blood test, an audiogram that tests amplitude perception and frequency response between 500 and 8,000 hertz, and an eye examination. If a recruit has faulty vision, even though corrected by glasses before enlistment, he is issued black-rimmed, shatterproof glasses ground to prescription and fitted on the premises. Contact lenses cannot be worn, for fear they will pop out during vigorous exercise.

The medical examination is the last of the processing formalities for members of Platoon 1036. Being the first of the four platoons (1036 through 1039) that will form Company B of the First Training Battalion, Recruit Training Regiment, their introduction to the Marine Corps is a leisurely five days instead of the three which Platoon 1039 will receive. Nevertheless, they won't be idle. Sergeants Bentley, Raymond, and Coleman will fill their time with "field days"—cleaning the barracks and Receiving area, marking clothing, studying their "knowledge"—basic recruit information, and practicing close-order drill. Before they leave Processing, they will have learned to respond to the commands Fall In, Forward March, Platoon Halt, and facing movements. They will learn to stand at attention, as still as statues, enduring the bite of Parris Island's myriad sand fleas and swarming gnats with immobile stoicism—or else.

Dear Mom:

Well, here's your favorite son Scott at Parris Island. So many things have happened in the past three days my head's swimming—haircut, shower-by-the-numbers, clothing issue, medical inspection, intelligence tests, close-order drill, filling out a zillion idiot forms. And getting chewed out by the drill instructors is a full time job all by itself. High school didn't prepare me for Sgt. Bentley and Sgt. Raymond. They're genuine tough eggs. And they are also, well, let's call it *impatient*. I've bet McGrath, he's my bunkmate, 50 cents worth of chits—we get chits instead of cash—that Bentley punches that crybaby Winters out before we leave Receiving. It's money in the bank.

They say we'll get an hour to write home every night before Taps, but this is the first chance I've had to sit down, let alone write. Sgt. Raymond says I should write home every week. I'll try, Mom.

Here at P.I., everything I do is wrong, and the D.I.s notice even the smallest mistake. If you don't hold your thumbs a certain way at attention, they shout at you and make you feel stupid. Well, I guess I *am* stupid. I joined the Marines, didn't I? Ha! Ha!

But then, so did fifty-nine other guys in this platoon. There are some foul balls, but most seem pretty nice. I've made friends with McGrath and Copper. One's black—here called a dark-green Marine—the other white, a light-green Marine. We've got one recruit lets everybody know he knows everything—we call him "The Perfessor"— but he doesn't know how to keep in step. The D.I.s love to quarterdeck him. Having the Perfessor in the platoon makes everybody feel good.

Taps in three minutes. Tomorrow we transfer from Receiving to B Company Barracks, First Recruit Battalion, and go on "schedule." That's the minute-by-minute routine we'll follow for the next eleven weeks.

P.S. Sgt. Bentley hasn't punched out Winters yet, so I guess I lose my fifty cents. But I can afford it. My $620.40 pay doesn't look like much, but with board and room and medical care taken care of, I can keep most of it. Not a fortune, but it beats pumping gas at that Texaco station on Vine Street. . . .

Platoon 1036 is above average, their drill instructors agree. Their estimate is based on recruit test scores, attitudes, military bearing, speed of response and learning basic drill.

The sixty men who pass to the next stage of recruit training, Forming, will within a week number fifty-eight, one being transferred to another platoon, another—the fearful one—being sent back to civilian life.

They are a slice of contemporary America. The oldest is 26, the youngest 17; their ages average 19.5 years. Their GT (standard intelligence test) scores average a respectable 109. All are U.S.-born except for three: a naturalized Korean, and a Cuban and a Romanian possessing the green cards of permanent U.S. residents. Languages spoken include Spanish, Romanian, Serbo-Croat, German, and Italian. In Platoon 1036 there are 47 whites, 12 blacks, and 1 Asian. Protestants number 34, Catholics 18, Baptists 2, Pentecostalists 2, nondenominationals 2, and Mormons and Jews are represented by 1 recruit each. Thirty-four recruits have enlisted as regular Marines for four years, and 10 for six years. Twelve are reservists, who will complete boot camp and schooling for an MOS, then return to civilian life committed to regular military training. Three have previous regular U.S. Army service, one a tour in the Army reserves. Six are married. Only 1, with 11 years schooling, does not have a high school diploma; 19 have attended college, and 1 is a university graduate.

By civilian standards, they have already come far. By Marine standards, they are 60 blobs of unformed clay.

The Legendary Leathernecks

From the beginning, the U.S. Marine Corps has been invested with an aura of improvisation and impermanence. In May, 1775, in Tun Tavern, a smoky sailor's hangout in Philadelphia, the Marine Corps' first recruits were lured into service with promises of bounty, pensions and glory—later, and plenty of free grog—now. Their first weapons were pikes, spears, flintlocks and Indian tomahawks. Although the motley one thousand-odd Marines distinguished themselves in the Revolutionary War, foreshadowing their future role by staging the first amphibious landing (on the island of New Providence in the Bahamas) in U.S. history, they were disbanded in 1784 along with the Navy, in what was to become the recurring practice of dismantling American defenses following victorious wars. Two centuries later, President Harry Truman and General Douglas MacArthur tried to repeat the folly, fortunately with less success.

The time soon came when Marines were again needed. The threat of war with France caused the Marine Corps to be reactivated, this time permanently. Though that conflict became merely a war of words, the Marines were ready when, in 1801, the Pasha of Tripoli (in today's Libya) declared war after failing to obtain an increased tribute from U.S. shipping in the eastern Mediterranean where his corsairs marauded. With reckless bravado, Marine Lieutenant Presley O'Bannion made a grueling desert march with a handful of men and mercenaries, and captured Derna. The pasha's capitulation in sight, soldier's victory turned to diplomat's defeat when President Jefferson's peace emissary was outmaneuvered by the Pasha. Lt. O'Bannion managed to save Hamid, the American candidate for the throne, who in gratitude presented O'Bannion his scimitar-like Mameluke sword. It became the model for that worn today by Marine officers, the oldest weapon in continuous use in the U.S. armed services.

In the War of 1812, the Marines played an heroic role in the battle which Oliver Hazard Perry immortalized with the words, "We have met the enemy, and they are ours . . . ," but at the cost of the Marine commander and half his men. Later, outgunned in the defense of the nation's capital, 500 sailors and Marines were overrun by 3,000 seasoned British troops, but they were avenged when their mates, fighting at New Orleans under Andrew Jackson, killed 700 British at a cost of 8 dead.

Despite its valor in battle, the Marine Corps was still a haphazard organization when, in 1820, thirty-seven-year-old

Lt.Col. Archibald Henderson became their fourth commandant. By that year the Corps had shrunk to 49 officers and 865 enlisted men. Uniforms featured a high, leather-reinforced collar, which won the wearers the name "Leathernecks." A private was paid from $6 to $10 a month, and a lieutenant $25. Lt.Col. Henderson immediately imposed a harsh training regimen that gradually transformed Marines into hardened, professional fighting men. Morale soared when, during a prison riot in Boston, Marines were called to restore order. Their commander, Major Wainright, ordered them to fire a volley into the air, after which he addressed the rebellious prisoners: "These men are Marines." He turned to face his men. "Exactly three minutes from now I will raise my hand. You will commence firing, and continue until you kill every prisoner who has not returned to his cell." Before three minutes had passed, the courtyard had emptied.

In the years preceding the Civil War, Marines were called upon to do the nation's nasty little chores no other service wanted. They waged a punitive expedition in Sumatra after the robbery of an American merchantman in Quallah Battoo. In Argentina, they stormed ashore to rescue Americans imprisoned for trading with the Falkland Islanders. They fought the Seminole Indians in Florida's Everglades and a mob of hired thugs, the "Plug Uglies," on the streets of Baltimore. They campaigned in Mexico in 1847, landing at Vera Cruz, and assaulting the Citadel of Chapultepec (the "Halls of Montezuma"), gallantly defended by teen-agers at the military academy located there. In 1852, Commodore Matthew Perry appeared with 200 Marines off the coast of Japan with their fleet of black ships, intimidating the Japanese into opening their ports to foreign commerce. During China's Taiping Rebellion in 1856, in which twenty million people were to die in history's greatest insurrection, U.S. ships were fired upon by forts guarding the Pearl River near Canton; Marines retaliated by assaulting, capturing, and destroying the forts. In 1859, seventy-six-year-old then-General Henderson, who had commanded the Corps through all these actions under eleven presidents, died, more than fifty years a Marine.

Henderson was a traditional Marine, straight, anvil-hard, and opinionated. In 1943, in the Washington, D.C., home of Marine commandants since 1805, incumbent General Holcomb signed an order establishing the Woman's Reserve. He remarked with a smile that "Old Archibald would turn over in his grave if he ever found out that females could become commissioned officers in his beloved Marine Corps." At that instant Henderson's portrait, hanging over the sideboard, crashed to the floor.

General Henderson died on the eve of the Civil War, which divided the nation and the Marine Corps alike. Roughly half of the Marines left their posts to form the Confederate States Marine Corps, while those who remained in the north played a distinctly subsidiary role in subsequent operations. They participated in the Battle of Bull Run, and aboard ship blockading southern ports, while their erstwhile mates manned Confederate blockade runners and commerce raiders. Disenchantment mounted as the war ground on, until during the last year the Union's roll of Marine deserters, nearly one thousand strong, vastly exceeded its Marine battle dead, which totalled only seventy-seven. On both sides, heroism was commonplace, glory rare.

The Spanish-American War was the nation's first to be heavily influenced by the news media, just as the Vietnam War was the latest. It was here that the legend of the indomitable dare-devil Marine took root, fueled by the passionate prose of writers like Richard Harding Davis and Stephen Crane. During one engagement Crane witnessed, a Marine detachment ashore discovered itself under fire by both friend and foe. Seizing a semaphore flag, Sergeant John H. Quick stood on the parapet, as Spanish bullets whizzed by and U.S. naval shells exploded around him, and coolly signalled for the ships to cease fire. For his bravery, Quick was awarded the Medal of Honor, to which he added the Distinguished Service Cross twenty years later for heroism in World War II.

On the other side of the world, in the Philippines, Marines had little trouble with the Spanish, but considerably more with the Filipinos, who had no desire to see their Spanish colonial masters replaced by Americans. They fought fiercely and well, and here Marines first became acquainted with the jungle warfare in which they later became expert. Unprepared, they experienced great hardship in the hot, steamy, malarial jungle. In one harrowing episode, fifty Marines were told off to pioneer a route across the rugged volcanic razorback mountains and steaming rain forests of Samar. Sick and debilitated by tropical disease, short of rations, deserted by their porters, their shoes shredded by the rocks, and fighting through one ambush after another, forty Marines finally arrived at their destination, having covered one hundred ninety miles in twenty-nine days. Out of respect for their awesome feat, it became the custom for the first Marine to perceive a survivor's entry into the room to command: "Rise, gentlemen. He served on Samar."

Until the middle of World War I, training of enlisted men had been a matter of apprenticeship and assimilation. Not until 1915 did training become formalized at boot camp, at Parris Island. In the course of the war, seventy-five thousand Marines would be trained there, and for a while it looked as though they might miss the war, for they didn't arrive in combat until March 1918, only eight months before the Armistice.

They quickly made up for lost time. Assigned to an "inactive" sector, they found themselves overrun by fleeing French soldiers and civilians hurrying to get out of the way of the German spring offensive. A French general explained to Marine Captain Lloyd W. Williams that a general withdrawal was in progress, and ordered him to take his Marines and retreat. "Retreat, hell!" Williams exploded. "We just got here."

The Marines deployed in a line of skirmishers, and started cutting down the advancing Germans with accurate fire. For twenty days, the reinforced Marines battled the Germans in tree-denuded Belleau Wood. It was during this action that an impatient Gunnery Sergeant, Dan Daly, who had already won two Medals of Honor, leaped out of his trench exhorting his men: "Come on, you sons-of-bitches—do you want to live forever?"

Many, in fact, wouldn't live out the month. At the Battle of Soissons, 50 percent of the Second Battalion, Sixth Marines, commanded by Major Thomas Holcomb, became casualties in the first thirty minutes. In another action, German-speaking Sergeant-Major Ulrich of the same battalion took off alone after forty retreating Germans. Some minutes later he appeared, .45-pistol at the ready, his forty prisoners with hands aloft. "They were willing to listen to reason," he explained laconically.

Marines fought three other pivotal engagements in the few months the war still lasted, winning ground, battles, and the nickname *Teufelhunden*—after the legendary wild "devil dog"—from a foe respectful of Marine fighting qualities after Belleau Wood.

The nineteenth-century European passion for colonialism finally infected the United States in the twentieth century, when it began a brief but far-reaching flirtation with intervention in the affairs of other states, notably in Latin America. The U.S. Marines were the favored instrument of this policy. They battled "bandits"—who protested, with some justice, that they were actually freedom fighters—in Cuba, Panama, Nicaragua, Santo Domingo, Haiti, Mexico, and other turbulent areas. There they defended "U.S. interests," which often turned out to be identical to those of the United Fruit Company. In doing so, they bore the brunt of an anti-*yanqui* suspicion and hatred that persists in most of Latin America to this day.

While the postwar Marine Corps shrank to a mere 15,000 men, its horizons expanded. It was an era when the individual mattered, and the Marine Corps was fortunate to have some remarkable individuals in its ranks. Unique was a junior officer named Earl H. "Pete" Ellis. In the early 1920s, he farsightedly realized that Japan's ambitions, fueled by the League of Nations' mandate of Germany's Pacific islands to Japan after World War I, would one day bring Japan and the

United States, the other Pacific power, into collision. Ellis
argued that the U.S. would have to fight Japan to gain control
of those islands when the crunch came. He even planned a
campaign that was followed practically to the letter in America's later conquest of the islands. He died under mysterious
circumstances while reconnoitering Japan's bastion of Truk.

In Nicaragua, Captain Merrit "Red Mike" Edson pioneered techniques of jungle fighting and invented the "fire
team," a closely coordinated handful of men reinforcing the
firepower of the Browning Automatic Rifle. Close air support
of ground troops, dive-bombing and air-evacuation of the
wounded were other techniques perfected by Marines in these
otherwise barren exercises in neocolonialism.

At home, Marine strategists evolved by slow and painful
experimentation the amphibious doctrines which would, in
World War II and after, be used by all U.S. and Allied
forces. Shallow-draft boats developed by Andrew J. Higgins
spawned generations of landing craft still in use today. Donald Roebling's *Alligator*, the prototype of modern amphibious
assault craft, was hatched in 1937, appropriately enough in
Florida. The Marines wholeheartedly supported both inven-
tors, when other "experts" dismissed their work as irrele-
vant.

Thus, when the Japanese attacked Pearl Harbor in December 1941, the Marines were not wholly unprepared. They
possessed the methods of warfare and models of machines
which would win the war in the Pacific, once America's industrial might and its pool of young manpower teamed up to
fight the Japanese.

The beginnings were tentative and bloody. In late 1942, on
Guadalcanal, the Marines learned firsthand the determination,
endurance, and ferocity of the enemy. Finally winning that
battle, the Marines drove northwestward up the chain of islands in a series of campaigns which would, in three years,
bring them to the threshold of Japan. Bougainville, Cape
Gloucester, Tarawa, Peleliu, Guam, Saipan, Iwo Jima and
Okinawa became fiercely contested and sanguinary stepping-
stones to American victory.

The closer to the Japanese homeland the Marines came, the more determinedly and courageously the Japanese fought. Iwo Jima, the penultimate conquest, was one of the most bloody battlegrounds in history, with more than five thousand American and sixty thousand Japanese killed in seventeen days of fighting over eight square miles of volcanic ash. Okinawa lasted even longer, and claimed more lives. Had not the atom bomb abruptly ended the war, the Americans were anticipating at least a million more casualties, many of them Marines.

In an economy drive during the next four years under President Truman, the Marines were emasculated along with the other services, and FMF (Fleet Marine Force) Pacific consisted of only eleven-thousand-odd fighting men, too scattered to respond effectively when ten North Korean divisions suddenly smashed southward across the 38th parallel in June 1950. A scratch force of six thousand five hundred, the First Provisional Marine Brigade, was hastily assembled and shipped to Korea, arriving just in time to stop the communists from overrunning the Pusan redoubt, the only real estate still unconquered.

In less than two months the Marines stabilized their front, and launched an offensive of their own, driving the North Koreans before them in a rout. A North Korean counterattack ended in another Marine victory. But a strong enemy and a stalemate still faced the Americans. To break it, Marines under General MacArthur made an historic landing at Inchon far up the peninsula, forcing the outflanked Koreans to a precipitate retreat. The Americans were driving swiftly toward the northern border when an overwhelming force of Chinese, whose presence American intelligence didn't even suspect, fell upon them. The Marines were forced into an agonizing thirteen-day retreat in sub-zero weather, from the Chosin Reservoir to the coast and protection of the American fleet, in a successful and orderly withdrawal.

But withdrawals don't win wars. No one, in fact, won the Korean War. An armed truce was finally hammered out, and the combatants have glared at each other across the original demarcation line for more than thirty years, not quite at peace, not quite at war.

The Marines were to fight an even longer, more demoralizing and catastrophic war in Vietnam. It was a war of political expediency, mistaken strategic assumptions, elusive aims, media management, cowardice, and hypocrisy involving the Eisenhower, Kennedy, Johnson, and Nixon administrations. After urgently counseling the French to get out of Indochina, which they reluctantly did after Dienbienphu, the United States picked up the fallen sword, as *quid pro quo* for French support of NATO. At the time, General de Gaulle warned President Kennedy with great prescience: "You Americans . . . want to rekindle a war that we ended. I predict to you that you will, step by step, be sucked into a bottomless military and political quagmire."

They were. With no clear military objective ever enunciated beyond compiling enemy "body counts," the President of the United States and his civilian aides calling B-52 strikes from the White House basement, the military ordered to take enemy territory at appalling human cost one day, only to be ordered to abandon it without a fight the next, the United States subsidizing a series of unpopular and inept South Vietnamese governments, and a rising disenchantment with the war among Americans who were systematically deceived by its leaders and publicity-hungry celebrities parroting communist propaganda, the war could only end in tragedy, as it did in 1975 after ten thousand days of fighting.

Marines were a significant proportion of the fifty-seven thousand American dead in Vietnam—valiant men who had never been told why they were fighting nor, in the opinion of most who survived, had been allowed to win by their indecisive civilian leadership. It is a war regarded with bitterness by the men who fought there—betrayed, they believe, by their government, and scorned by fellow citizens for whose security they thought they were fighting.

During the next decade, Marines were dispatched on two missions, one that couldn't fail, the other that couldn't succeed. In 1982 they were sent to save the Caribbean island of Grenada from Cuban domination, the swatting of a fly with a sledgehammer. The same year they were also sent to Lebanon. Marines whose whole history has been one of slashing attack—and success—against clearly defined objectives were ordered to wait like sacrificial lambs in exposed positions until the enemy, happily realizing they could do so with impunity, slaughtered several hundred of them.

The lesson, if there is one, is that although the U.S. Marines are one of the premier fighting forces in the history of warfare, even they can't fight City Hall.

FORMING

Total Immersion

The parade ground between Processing barracks and the First Recruit Training Battalion area at Parris Island is a mere two hundred yards across, yet it divides two worlds, the civilian and the military.

During the past five days the men of Platoon 1036 have shed, one by one, the last vestiges of civilian life—long hair, the cigarette and gum-chewing habits, faded jeans, casual behavior, leisurely showers, idle chatter, unpunctuality, indifferent manners. Stripped of individuality, they are human clay ready to be sculptured into Marines.

The process begins in Forming.

At 0430 on 27 February, the sixty men are rousted from their racks, and at 0500 proceed through the pre-dawn darkness to the mess hall. Half an hour later, their bulging seabags transported ahead by truck, they are mustered and marched across the great expanse of asphalt to Bravo Company barracks, First Battalion. From this day on, they will march to a different rhythm—*presto* and *staccato* instead of *lento* and *legato*, to the *fortissimo* of drill instructors determined to forge disciplined, hard-muscled fighting men from soft civilian flesh.

Seated in a tight sixty-pack on the third-deck squad bay, the young men of Platoon 1036 witness the Series Commander, First Lieutenant Greenburg, administer the Drill Instructor's Oath to the drill instructors. These three experienced Marines, assisted by specialists, will be with the recruits twenty-four hours a day for the next eleven weeks.

Their objectives are well-defined: to develop self-discipline, self-reliance, and a willing obedience to orders; proficiency in basic military skills, including marksmanship; physical fitness and endurance; high standards of hygiene and military bearing; and *esprit de corps*, the shared values and striving for excellence which animates all Marines.

These objectives, and the means by which they will be achieved, are encapsulated in the Drill Instructor's Covenant which the Senior Drill Instructor, standing stiffly at attention, now recites to his platoon:

"My name is Staff Sergeant Dawson. I am your Senior Drill Instructor. Along with Staff Sergeant Gladden and Sergeant Montgomery, our mission is to train each one of you to become a Marine. A Marine is characterized as one who possesses the highest in military virtues. He obeys orders, respects his seniors, constantly strives to be the best in everything he does. Discipline and spirit are the hallmark of a Marine, and these qualities are the goals of your training here. *Every recruit here,* whether you are fat or skinny, tall or short, fast or slow, can become a Marine if you can develop self-discipline and spirit. We will give every effort to train you, even after some of you have given up on yourselves.

"*Starting now,* you will treat me and all other Marines with the highest respect, and you will obey all orders without question. We have earned our place as Marines and we will accept nothing less than that from you. I will treat you just as I do my fellow Marines, with *firmness, fairness, dignity and compassion.* As such, I am not going to threaten you with physical harm, abuse you, or harass you, nor will I tolerate such behavior from anyone else, Marine or recruit. If anyone should abuse or mistreat you, I will expect you to report such incidents to me. Further, if you believe that I have mistreated you, I expect you to report it to the series commander, First Lieutenant Greenburg. My drill instructors and I will be with you every day, everywhere you go.

"I have told you what I and my drill instructors will do. For your part, we will expect you to give 100 percent of yourself at all times. Now, this is specifically what we expect you to do:

"You must do everything you are told to do, quickly and willingly.

"You will treat all Marines and recruits with courtesy and respect.

"You must be completely honest in everything you do. A Marine never lies, cheats, or compromises.

"You must respect the rights and property of all other persons. A Marine never steals.

"You must be proud of yourself and the uniform you wear.

"You must try your best to learn the things you will be taught. Everything we teach you is important and must be remembered.

"You must work hard to strengthen your body.

"Above all else, you must never quit or give up. We cannot train you and help you unless you want to become a Marine—unless you are willing to give your very best. We offer you the challenge of recruit training—the opportunity to earn the right to be a United States Marine."

This somewhat utopian conception of what it means to be a Marine recruit is delivered with utmost solemnity, and it is clear that to S/Sgt. Dawson, the D.I. Covenant is Holy Writ.

The process of converting recruits to believers begins immediately. In Processing, the recruits have adapted to radical changes in dress, posture, manners and daily routine. Now their very language undergoes a transformation.

Sgt. Montgomery stands before the platoon, and with jabbing finger to punctuate his words, gives them their first lesson in Marine terminology.

"I'm standing on a *deck*, not a floor. To the right and left are *bulkheads*, not walls. In the bulkheads are *ports*, not windows. Above us is an *overhead*, not a ceiling. We are in the *squad bay*, not upstairs, but *topside*. Downstairs doesn't exist: it's *down below*.

"Directly ahead of you is the *quarterdeck*. Off the quarterdeck to the right is the *head*, and don't let me hear you calling it the toilet or latrine. To the left is the *D.I. House*, not the office. You are facing *forward*. Behind you is *aft*. Facing forward, the left is *port*, the right *starboard*.

"Your bed is a *rack*. Hurry up is *on the double*. Your clothes are *stowed* in your *seabag*. Now, then, I want you to empty your seabags on your racks, on the double!"

> . . . I feel like a catcher's mitt, they keep throwing stuff at you. Our S.D.I., S/Sgt. Dawson, made a nice speech about how nobody was going to abuse us, but ever since then he and S/Sgt. Gladden and Sgt. Montgomery have been pushing us right up against the wall. They don't let up for a second. I think they're doing it to make the wimps drop out, so they don't have to waste time on guys who won't make it, anyway. . . .

The recruit's first clothing issue comes out of the seabag just as it went in, in a jumble. Ranged in lines in front of their double-decked racks, the recruits once again perform what will soon become a familiar, dreary ritual, the inventory.

"Get three utility caps," commands S/Sgt. Gladden. "Hold one in each hand, one between your teeth."

He scans the two long lines, determines that all have three utility caps, then passes on to the next item. To the recruit, who has already suffered through half a dozen inventories, it's all a tedious waste of time. But, as invariably happens, squad bay sorcery has spirited somebody's gear into another's seabag, and fast switches must be made to achieve the proper count.

At 0705, Platoon 1036 is sent to the showers. Four minutes later the sixty men, still dripping, are lined up again at attention before their racks. The Series Commander walks down the ranks, inspecting each man for burns, cuts, abrasions, skin eruptions, scars and scratches. These are noted on the recruit's record, as well as evidence of acne, moles, ring-worm or other skin defects. These precautions alert the S.C. (Series Commander) to the need for medical treatment, and protect drill instructors from allegations of mistreatment.

During the inspection, Private Atkins, who has been stand-ing rigidly at attention, passes out, striking the back of his head on a foot locker. Within five minutes, two Navy hospi-tal corpsmen have appeared, inspecting and dressing the su-perficial wound. They take Atkins' pulse and blood pressure, and wait for him to recover fully before radioing the depot sick bay with their report. The D.I.s again counsel the re-cruits against standing with locked knees.

The rest of the day passes in a blur of marking laundry, close-order drill, demonstrations by the D.I.s on the proper methods of making a rack, shaving, brushing teeth, stowing gear in a regulation manner in the foot locker, asking for permission to speak. Nearly every movement is done by the numbers and performed by every man in the platoon in uni-son. Even head calls are performed in a military manner. After each meal, the recruits are lined up before their racks, each with toothbrush and paste in their left hand, elbow tucked in, forearm parallel with the deck.

"For a head call!" booms the D.I.

"For a head call—aye, aye, sir!" respond the recruits, adding, "Recruit's canteen filled?" [They quickly check the canteens at the foot of their racks and step back into place.] "Aye, aye, sir!"

"Ready, step."

The starboard rank steps one pace forward, shouting "Step!" "Freeze!" (snap to attention), "Cock!" (turn left), "Drive!" (come again to attention), "'C', Lock!" (put the right foot behind the left for a hundred-and-eighty-degree turn) "—and ease about!" (execute the about face and come again to attention).

"Forward, march!" commands the D.I.

The recruits on the port side execute the same evolution in mirror image, and fall in behind the starboard side. Presumably, each recruit's internal functions are expected to perform in the same military manner and, to the recruit's astonishment, in a very short time they generally do.

> . . . I'm becoming bi-lingual, English and Marine, and learning to do everything "by the numbers." Bathroom is "head," and would you believe it, we go to the head by the numbers! But maybe that's the only way to get 60 men through their five S's—shine, shave, s----, shower and shampoo—in 15 minutes. . . .

Lights are extinguished promptly at 2100—9:00 P.M.—after brief devotions conducted by lay leaders instructed by their respective chaplains. In Processing, a number of recruits complained of disturbed slumber and bizarre dreams. Here complaints vanish: the high level of activity produces exhaustion by lights out. The only sounds heard thereafter in the darkened squad bay are the regular breathing of sleeping men and the soft footfalls of the fire watch, two recruits alternating duty with mates at two-hour intervals, alert to carry out their eighth General Order: "To give the alarm in case of fire or disorder."

For the remainder of boot camp, reveille for recruits will sound between 0330 and 0500, except on Sunday, when they are allowed the luxury of remaining in their racks until 0600. The first hour of morning routine is invariable: a quick head call, making up the rack, dressing, policing up the squad bay, and chow down. Recruits dress on their feet, including the awkward balancing act of lacing up their boots; after all, bivouacs do not come equipped with footstools.

By 0600, Platoon 1036 begins a day of unremitting activity. In Forming, the schedule is determined by the drill instructors' assessment of what the recruits most need to know. It is axiomatic, of course, that recruits know nothing at all, and that only the combined and constant efforts of their three D.I.s will dent their ignorance.

Close-order drill exemplifies the D.I.s' method. It is a straightforward progression from the simple to the complex, the slow to the swift, the approximate to the precise. The recruits have already been taught Attention; Forward, March; Halt; and a few other simple evolutions during Processing. These commands are repeated, with greater attention to detail reinforced by endless repetition. Gradually more difficult commands are introduced, such as column movements. With each day's drill, the ranks appear less ragged, the response more clipped and confident. With improvement in technique comes an unconscious effort by each recruit not to be the one to destroy the platoon's symmetry, rhythm and snap. The group spirit that close-order drill engenders is, in fact, its principal benefit. Drill evolved centuries ago when slow-firing musketry demanded absolute discipline of movement for maximum effect against attacking troops. Today drill, whose original purpose vanished with the advent of rapid-fire weapons, is still the most effective method of instilling unit solidarity. So long as regular armed forces exist, close-order drill will probably remain an important element in their training.

Drill is taught with the help of elementary psychology. The S.D.I. gives the commands. When they are not carried out impeccably, Sgt. Dawson's righteous anger is always tinged with sadness, as though he has been betrayed by those in whom reposed his entire trust. "I'm easy to please," he points out. "All I want is perfection." The platoon, as a result, suffers feelings of guilt which they try to purge by better performance next time 'round.

Sgt. Montgomery, the "Second Hat" or "Heavy A," then follows up the dereliction by summoning the worst transgressor from the ranks and giving him the rough edge of his tongue, then schooling him individually and repeatedly in the movement. When necessary, he demonstrates it in slow motion until even the dimmest witted cannot but understand what he must do.

Invariably, despite their best efforts, and regardless of the number of repetitions or the simplicity of the drill, an infraction large or small—a bent leg that should be absolutely straight, slumping shoulders, wandering eyes—is committed, and the "Third Hat" takes charge. His role is frankly punitive. He showers the hapless recruit with imaginative invective that, by its ferocity, never fails to inspire dread. Nose-to-nose with the recruit, the "Third Hat" threatens dire punishment, and promptly proceeds to carry it out, usually by means of "Incentive Physical Training" (IPT) in the Pits. Where the S.D.I.'s weapon is to inspire guilt, the "Heavy A" relies on bone-numbing repetition, the "Third Hat" on raw fear and pain.

By such various means to do the D.I.s whip the platoon into shape. No psychological weapon is neglected. Group shame, individual guilt, pride of accomplishment, ridicule, fear of failure and suffering, hope of improvement—all are applied to produce quick and automatic compliance to orders.

To some civilians, the method smacks of sadism. Marines know better. Unless high standards of performance are observed scrupulously by every man in a unit, without exception, unless orders are obeyed without question, doubts about whether the man on either side is pulling his weight distract the individual from his own job. The resulting hesitation inhibits decisive, determined action, loses time, destroys confidence, cooperation and cohesion, imperils the unit's mission, and causes casualties. Distasteful as is the sacrifice of "individuality," the history of war both ancient and modern proves repeatedly, nevertheless, that the individual has the best chance of achieving his objective and surviving as a member of a disciplined fighting formation. It is this type of unit that the Marine Corps strives to build, starting in boot camp.

Morning sick call is the refuge of those recruits who have ailments which will prevent them from giving their best in the full day ahead. Blisters and sore throats are the recruit's most common complaints. Regulations prohibit the D.I. to do so much as apply a band-aid to an abrasion or prescribe aspirin for a headache. These are among the functions of the nearby

battalion aid station. Every recruit and Marine has the in-
alienable right to make sick call, despite a D.I.'s suspicion,
often correct, of malingering. Most complaints are, in fact,
trivial. During the first six months of the past year, of the
16,500 recruits seeking treatment at the aid station, only
1,500 had maladies sufficiently severe to be referred to the
Depot Sick Bay. Of these, 1,000 were hospitalized at the
Naval Hospital in neighboring Port Royal.

Appearing at sick call this last day of February is the recruit who has pleaded to be allowed to go home. He is sent,
along with the blisters and sore throats, to the aid station
where, after a brief interview, he is referred to the NPU
(Neuro-Psychological Unit). He returns to the squad bay in
tears, but the D.I.s are unable to comfort him: getting out of
the Marine Corps, at this stage, is harder than getting in.

Three other recruits are also on the razor's edge. Yesterday
they confided to the S.D.I. that they wanted out. He diag-
nosed their ailment as Forming Week jitters and dismissed
them. Nonetheless, for the next few days, he keeps a careful
watch on them. He is rewarded to find that his diagnosis is on
target: their fear evaporates and he hears no more about the
matter.

Without their realizing it, the recruits' pace has quickened.
On their first day in Forming, it took from 0430 to 0500 to
make their racks and dress. By the third day, that thirty minutes has shrunk to ten, and will sink still further. Part of their
increased speed comes from habit, teamwork with their bunkmates, and shortcuts like preparing their clothing the night
before in the order they will don it. They are also spurred on
by the D.I.s, who allow an interval they judge slightly less
than needed for each operation, then begin a rapid countdown
from ten. After the count of "zero," the recruits shout
"Freeze, recruits—*freeze!*" and become statues. If the D.I.s
feel that the job wasn't done right or fast enough—usually
it's both, they order the recruits to undress or tear up their
bunks and begin all over again.

During Processing, Platoon 1036 gained only a general

idea of what was expected of them: instant obedience to orders, movements performed like "green amphibious blurs," strict attention to hygiene, and respect for senior officers. In Forming, they come into collision with the details.

The mass of detail is as intimidating as a D.I. seven feet tall. What every recruit must learn is embodied not only in their D.I.s' verbal instructions, but in "knowledge." This consists of a set of books and pamphlets issued each recruit: The 426-page *U.S. Marine—Essential Subjects*; the 495-page *Guidebook for Marines*; the 56-page *M16A1 Operations Manual*—the "Green Monster"—an inch-thick study guide; and a notebook and workbook to record wisdom passed down in several dozen formal lectures.

Recruits spend every minute not otherwise scheduled studying their knowledge. Foot lockers are aligned at the edge of the squad bay's central passageway—exclusive D.I. territory except during lectures—with their books neatly stacked and filled canteens alongside them. Sitting on one end of their foot lockers, the recruits peruse their books, only their lips moving silently as they commit to memory the myriad facts, charts, tables, and orders they must know by heart. At irregular intervals each day, the recruits, standing at attention in facing ranks in the squad bay, will heed the D.I.'s command to spout knowledge such as General Orders.

"Sir," they bellow in concert, "the recruit's First General Order is 'To take charge of this post and all government property in view,' sir! Sir, the recruit's Second General Order is 'To walk my post in a military manner, keeping always on the alert, and observing everything that takes place within sight or hearing,' sir! Sir, the recruit's Third General Order is . . ."

> . . . Fifty years from now I'll remember my General Orders letter perfect, that's how they've drummed them into us. I can recite them in my sleep. They're just one of the dozens of things we have to learn by heart, like the characteristics of the

M16 and the chain of command. The twelfth
General Order, the one they don't teach us, is the
one that makes most sense: "Don't get
caught. . . ."

Similarly, they learn and recite the names of the ten persons in their Chain of Command, beginning with "Sir, the
first person in the recruit's Chain of Command is *Senior Drill
Instructor Staff Sergeant Dawson,* sir!" and ending with
". . . the President of the United States, the Honorable
Ronald Reagan, sir! Sir, this is the recruit's Chain of Command." Inevitably, some recruits try to camouflage their ignorance in the thundering chorus, silently moving their lips as
their minds grope for the words. D.I.s are not deceived. Such
stratagems are rewarded with instant IPT (Incentive Physical
Training) on the quarterdeck.

IPT is one of the few methods by which D.I.s can enforce
discipline, since the Marine Corps outlawed even the mildest
forms of bodily contact under congressional pressure following hearings in 1975. The most common exercises are bends
and thrusts, leg lifts, side lunges, mountain climbing, running
in place, side straddle hops and push-ups, done at as fast a
pace as the D.I. can exact from the recruit. Bends and thrusts
require the recruit to drop to the deck, body extended in the
push-up position, then spring back to attention, repeated
without pause. Mountain climbing mimics the motions of
running on a fast-moving treadmill, but with the hands on the
deck. When running in place, the recruit must raise his knees
to waist level—and fast. Doing push-ups, the recruit must
keep his back perfectly straight, extend his arms to the limit,
and pray for the D.I.'s clemency.

It is never forthcoming, although Marine Corps regulations
prohibit more than five minutes of IPT, broken midway by a
thirty-second rest, every hour. The "incentive" is at its maximum during the first two weeks of boot camp, when recruits
coming from civilian life are usually in poor physical condition. But as the days go by and muscles harden, IPT becomes

less of a punishment and more of a diversion. By the end of the Third Phase, the platoon's "Tail-End Charley" will be able to do five minutes of IPT without even breathing hard.

The reason for this enhanced endurance becomes apparent at 0900 on 2 March, when Series S.D.I. Gunnery Sergeant Lyon lectures Platoons 1036 through 1039 on the conditioning program which they will pursue—and which will pursue *them*, during the next eleven weeks.

> . . . They call it "Incentive Physical Training," but we call it Intensive Physical Torture. Push-ups, mountain climbing and bends and thrusts are tearing up every muscle in my body. It's not human, but neither are D.I.s. They're like machine tools in an automobile factory, only P.I. is the factory, and here they're turning out Marines. They don't care where you came from, or about your color or education, only whether you've got what it takes. Remember that Marine recruiting spot on TV where they're forging that officer's sword? Well, now I know what it feels like to be between the hammer and anvil. . . .

On nearly every training day they will perform six limbering exercises, followed by the "daily dozen"* to build strength and stamina, each of up to 15 repetitions, up to three sets. This daily one-hour routine concludes with runs building up from one and a half to five miles. The daily exercise prepares the recruits for the Circuit Course, involving running, weight lifting, pull-ups, sit-ups, and so on, done at full speed. In addition, an Obstacle Course and a Confidence Course challenge recruits to test their developing muscles and agility by climbing ropes and high obstacles; traversing water barriers

---

*Side-straddle hops, bends and thrusts, rowing exercise, side benders, leg lifts, toe touches, mountain climbing, trunk twisters, push-ups, bend and reach, body twists, squat benders.

on ladders hand-over-hand; sliding down a long rope from a height of ten meters, over water, twice changing position; and similar tortures devised to fashion the fearless spirit and to demonstrate that Marines can, after all, do anything to which they put mind and muscle.

All Marines are trained first as infantry. These recruits will get a taste of the grunt's life, Gy/Sgt. Lyon tells them, in conditioning marches of up to ten miles during which, depending on the phase of training, they will wear a steel helmet and carry a rifle, two full canteens, and a forty-pound pack with all the gear needed for eight days in the field.

By 1000, the 240 benumbed recruits in 1036 Series are beginning to feel there is no justice. Being recruits, they are wrong: there is a full hour of it coming up—a lecture by SC Lt. Greenburg on the provisions of the Universal Code of Military Justice (UCMJ). He discusses the rights of recruits, which closely parallel those provided by the civilian judicial system, to know the charges brought against them, to have counsel, to remain silent, to call witnesses, to appeal court-martial decisions and so on. They are also instructed on the various stages of military justice, beginning with Office Hours by the commanding officer, and ranging up to a General Court Martial. It is human nature to assume that only the other fellow will get into trouble with the law, so it is not surprising that, during classes on UCMJ, recruits' eyes tend to glaze over and that, as a result, their lowest academic scores will be made on tests in this subject.

By Monday, 4 March, the last day of Forming, the recruits of Platoon 1036 have lost their initial terror—the great majority will sheepishly admit, after graduation, that they feared savage beatings at the hands of their D.I.s—and look forward to Training Day One, which will begin on the morrow. They have learned the BDR—Basic Daily Routine, the rudiments of close-order drill, uniform maintenance, how to shave, bathe and brush their teeth the Marine Corps way, how to spit-shine boots, polish brass, stow their foot lockers, respond to fire drill, go through chow line, recognize if not always use the esoteric Marine nomenclature and, of course, climb mountains. Their teeth have been x-rayed, drilled, and plugged. Their denuded heads have been crammed with information, their muscles stretched with IPT, their endurance tried with the repeated making of ripped-up racks.

Altogether, they are feeling quietly pleased with themselves, until the S.D.I. brings them down to earth, after a spectacularly clumsy evolution, with the brutal taunt: "Get that trash out of your minds about being honor platoon—you're the worst bunch of foul-ups it's ever been my misfortune to have inflicted on me. Take a good look at the men on your right and left, because I can guarantee that in eleven weeks one of them won't be here."

To which, in every recruit's burning heart, comes the echo: "We'll show him!"

"We"—not "I." Already they're beginning to think as a unit.

P. I.

Parris Island is a place about which Marines who have trained there know virtually nothing, yet remember virtually everything. Its history, traditions, command structure, facilities, and flora and fauna are aspects of the Marine base recruits never discover, concentrating as they must on important matters like close-order drill, rifle maintenance, Incentive Physical Training, and avoiding the D.I.'s bark while enduring the sand flea's bite.

Recruits arrive at Parris Island, spend eleven weeks in ceaseless training, and depart, blissfully unaware that they trod in the footsteps of conquistadores, that they dwelt among the ruins of outposts of empire of three different colonial powers—France, Spain, and England.

Suffering, as every recruit will attest, is what Parris Island is all about. Indeed, human hardship began with the very first attempt at settlement more than four centuries ago, when the Huguenot Jean Ribaut left twenty-eight men to construct and hold a bastion on what is now Parris Island, which he called Charlesfort to honor King Charles IX, while he returned to France for reinforcements and supplies. Within six months the settlers—hungry, homesick, and disheartened—bravely launched a vessel of their own construction for a winter crossing of the tempestuous Atlantic. Before they were rescued off the coast of England, they endured agonies of exposure and hunger, and only the sacrifice of one saved the others from starvation.

Within four years the Spanish, beguiled by visions of a North American empire to match their Mexican conquest, pre-empted a French return by building Fort San Felipe on the island. A decade later the Indians drove them out and burned the fort, but the persistent Spanish returned the next year to rebuild the stronghold, calling it Fort San Marcos. Only when Sir Francis Drake burned St. Augustine in 1586, threatening their northern flank, did the Spanish abandon their grandiose imperial designs. Parris Island, named after Colonel Alexander Parris, who was granted the area by royal writ, thus fell by default into the British colonial orbit, along with the future state of South Carolina of which it is a part.

The U.S. Marines made their first appearance on Parris Island when Union Captain Samuel F. Dupont, commanding the Atlantic Blockading Squadron, seized neighboring Port Royal during the Civil War and used it as a naval base for the remainder of the conflict. In 1891, the construction of a dry dock at Parris Island attracted a large number of laborers, "many of them very vicious characters from cities in the vicinity," as one chronicler put it, with the result that a Marine guard was posted to protect the government's interest. The Marines, who lived in leaky tents during the inclement winter of 1891–92, contracted so many illnesses that a medical officer recommended more permanent housing. The naval station commandant acted at once, transferring the Marines to drier and more spacious quarters—in the coal shed.

Not until New Year's Day 1909, with the establishment of a Marine Officers School and the graduation of a first class of twenty-seven second lieutenants the following December, did Parris Island begin to fulfill its destiny as the forcing house of the U.S. Marine Corps. In November 1915, the Recruit Depot began operations at Parris Island, and in the intervening seventy years its mission has been unchanged: to transform young civilians into the world's premier fighting men.

The island's history since the eve of America's entry into World War I has been one of volcanic expansion followed, once war ended, by equally violent contraction, accompanied by the lulling siren song of peace everlasting.

In Spring 1917, the 835 men training at Parris Island suddenly ballooned to 13,300 men under arms as the war heated up, then deflated to a mere 4,000 by Armistice Day. Of the 58,000 wartime recruits, Parris Island trained 46,000—the remainder being molded into Marines at Mare Island, in the state of Washington.

The training program for Marines of that era was not markedly different from that of today, illustrative of the unchanging demands of war. Close-order drill, physical exercise, bayonet fighting, swimming, personal combat, and rope climbing, followed by three weeks on the Rifle Range, were the core of the eight-week curriculum. Academic subjects were not emphasized due to the generally low level of formal schooling of the average recruit.

After the Armistice, Parris Island, which had got along with a meager 58 acres of dry land, fell heir to its present

8,000-plus acres (of which 4,400 are suitable for training, the rest being estuarine marshland) by presidential proclamation. This period also saw a construction boom during which more than 230 structures accommodating 5,000 men were built (another 2,000 were quartered in a tent camp). Some of those buildings are still in use today.

Between the two great wars, recruit strength and training periods fluctuated according to the national economic situation. As the Depression deepened, training time shrank from twelve weeks to twenty-four days, while during the mid-1930s only 300 recruits were undergoing training each month at a near-deserted Recruit Depot. But the rainclouds of approaching war in Europe brought an end to the drought for America's armed services, as the nation again girded itself for war. An increase of 5,000 Marines was authorized for 1938, and it was necessary to pitch tents on the parade deck to accommodate the rush of eager recruits.

On 8 December 1941, the day after Pearl Harbor, the spate became a flood. During the next twenty-two days, 10,224 men enlisted in the Marines, and in January, double that number. The Corps' authorized strength shot up to 104,000, quintuple peacetime numbers. Parris Island, which had been training 1,600 men per month, was suddenly called upon to train 6,800. The training cycle dropped to six weeks, then to five, but by early 1944 was back up to eight weeks, followed by another eight weeks of basic field training.

The end of the war predictably brought a speedy retrenchment in recruitment and training, as was later to occur in the aftermath of the Korean and Vietnam wars.

Meanwhile, training had become systematized, and though still very much an art based on personal leadership by the drill instructor, became infused with scientific and pedagogical elements proven to mold better Marines. As a first step in that direction, a Drill Instructors School was opened in 1956, with a two-week curriculum consisting mainly of briefings by veteran D.I.s. By the post-Korean War period, specialists began to relieve the D.I.s of instruction in strictly academic subjects, giving them more time to inculcate their troops with the intangibles of pride, teamwork, discipline, hygiene, *esprit de corps*, loyalty, self-confidence, initiative, adaptability, and fighting spirit.

Gradually the D.I. School evolved in rigor and scope and quality. Today it lasts nearly ten weeks, accepting only outstanding Marines as D.I. candidates. Its graduates are marked for rapid career advancement; its alumni enjoying the reputation of being smart and tough, ruthless against slackness and swagger, yet compassionate and patient with recruits who strive seriously to become Marines.

Peacetime P.I. is an island of tranquillity and order, or purposeful frenzy, depending on the time of day. During daylight hours, the parade deck resounds to bellowed orders, the clash of arms, and the crash of booted feet. At dusk, however, a sudden hush falls over the depot like a leaden shroud, streets empty, and arc lights glare out across the unpeopled darkness and thoroughfares bearing names that conjure up the thunder of artillery and the stink of burning cordite: Wake, Guadalcanal, Iwo Jima, Panama, Pelileu, Midway, and Nicaragua—where Marines have fought eleven times in this century, and may fight again.

Parris Island lies low to the sea, at no point being more than twenty feet above high tide. It has been ravaged by hurricanes blowing up out of the Atlantic, and in 1973 was covered by six inches of snow. Each year, some fifty inches of rain fall, producing a suffocating summer humidity to baste the base in temperatures that often soar past one hundred degrees. Surrounded by Port Royal Harbor and the Beaufort and Broad rivers, marshland and deep water are never far away, inhospitable to man but teeming with fire ants as well as all four of North America's poisonous snakes—the water moccasin, coral, copperhead and rattler—and sharks and alligators. Though the latter seldom stalk the parade deck as in years past, they still provide a powerful disincentive to recruits who contemplate heading homeward without benefit of leave. Less lethal are the rabbits, squirrels, raccoons, deer, otter and pelicans which abound in the outer reaches of the base among stands of red cedar and slash, white and loblolly pine, but which are sometimes themselves in jeopardy from a vicious hook or slice from a dub's club on the Depot's eighteen-hole golf course.

Despite its geographical remoteness from American population centers, Parris Island is perhaps the most visible and accessible U.S. military training facility. Almost any individual or group is given the run of the place—allowed to visit, inspect and photograph any feature of recruit training save the private precincts of the platoon squad bay. Visitors, who come at the rate of one thousand a week, include parents and relatives as well as groups of educators, aldermen, high school students, career counselors, veterans, businessmen, police chiefs, foreign dignitaries and military observers. Among the latter may be found note-taking, picture-snapping army and navy officers from the communist bloc. Well, that's democracy.

WEEK ONE

Guerra:
A Private War

As a Marine recruit he's aptly named, for in Spanish *guerra* means "war." But wars he may one day be called upon to fight are a distant concern; his present battle is simply to stay in the Marine Corps. The enemy that may keep him from this goal—"my last chance to make something of myself," he says—is one that afflicts many young Americans: fat.

Weighing in at 206 pounds, 5'11" Francisco Guerra was not able to do a single pull-up in the Initial Strength Test (IST) that took place on Training Day One. Senior Drill Instructor Dawson thus had the option of transferring Guerra, along with three others who failed the IST, consisting of pull-ups, sit-ups, and a one-and-a-half-mile run in under 13:30, to the Physical Conditioning Platoon. Nevertheless he kept all four: each had demonstrated the clenched-jaw determination that is, in boot camp as in the world outside, the indispensable key to success.

Guerra has had little success so far in life. A twenty-one-year-old immigrant from Cuba, in the United States only four years, he has spent the last three in the frustrating dead end job of assistant store manager, earning too little to finish his degree at Miami-Dade Community College, where he accumulated three semesters of credit. To him, the Marine Corps offers a career as aviation mechanic, one which combines a valuable skill with service to his adopted country. First, though, he'll have to shed more than twenty-five pounds in order to pass the increasingly rigorous physical fitness challenges that comprise an essential part of a boot's life. Immediately put on half rations, ordered to eat only vegetables, salad, meat and fish, Guerra faces Training Week One with resolution. No matter what happens, he won't quit.

Guerra and his fifty-eight fellow recruits have ahead of them fifty-six more ten-hour training days divided into three phases. Phase I is basic Marine orientation; Phase II: Rifle Range, Mess and Maintenance and Individual Combat Training; Phase III: preparation for final inspection and graduation.

The "ten-hour day," recruits soon learn, is illusory. Actually, in addition to their scheduled program, they are kept busy with drill, field days—squad bay housekeeping, rifle maintenance, personal leather and brass polishing, IPT, study of their "knowledge," personal hygiene and inspections from reveille at 0500 until taps at 2100—sixteen hours of ceaseless activity broken only by three twenty-minute intervals of relaxation at meals.

Consuming the greatest portion of their time will be 110 hours of "administrative" chores—dental and medical examinations, clothing and weapons issue, religious services, inspections and tests. Physical conditioning will convert flab into sinew during 92 hours of vigorous exercise over the next 11 weeks; 17 hours more are alloted to recovery from their exertions. Meals lasting a total of 84 hours will provide energy for their PT, as well as for 77 hours of classroom study. Marksmanship training takes 71.5 hours, combat techniques in the field another 63, and drills and ceremonies surprisingly a mere 41 hours, although much of the 23 hours earmarked for "commander's time" may be devoted to close-order drill. During the one "free" hour before Taps, recruits find time to shoot the breeze and write home, but the forethoughtful make sure their rifles and gear are ready for a crowded morrow.

The most urgent duty of recruits is to get into shape, and ten full afternoon hours during the first week of training are devoted to this mission. Dressed in red shorts, yellow T-shirts emblazoned with a bold USMC, and running shoes, Guerra and his mates of 1036 Series (comprising platoons 1036 through 1039) will fall out for two and a half hours of PT four times this week.

Forming up by platoons on the black-topped parade ground outside their red-brick barracks, the two hundred forty men are mustered, face right and, at double-time, charge off toward the grass exercise field a quarter of a mile away. Behind the yellow guidon bearing their platoon number, each platoon chants as it goes. The drill instructors, running with the platoon—and twenty-seven-year-old Lieutenant Greenburg bringing up the rear, although he can outrun anybody in the series, recruit or D.I.—bellow the lines of an apparently bottomless seabag of chanteys, and the recruits roar them back, line by line. On 5 March, their first day on the field, they chorus,

> Mothers of America, meek and mild,
> Say good-bye to your sweet child.
>   We're gonna make him drill,
>   We're gonna make him run.
> We're gonna make some changes in your sweet son.

By the time they reach the PT field, they're panting, but they're panting in doggerel:

> Lift your head and hold it high,
> Platoon ten thirty-six is running by.
> Lift your head and hold it proud,
> They're running hard and yelling loud,
>
> Look to the right and what do I see?
> A bunch of civilians looking at me.
> So lift your head and hold it high;
> The pride of the Corps is running by.

And run they do, at one hundred twenty thirty-inch paces a minute, all in step, two hundred forty young men in four compact ranks heading for what will be for some the hardest work they've ever done.

On the field, now in extended order, Series S.D.I. Gy/Sgt. Lyon greets them with a cheery "Good afternoon, recruits!"

"Good afternoon, sir!" they shout, but not, of course, loud enough for the Gunny, who cups hand to ear.

This time they thunder it back and, placated, he nods. They will begin, he says, with 6 limbering exercises. He demonstrates each in turn. Then, with the D.I.s leading their platoons, he starts with 10 side-straddle hops, counting as he goes. Recruits who do 11, or malinger in the hope they will blend with the landscape, are sentenced to 10 push-ups while those who can count take a thirty-second breather. Then come ten repetitions of shoulder rotations, chicken wings (straight arms extended to their backward limit), toe touches, bends and thrusts (squatting with arms thrust to the rear between the legs) and other muscle-loosening drills.

Now warmed up, the recruits' real exercise begins. The men line up under 16 chinning bars, and each man does his maximum pull-ups, then falls back into line to repeat the effort.

The platoons next move to form a human cross, four files deep, with Gunny Lyon on a padded table at eye-level in the center, visible to all. Again he demonstrates the exercise, again the recruits follow, counting the repetitions at the tops of their lungs. No one is punished if he gives his all and fails, but quitters soon develop bulging shoulder muscles from push-ups seemingly without end. In this first session, Gunny Lyon is merciful: only 10 leg lifts, 10 rowing exercises, 10 mountain climbers, 10 push-ups and 40 bent-knee sit-ups. Within a week, they will be doing exactly double that number. By the end of their training, they will run off three sets of the entire daily dozen, a total of 435 separate exercises.

The field resounds with the din of shouted counting—never loud enough for Gunny Lyon—and the tiger's snarl that leaps from every throat as they "run it out" after each exercise.

The loudest platoon gets Lyon's accolade, a pistol-pointing finger, after each exercise, and woe to the platoon that fails to win its share: after PT, they will likely find themselves kicking up clouds of sand in the Pit behind the barracks, to the encouragement of the D.I.—audible city blocks away.

Now that they've worked up a little sweat, the four platoons fall in for a mile-and-a-half jog around the exercise field. Before he has reached the half-mile mark, Guerra is in pain. He wants to give up. His feet ache, his heart pounds, his yellow shirt is soaked, his leaden legs protest. But he keeps going. The hypnotic chanting helps divert his mind from the agony that is his body. So does the vocal prodding of his shipmates. After what seems an eternity, the lung-searing run is over. Each platoon picks up its grounded canteens and forms a large circle—the "wagon wheel." For the next ten minutes, the recruits plod behind one another like processionary caterpillars, sipping from their canteens, cooling off.

On their run, a first aid truck has followed at a fifty-yard interval, ready to minister to drop outs. Regulations forbid exercise without such a truck present. Even now the D.I.s watch their recruits closely for signs of excessive fatigue, especially those who, like Guerra, wear shirts bearing two broad horizontal red bars. These recruits are either obese, have a history of heart problems, previous open-heart surgery, sickle-cell anemia, or pallid skin predisposing to sunburn or sunstroke. In Platoon 1036 nine recruits wear them. Forbidden PT absolutely are those on light duty due to a physical ailment and those receiving medication of any kind.

Twelve "don'ts" govern all physical activity, including prohibitions against exhausting recruits, giving IPT after inoculations, one-half hour before or one hour after meals, or twice during one hour. Six "do's" enjoin close observation of exercising recruits, giving short periods of rest, assuring that recruits drink plenty of water, and other safety measures. Showers on the open field provide instant cooling in case of heat exhaustion, and on hot days the runners jog through them on every lap. Should a recruit suffer heat stroke, he will be rushed by an aid truck to the depot sick bay, there to be immersed in a special ice water bath to bring his body temperature quickly down to normal. From 1 April until 15 October the ice bath is constantly kept filled for emergencies.

At least once a week, after the quick shower following regular PT, SC Lt. Greenburg or Assistant Series Commander Lt. Herrera holds a hygiene inspection to detect injuries.

> . . . You've got to hand it to them—the D.I.s do everything they order you to do, and then some. They run so fast and do the PT with so little effort they make us ashamed. They can't hit you, so all they can do is make you feel like a soft-handed girl if you don't measure up. That, and scream at you. But once you realize they aren't going to belt you one, the shouting scares only the Nervous Nellies. Knowing that, some recruits are resting on their oars. They need a swift kick in the slats. But that's against regs, so they're a drag on the whole platoon. . . .

By the end of Training Day Five (TD-5), the muscle tone of the recruits is visibly better than on TD-1, when they took the IST—Initial Strength Test. The test required minimal performance: 2 pull-ups, 35 sit-ups in two minutes, and one and a half mile run in 13:30. Even so, 20 recruits of the 236-man series failed. Guerra, unable to lift his chin over the bar even once, was the worst of the four in Platoon 1036. His reprieve by S/Sgt. Dawson from assignment to the Physical Conditioning Platoon would last only a little more than two weeks. Then, on TD-16, in a retest, he would be required to do 3 pull-ups, 40 sit-ups in two minutes, and a three-mile run in under 28 minutes.

Even though PT, like most things in recruit training, is done by the numbers, it lacks the precision demanded of other activities. Everything else is strictly by the book, and by the clock. The First Phase BDR (Basic Daily Routine) for

training days is unvarying: 0500 (or earlier), Reveille; 0500-
0650, chow and clean up; 0700-1700, classes, meals, drill
and PT; 1935-1950, D.I. hygiene inspection; 1950-2050, free
time; 2050-2100, final muster and devotions; 2100, Taps. Except in their free time—and frequently even then, recruits are
engaged in scheduled training to promote their "knowledge"
and efficiency as Marines.

During the first training days, for example, the recruits
memorize the sequence of facing movements in making their
head calls. By the end of the week, head calls are integrated
into the training routine by driving home the firing sequence
of the M16A1. After the starboard section has had sufficient
time in the head, usually three to four minutes, the D.I. orders:

"Clear the head!"

"Clear the head!" respond the recruits standing at attention
on the port side of the squad bay. "Aye, aye, sir! Firing . . .
unlocking . . . extraction . . . ejection . . . cocking . . .
feeding . . . chambering . . . locking. Freeze, recruits,
freeze!"

And freeze they do. Laggard starboard-siders caught between head and ranks can look forward to IPT on the quarterdeck, spurring them to respond more quickly to orders the
next time.

The firing sequence of the M16A1 is but one of the myriad
facts to which the recruits are exposed the first week in fifteen
hours of academic work in seven subjects.

Predictably, the M16A1, the principal tool of the Marine's
trade, receives the most emphasis, four hours the first week
being devoted to its description, operation, capabilities and
maintenance. Recruits commit its characteristics to memory:
"The M16A1 is a 5.56 millimeter lightweight, air cooled,
gas operated, magazine fed, shoulder weapon capable of both
automatic and semi-automatic fire . . ." They must, as well,
memorize its range (2,653 meters), muzzle velocity (3,250
feet per second), chamber pressure (52,000 psi), rate of fire
under various conditions, and how to field strip its seventeen
major components at speed.

From now on, the recruits will be required to maintain the weapon in optimum operating condition by stripping, oiling and cleaning, a process that can easily wipe out an hour a day. A Marine must know where his rifle is at all times. When it is not in his hands, it must be secured by steel cable and combination lock to the recruit's rack, in a squad bay patrolled by two sentries. The loss of the rifle is a court-martial offense only marginally less severe than desertion.

Recruit instruction is divided between the squad bay and Building 602, the academic center across the parade ground from the barracks. There, D.I.s assigned this duty for six to twelve months specialize in the various academic areas, such as guard duties, life-saving and Marine Corps history, and teach each series of recruits in turn. Instructors from this section are also responsible for teaching recruits swimming, individual combat techniques, hand-to-hand combat and administering tests. While recruits may gain from the greater knowledge of their special instructors, however, the system of divided instructional responsibility dilutes the authority and effectiveness of the series D.I.s, fortified by uninterrupted personal contact with the recruits.

Marine Corps history is considered perhaps the primary motivating influence on recruits. In active campaigning on foreign shores for more than half the two-hundred-plus years of its existence, the Marine Corps has compiled a record of enterprise, valor and accomplishment it believes unequalled by any other military service. This tradition of endurance and sacrifice is the subject of three hours of lectures during the recruit's first training week, with many more to follow before graduation.

At this stage, history instruction almost totally ignores such matters as weaponry, logistics, organization, manpower and geopolitical factors. Instead, it focuses on symbolism—the origin of the officer's Mameluke sword, the Marine emblem, the motto *Semper Fidelis*, the Marine nicknames "Devil Dog" and "Leatherneck," and on the colorful campaigns which the Marines fought.

The campaigns are legion and, to all Marines, legendary.

Recruits learn about the origins of Marine amphibious traditions which began with their very first campaign in the Bahamas under Captain Samuel Nichols. From that day in 1776, Marines have engaged in conflicts ranging from short, sharp, nasty jungle actions in Latin America to major conventional wars in Europe and Asia. Recruits are not burdened by discussions of the political or economic factors behind their participation. As Marines, they are told, they have the responsibility to go where sent by the President and perform whatever mission he assigns.

To fulfill this function requires high standards of professionalism, the core of which is leadership, a quality in which Marines take exceptional pride. By tradition, unit commanders cannot merely designate objectives for their troops to capture, but must personally lead the attack. In two hours of lectures on this subject, Platoon 1036 learns that leadership personifies those qualities which inspire trust and emulation: military bearing, courage, decisiveness, dependability, endurance, enthusiasm, initiative, judgment, integrity, justice, knowledge, loyalty, tact and unselfishness.

This catalog of virtues never fails to overwhelm recruits, until it is explained that no one individual is expected to embody them all. They are, rather, the ideal toward which Marines should consciously aspire. Their place in Marine history is illustrated by the recitation of feats of arms by Marine heroes—usually bravery, intrepidity or self-sacrifice under fire. The reading of Medal of Honor citations to leadership classes illustrates exploits of ordinary men once recruits like themselves, who became Marines by rigorous, dedicated training. The unspoken implication is that, once their own training begun at Parris Island is completed in the Fleet Marine Force, each will be fully qualified to add his name to the Marine pantheon when the occasion demands.

In practice, the Marine Corps judges leadership of a unit by four characteristics of its members: discipline, morale, efficiency and *esprit de corps*. The latter quality, regarded by Marines as the linchpin of the Corps, is based on an intense respect for the tradition of courage and perseverance established by their predecessors. Boot camp is too short a period to develop all these traits, but long enough to instill discipline, provided recruits can be made to appreciate that discipline is indispensable to a unit's morale and efficiency and, in the longer term, to its *esprit*.

Two classes are given on Interior Guard, which, paradoxically, is usually *exterior* guard. Even as recruits, the men of Platoon 1036 will walk post outside the barracks, and stand fire watch in the squad bay and sentry duty during ICT (Individual Combat Training) in the field. The eleven General Orders which they have by now committed to memory apply to this and all other guard duty. Supplementing them are special orders applicable to particular situations or posts involving challenges, passwords, countersigns and the use of deadly force. Impressed upon every recruit is the absolute prohibition against surrendering his rifle to anyone—even the base commander—except their three D.I.s and officers of the watch, since he might inadvertently be handing over his weapon to criminals or terrorists masquerading as officers. The cardinal rule is, "A Marine on guard has no friends."

Especially his feet, thinks Guerra. He is being trained to kill, but meanwhile his feet are killing *him*. Whether he's running, marching or standing at attention—and his days are filled doing one or the other—his heavy black boots are vessels of pain. The real Marine, he knows, is the infantry grunt, but he can't help thinking how pleasant an assignment to Motor Transport would be.

The week's academic studies are rounded out by one-hour classes on the "Tailoring, Maintenance and Laundering of Uniforms," "Life-Saving," and the "Marine Corps Promotion System." Promotion may come through graduation from service schools, professional achievement—based on such factors as rifle, physical fitness and EST scores, proficiency marks and time in grade—and for meritorious achievement. Avoidance of disciplinary problems and excessive debt as well as the display of initiative and off-duty schooling at all levels also enhance a Marine's promotion prospects.

. . . Lectures are getting to be a pain in the neck. We're herded into a big classroom, they dim the lights so we can see the Marine on stage reciting his memorized speech, and pretty soon somebody falls asleep. The D.I.s are watching. When they spot a drooping head, they order the recruit to stand at the back of the hall. On a warm day at a boring lecture, like the one on "Uniforms," we'll have thirty or forty guys swaying on their feet, like elephants at a zoo, struggling to stay awake. One thing I've learned at boot camp: if you're tired enough, you can fall sound asleep, standing up, with your eyes wide open. . . .

Whether a recruit's classes are given in Building 602 or the squad bay, they serve merely as an introduction to the subjects covered. Details, examples and supplementary information are provided in his "knowledge," which he is supposed to study in intervals between drill, classes and other duties, even when standing outside in the rain while awaiting the appearance of his D.I. During the free hour recruits have each evening, some will be studying their "knowledge," preparing their gear, practicing difficult drill movements, stripping and cleaning their M-16s or doing pull-ups on one of the six high bars in each squad bay; others will be shooting the breeze, writing letters, daydreaming while staring blankly at the bulkhead, or participating in barracks-room japes. The former will excel, the others scrape by or fail.

For both, the high point of the day is Mail Call, which comes after evening chow. Predictably, it is by the numbers.

The D.I. calls the name of the recruit.

The recruit yells "Here, sir!" and double-times to the quarterdeck, stopping at attention before the D.I.

"Recruit Three-Thumbs reporting for Mail Call as ordered, sir!" he bawls. The letter extended, the recruit slaps it between his hands. "Mail received, sir!" he proclaims, and darts back to the ranks, which remain at attention until the last letter is distributed.

This week the mail brings one recruit a suspiciously thick letter which, on inspection, is found to contain pornographic pictures and four dilapidated cigarettes, which the recruit surrenders wistfully. Sgt. Montgomery tells him to write his "friend" to say he's doing the recruit no service by sending such missives. At least the sender wasn't a parent, one of whom sent a recruit some cigarettes concealed in the false bottom of a cake box. In suspicious cases, a D.I. can ask to examine a package's contents, a request the recruit can refuse. The D.I. must then apply in writing for permission to the series commander, who kicks it up through channels to the battalion commander, who has the authority to issue what is, in effect, a search warrant allowing the D.I. to inspect the package for contraband.

A final chore on those evenings before inspections is the field day. With his own scrub brush each recruit begins by sweeping dirt and dust from beneath his bunk to the center of the squad bay. There the accumulation is swept up by other recruits with brooms. For the next two hours, the platoon scrubs decks, bulkheads, showers, ports, toilets and urinals— everything in their area. Sixty men spending two hours cleaning a single room should leave it spotless but, as recruits soon learn, the inspecting officer's probing hand is a magnet for any overlooked patch of dirt, or "holiday."

For Francisco Guerra, that's the only kind of holiday in sight. The first five training days have sped by, with Guerra running hard to catch up. So far, he's still eating dust, but he has made progress. From zero pull-ups on TD-1 he has raised himself and his score to six, and has reduced his weight by an equal number of pounds, to an even two hundred. Unlike most recruits, he wishes he had more PT.

A few clouds still hover on Guerra's blue horizon. He still has trouble with his feet, despite the issue of prescription orthotics from the depot sick bay. The rank structure does not fall trippingly from his tongue, and the legal niceties of the

Uniform Code of Military Justice are hard to unscramble. Marine Corps jargon, overlaid on his recently acquired English, is only slowly becoming comprehensible. Like his shipmates, he has difficulty remembering to address himself and everybody else in the third person; completely eliminating the "I's" and "you's" from his vocabulary is a distant goal.

All the same, he is heartened by having survived thus far. "I have—" he begins, then corrects himself, "—this *recruit* has more confidence in himself. And when this recruit was singled out by the D.I. as one who refused to quit—well, for me, coming from S/Sgt. Gladden, that was incredible."

D. I. from P. I.

In another age, they might have been Knights Templar, monkish men trained in the art of war in order to do battle for a consuming, transcendent ideal. They are the D.I.s, the snappiest, proudest and most thoroughly indoctrinated men in the Marine Corps. They have to be, to turn such apparently unpromising material as Francisco Guerra into hard-muscled, motivated and professional fighting men.

Only a select handful of men and women qualify for the six classes each year at the Marine Corps' East-coast Drill Instructor School at Parris Island, founded in 1956. There is a virtually identical D.I. school based at the Recruit Depot in

San Diego. To be considered for instruction, the candidate must be twenty-one to thirty-five years old and a high school graduate, or possess a GED-GCT equivalent above 90 (the actual average is 112), and rank from sergeant to gunnery sergeant. A single court martial, or more than two nonjudicial punishments during the previous twelve months, is disqualifying. He must be medically fit, consistently pass his physical fitness tests, live within his means, and have no history of explosive or uncontrollable behavior.

Recruiting teams visit posts in the United States each year to screen all qualified Marines who have not previously had drill instructor assignments. Approximately half of those eventually chosen will be volunteers, the others ordered to this difficult and demanding duty. In Drill Instructor School, as in boot camp, motivation is a decisive factor: of the volunteers only a small percentage fail. The overall attrition rate is about 40 to 45 percent, of which medical and neuropsychological disabilities disqualify 20 percent; academic and physical training deficiencies eliminate the remainder.

Drill Instructor School is considerably more exacting than boot camp. In a nine-and-a-half-week course, the student receives 33 hours of instruction on basic military subjects, 63.5 hours on Standard Operating Procedure—the D.I.'s guide to handling recruits, 9.5 hours on recreation supervision and evaluation, 12.5 hours on leadership, 17 hours in weapons and marksmanship training, 35 hours in close-order drill (actually double that ration, in unscheduled sessions during Commander's Time and on Sundays), 42.5 hours in physical training, 30 hours in individual combat training, and 49 hours in evaluation. These 40-hour weeks do not, of course, include long evening hours given to study in barracks, rifle maintenance, uniform and inspection preparation and administrative duties.

The program proceeds at a forced-draft pace, so contrived that no student can possibly fulfill all the requirements. The pressure is deliberate: it subjects the candidate to even greater stresses than he will experience on the street, drilling recruits. If he can't tolerate these stresses in Drill Instructor School, he'll not graduate to handle recruits. Attempting to keep up with the work load, many students skip meals, and a twenty-pound weight loss among men already trim is not uncommon during the nine and a half weeks.

Sergeant Michael Edward Montgomery, Heavy A of Platoon 1036, like all other D.I.s at Parris Island a graduate of Drill Instructor School, was a typical D.I. candidate. A native of Rome, Georgia, he attended college briefly before deciding, at eighteen, that the Marine Corps offered more scope for his restless energies. After boot camp he was selected for avionics school, then served on deployments in the Caribbean and the Mediterranean. Meritorious promotions to Pfc and corporal made firm his resolve to be a career Marine, during which period he intends to complete his university studies at night school and hopes to achieve warrant-officer rank in the field of Intelligence.

Like his classmates, Sgt. Montgomery underwent fourteen uniform and personnel inspections—half of them un-scheduled—and had to pass twenty-nine performance exams in everything from the basic subjects to platoon movements, conduct of drill, sword evolutions and physical training. In the latter test, he was required to run three miles in under twenty-four minutes. All students must meet this standard, regardless of age—no problem for motivated and superbly conditioned Marines whose average PFT score is 275 out of 300. In addition, in order to be considered for the Drill Instructor School diploma, Sergeant Montgomery had to demonstrate good conduct and a high degree of personal organization and management skills, be certified as emotionally well-balanced by the neuropsychological unit, negotiate all the obstacles on the obstacle course, and pass an interview with the school's commanding officer. Predictably, he surmounted all obstacles—physical, psychological and intellectual. Predictably, he spent every waking hour studying or at drill, with only minutes at a time in the mess hall. Predictably, he lost twenty-two pounds.

Drill instructors take pride in doing everything they ask recruits to do—but better, faster and more often. Their inspiration is fed by the photographs and citations of all Marine Medal of Honor winners, which line the corridors of their modern but austere school. As a group, they are the kind of students professors dream about but rarely get: immaculately groomed, disciplined, eager, mannerly, questioning, hardworking and erect in bearing.

The 300 to 400 who graduate annually from Drill Instructor School are, by service standards, privileged young men and women. They are awarded the coveted D.I. MOS 8511 in addition to their basic MOS, along with superior-performance pay of $165 monthly for the first six months of D.I. duty, and $220 each month thereafter. They receive a supplementary clothing issue, and free laundry and cleaning services. Upon completion of their tours, they will be able to choose their next duty stations. All receive preferential consideration for promotion and, in fact, meritorious promotion to staff sergeant and gunnery sergeant is available *only* to drill instructors, recruiters and embassy security guards.

The symbols of their new status are the broad-brimmed campaign ("Smoky Bear") hat, and the wide green web belt, worn by assistant drill instructors. Starting as Third Hat with a platoon on graduation, whatever his rank, the D.I. can look forward to promotion after one or two series to Heavy A, and after several more, to senior drill instructor. The mark of the S.D.I.'s office is the black fair-leather belt. His is a face, a voice and an air of command the recruit will always remember, usually with nostalgic affection.

Drill instructors have perhaps the most demanding and responsible job in the Marine Corps. Once assigned to a platoon, they can expect weeks of up to 110 hours working or on duty, while the platoon is in its formative stage. In the Second Phase, the weekly training routine typically consumes 95 to 105 hours, while in the Third Phase the toll rises once again.

Parris Island's drill instructors work in teams of three, and their duties are so complementary that they must function in complete harmony to turn out well-rounded Marines. The senior is "Big Dad," the "Omnipotent and Omniscient One," the "Father Confessor," the only one who may occasionally laugh, who whipsaws the platoon into shape with alternating praise, cajolery, sarcasm, ridicule, indifference, contempt, and rage. Everything must be keyed to the slowest man in the platoon, yet the S.D.I. must make sure that the measured pace of learning does not bore the bright and quick. He must consider carefully the implications of his words, which from experience tend more to the literal than the figurative. One S.D.I., for example, told his men to "Shave everything between your ears and shoulders," only to have a recruit report with eyebrows shaved off. Now he adds "—*except* your eyebrows."

More driven even than the S.D.I. are the Heavy A and the Third Hat, who must adhere to a program of instruction (carried in the crowns of their hats) listing the minute-by-minute schedule of each of the fifty-seven training days. The Heavy A is responsible for teaching, the Third Hat for discipline. Neither smiles: D.I.s believe that any sign of levity while instructing recruits in the martial arts weakens discipline. Their job is to train men to kill, and death is no laughing matter.

In recent years, more and more instruction is being carried out by specialist drill instructors. During individual combat, swimming, hand-to-hand combat, marksmanship training and most academic lectures, a platoon's drill instructors are present to enforce discipline, but take no active part in training.

It was not always so. The process of making a drill instructor, today almost an exact science, was once a most inexact art. Toughness and an unbending sense of duty and discipline were the indispensable virtues, along with basic military skills, and the means by which the D.I. forged the singing sword from base metal was left pretty much up to the individual. Over the years, a wide variety of instructional and disciplinary methods were tolerated.

On the eve of World War II half a century ago, for instance, recruits with two left feet might be required to duck-walk—tucking the rifle behind the knees and in the crook of the arms and waddling the one-mile perimeter of the parade deck, a procedure at once exhausting, humiliating, and sometimes permanently destructive to the cartilage of the knees. Anyone caught eating ice cream—forbidden fruit—was ordered to buy a quart of it, balance the paper carton upside down on his bare head under the summer sun, and stand at attention until it melted completely, a feast for the flies and sweet misery for the recruit. Dropping a rifle incurred the penalty of having to don three rifles beneath the underclothes and sleeping on them. A speck of dust on the two-man tent deck—permanent barracks had not yet been constructed—was the prelude to a thorough scrubbing of the whole wooden deck with a toothbrush. Talking in ranks was rewarded more or less in kind: the recruit had to stand at attention at one end of the parade deck with a bucket over his head and scream obscenities—and God help him if they were not sufficiently obscene—about his mother, sister and girlfriend, loudly enough to be heard at the opposite end of the field. The recruit who failed to take the obligatory daily shower was spread-eagled naked on the company street, held down by four stalwart shipmates while two others scrubbed his body with street sweeper's brooms with buckets of sand in lieu of soap; thereafter the habit of personal cleanliness was quickly and permanently acquired.

Until approximately a decade ago, drill instructors were given wide latitude, and used it freely. Lackadaisical recruits could be peremptorily assigned to a "motivation platoon," where they labored from sun-up to sun-down, waist deep in a muddy ditch, shoveling muck from one pile to another; after a single day, a revival of motivation was sudden, dramatic and lasting. A prod in the ribs with the D.I.'s elbow concentrated the attention of a recruit with a wandering mind. A smart swat across the buttocks by a D.I.'s improvised swagger stick—a golf club with the head sawed off—was a great spine straightener. On the firing line, a recruit whose

loaded pistol's muzzle inadvertently strayed toward his shipmates could expect swift and certain retribution: a kick in the
leg which on occasion removed a rasher of flesh.

Abuses of their almost unlimited powers sometimes occurred, and a few D.I.s were indeed certifiable sadists. They
seldom lasted long: boot camp has in all eras been a place to
train men to fight and survive, not to indulge the cruelty of a
few warped individuals, and officers didn't hesitate to remove
or even court martial those D.I.s who abused their considerable authority. In general, among either D.I.s or recruits,
there was little outrage or even resentment at peremptory punishment, judiciously applied. Both knew that the overriding
aim of the overwhelming majority of D.I.s was to turn their
charges into tough, disciplined, efficient fighting men. Were
they ever treated unjustly? Of course, most recruits admitted,
but then war itself was unjust, and the sooner they became
inured to discomfort and physical pain, the better their
chances of survival on the battlefield. To just such training
can be attributed the survival of so many Marines in some of
war's most brutal campaigns—Guadalcanal, Tarawa, Peliliu,
Iwo Jima, Chosin, Khe Sanh.

With the elimination of conscription coinciding with the
rising agitation for "human rights," though, the Marine
Corps slowly, often reluctantly, began to moderate the rigor
of its training. The 1956 night-training accident at Parris Island in which half a dozen recruits drowned, and the killing
of a recruit during pugil stick training at San Diego just
twenty years later, in another service would have been one-
day wonders in the American press. In another country they
would have gone unnoticed, part of the price a nation pays
for preparedness. But the Marine Corps now paid dearly for
its high visibility and its genius for self-promotion. During
the ensuing hearings on Capitol Hill, various congressmen
hinted heavily—as General Douglas MacArthur and President
Harry Truman had done before them—that the Marine Corps
should be disbanded or absorbed by the Army.

In a desperate rear-guard action, the Marine Corps insti-

tuted regulations calculated to insure that such tragedies were
never repeated. Swinging from frontier justice at boot camp
to the opposite extreme, the Corps has progressively shorn
D.I.s of nearly all initiative. Regulations forbid them to swear
at, or even in the presence of, recruits. ("Damn" and "hell"
are considered swearing; "Doggone it!" and "Gee whiz!"
are tolerated.) Recruits are encouraged to report D.I.s for
physical or verbal abuse, and a D.I. so accused is relieved of
duty at once, and remains in limbo until an investigation is
completed.

"Verbal abuse" reported, investigated and punished at P.I.
during the period Platoon 1036 was in training involved one
recruit being called a "slimebag" and another a "clown."
"Truck driver," "appleneck," and "crybaby" were also
names used by D.I.s for which they were reported. A D.I.
called another recruit a "quitter and a weird one," for which
offense he was fined $200. A D.I. who called a recruit "hu-
man jello" was put on report. A D.I. who "threatened a
recruit by raising an unsecured rifle in front of the recruit,
with no contact made or intended," was reduced to corporal
and fined $500. An outstanding D.I., being considered for
meritorious promotion, committed the sin of telling a
bemused recruit, "Goddamn it, get your head out of your
ass," and was denied promotion and relieved of training duties for two months. Other subjects of abuse were a recruit
solicited (by a non-D.I.) for $70, and a recruit relieved as a
scribe "because [allegedly] he was ugly."

Major Alfred A. Cortez overheard Gunnery Sergeant Vansweringen using profanity; Vansweringen was fined $100.
"Get your goddamned ass over to church" was the occasion
for another allegation, as were the epithets of "Curley Tur-
key," "boy," "freak," "sweet pea," "brainstorm," and
"stupid." A recruit made an allegation against his D.I. for
saying, "So you're a druggie, eh?" (It turned out that the
recruit *was* a druggie and was under investigation for fraudulent enlistment.) Another recruit made an allegation against
his D.I. for "yelling at" him.

Incidents of "physical abuse" during the same period included excessive IPT; closing a hatch on a recruit's finger, breaking it; throwing a lockerbox tray on the deck, hitting a recruit on the foot; denying a recruit with a broken arm permission to go to the sick bay; "touching" a recruit; "touching a recruit's face"; bumping a recruit with an elbow; running into a recruit with his chest; "making it rain" by ordering recruits to throw sand in the air while on IPT; placing a hand on the back of a recruit's neck; and pulling on a recruit's jacket sleeve because his long-john sleeve was exposed. All those convicted of these heinous acts were punished with the full rigor of the Uniform Code of Military Justice.

In all, during the first six months of 1985, the Recruit Information System (RIS) established to process allegations of physical and verbal abuse by drill instructors, of which those described above were the most serious, confirmed thirty-nine cases and dismissed thirty-three, in a recruit population exceeding twelve thousand.

During their sixty-three and a half hours on Standard Operating Procedure, Sgt. Montgomery and his classmates are intensively indoctrinated to avoid such incidents, any one of which can destroy their careers as Marines. They are indoctrinated to "cover ass," to forecast the consequences of every action before it is taken, to be able to justify it by some regulation in the event it turns sour. And so Marine officialdom, coerced by the Congress which holds its purse strings, trains the new breed of D.I.—defensive, cautious, litigious, wary of taking initiative, content to accept the minimum performance, while praying that he never has to lead these undertrained, mollycoddled men into battle, if indeed they'll consent to go.

"Risk aversion" is the contemptuous name given by veteran D.I.s to the cowardice of officers and NCOs who cling to the letter of the *Standard Operating Procedure for Recruit Training,* sacrificing the substance of training for empty ritual which will not jeopardize their careers. Gun-shy "leaders" now devote hours to trivia—stress management classes ("bring your wife"), sexual awareness classes (to avoid the suggestion of sexual harassment), leadership discussions on race, and pencil whipping—which were never factors when the U.S. Marine Corps was true to its traditional structure and training methods. Such officers and NCOs prosper; recruits are shortchanged.

Many D.I.s fight the system by living on the razor's edge, pushing their recruits well beyond what they had conceived to be their limits, demonstrating that real Marines *recognize* no limits, and winning the respect and gratitude of recruits who joined the Corps expressly to make that exhilarating discovery. Such recruits can be—and on occasion are—jostled, cussed and pushed around. They accept it with the stoicism it is supposed to induce, knowing it is for their own eventual good. Others, however, spoiled by civilian ease and truculently assertive of their "rights," protest and are heard. A common result is that first-rate Marine drill instructors are sacrificed, that the weak and worthless may prevail.

For these reasons, well understood by aspirant D.I.s, the emotional demands of Drill Instructor School are no less formidable than the physical. Six- or seven-day weeks, competition between their platoon and others of the series, and many additional duties such as watch standing, keeping their basic MOS current, attending classes in CPR and first aid, and requalifying annually with the M-16, take a heavy toll. Due to the strain of long and irregular hours, divorce rates among drill instructors are the highest in the armed forces. The combined pressures lead to the familiar drill instructor malady "burnout," characterized by irritability, impaired judgment, loss of weight and other symptoms of chronic stress. These symptoms are seldom alleviated by the four or five days off the drill field instructors usually enjoy between series—usually, because during the heavy summer season, D.I.s often graduate a platoon one day, and pick up a new one the next.

Recruit Depot policy is to transfer drill instructors displaying the first symptoms of burnout, which generally appear after the second or third consecutive series, to the Support Battalion. There, "on quota" for six months, keeping shorter and more regular hours, a drill instructor works as a swimming coach, clothing inspector, clerk or processing NCO, and becomes reacquainted with his family. Even so, the harsh demands of the intensely competitive job, and the commitment of the drill instructors to their recruits, is responsible for high levels of stress and turnover among drill instructors.

The D.I.s' task is complicated because, in order to make Marines—disciplined fighting men who put the welfare of their unit above personal concerns—they must re-form the recruits' cultural values. In today's society, these often include the me-first ethic, the recruit's belief in the right to do whatever he pleases, systematic shirking of responsibility, immunity from punishment for antisocial or even criminal behavior, and the recruit's conviction that his every whim should be immediately gratified and every material acquisition within his grasp—now.

Nevertheless, the drill instructors try, and try mightily. How well they do their job will not become apparent until their new-hatched Marines join the very profane and very professional Fleet Marine Force, where the attitudes and skills learned in boot camp will make or break them. Meanwhile a drill instructor like Sgt. Montgomery must be content with the verdict of the stunned parent who, on graduation day, warmly shakes his hand, saying, "I can't believe it— you made a *man* of him!"

WEEK TWO

Hall:
A Matter of
Motivation

"You're lazy, apathetic, immature and shiftless—and those are your *good* qualities," says a disgusted S/Sgt. Dawson to Recruit Calvin Hall. "You don't belong here."

Hall is inclined to agree, but observing the fire in S/Sgt. Dawson's eye, doesn't think it politic to say so. All the same, he is a man with a weighty grievance: he feels betrayed by circumstance.

At twenty-three, Hall has worked briefly as a waiter and as an assembler of circuit boards, and studied at North Carolina State and Dillard University, where financial need forced him to drop out after two and a half years. Married but jobless, with a newborn child, Hall sought a measure of security in a career in the Marine Corps Reserve. His educational background and job experience brought him the guarantee of specialization in electronics and the possibility of officer training. But during the ten-month interval between signing up and being called to duty, Hall had found a good job with an electronics firm he was loathe to leave in order to fulfill his military commitment. Ever since he stepped off the bus in Parris Island nearly three weeks earlier, Recruit Calvin Hall had been plagued by second thoughts.

He paraded them. He displayed a street cool at all times, declined to sound off, marched out of step, fidgeted and looked around in ranks, and moved at a languid pace not to be confused with a Green Marine Blur. He became a regular in the Pits, churning up clouds of sand as he climbed mountains with peaks lost in the mists of never-never land.

Meanwhile, his mates in Platoon 1036 were grappling with more important challenges than personal discontents. During the second training week, they would have to absorb some sixteen hours of lectures concentrating on first aid, Marine history, and bayonet techniques. They would have, in addition, some eighteen hours of drill, one half held by demanding D.I.s on the parade deck, the other half—for those who needed it—by men in white jackets at dental recall.

Some recruits beginning this second week are destined not to finish it. Their failure does not surprise D.I.s who have learned to forecast a platoon's performance with remarkable accuracy. Experience has taught them that, after a few weeks at Parris Island, recruits lose their initial dread of being subjected to physical and verbal abuse, having discovered that the D.I. Covenant, about which many harbored a healthy skepticism, will be observed by most D.I.s to the letter.

Some recruits presume on their immunity. They become belligerent, or malinger, talk in ranks, display dumb insolence or even disobey direct orders. Punishment follows swiftly, meted out to the entire platoon, all being punished for the misconduct of the few. Such mass punishment is manifestly unjust, but D.I.s inflict it purposely to bring home to every recruit that the military unit, for better or worse, is indivisible. In the field, every man is responsible for, as well as dependent upon, his shipmates. The platoon is more than a random collection of men: it is a living, functioning organism.

Some recruits cannot accept this and other stark realities, and soon depart.

In Platoon 1036, the first to go is Stanley Winters, the nervous young recruit given to tears and sudden terrors. The Neuropsychological Unit (NPU) decides that, for his own good—and that of the service—he should be returned to civilian life. Winters is sent to Casual Company for Entry Level Separation—Defense Department new-speak for discharge.

On Training Day Five, Clinton H. Hardison, a husky, apparently healthy recruit, passes out on the parade deck after drill. Revived, and seemingly suffering only from mild dehydration, he resumes his place in ranks. The following day, Sunday, 10 March, he is found face down on the deck in the head, unconscious and cyanotic. Sgt. Montgomery comes running, and orders an ambulance summoned while he extricates Hardison's swallowed tongue and gets him breathing again. Rushed to the sick bay, Hardison is transferred to the Naval Hospital in Charleston for observation. There, doctors learn that he recently suffered a near-fatal automobile accident, a fact he concealed from recruiters. Within the week Hardison, too, is on his way home, for fraudulent enlistment.

After lunch this same Sunday, Murray K. Stone, an alert and intelligent recruit, returns from the mess hall with a stolen knife and fork. He declares matter-of-factly that he intends to use these implements to commit suicide. He cannot, he complains, "put up with the environment." "Besides," says Stone, who enlisted for six years and is guaranteed promotion to Pfc on completion of training, "my girlfriend is about to go into the Israeli Army, and I want to go see her."

The NPU is closed on Sunday, so Stone is put under round-the-clock surveillance until the morrow. Transferred the next day to the Casual Company for ELS after convincing a psychologist of his sincerity, Stone is observed studying a borrowed New Testament, issued to all Christian recruits. His fingers tiptoe through the Gospels. Suddenly his eyes are aglow. To all who will listen he quotes Matthew 10:36: "And a man's foes shall be they of his own household." He explains that obviously this is a warning from heaven that the members of Platoon 1036 are his enemies. Stone has found a biblical rationale for his breach of contract, and he is content. . . .

Recruit Halsey Congreve isn't. Assigned to keep watch over the would-be suicide Sunday night, he sits down on Stone's foot locker in the darkness and daydreams of home. An hour later, the corporal of the guard finds him asleep. In wartime, the penalty for sleeping on watch can be death, but the death sentence is passed only on Congreve's Marine career. He is sent to join his three failed shipmates at Casual Company. In two weeks he will be back home, where his heart is.

Morale and discipline are slipping fast, and not only in Platoon 1036. Other platoons in the series have had similar problems. The recruits don't know it, but lightning is about to strike.

> . . . Not a shot's been fired, but already Platoon 1036 is taking casualties. The foul balls are beginning to show themselves, and the D.I.s are belting them into the bleachers. We've got all kinds—the gutless ones, the lazy ones, a couple whose upstairs isn't fully furnished. Once all the misfits get separated, 1036 will be a better platoon. Fewer punishments, more team spirit. Nobody's crying for the dear departed. In fact, the platoon would be happy if the earth opened up and another ten or fifteen eight balls disappeared. . . .

On TD-9, the 240-man series is assembled in 1036 squad bay and seated on the deck, shoulder-to-shoulder—all except three of their number who wait, apprehensively facing an empty chair and blanket-draped table on the quarterdeck.

The door to the squad bay opens and Bravo Company commanding officer Captain Michael E. Ratliff appears. He takes his place at the table. His manner is forbidding, his face grim.

Bravo Company First Sergeant Collins orders the three men before him to attention as the CO (Commanding Officer) enters and takes his seat at the table.

"This proceeding is Office Hours," Capt. Ratliff tells the three recruits, "or nonjudicial punishment. You are here on charges of violating Article 90 of the UCMJ—willfully disobeying a superior commissioned officer, and Article 91, insubordinate conduct toward a non-commissioned officer. Before I ask you to plead to these charges, I will read and explain your rights under the Uniform Code of Military Justice."

It takes quite a while. They have the right, Capt. Ratliff says, to be considered innocent until proven guilty, to remain silent, to protection against double jeopardy, to call witnesses, to a speedy public trial, to be informed of all charges against them, to protection against illegal search and seizure, to trial by court martial at which they can be represented by counsel, to review of sentence by higher authority, and to a number of other constitutional safeguards.

Each recruit signs a statement that he has read and understood his rights. Each pleads guilty.

Wentworth, guilty of three charges and specifications of insubordination, is sentenced to lose $130 in pay and to immediate discharge.

Maklovich, guilty of making an unauthorized telephone call, is fined $75 and recycled to TD-1 with another platoon.

Richards, a tall, healthy young man, refused repeated orders to undertake physical training with his platoon, complaining of fatigue. He loses $130 in pay and will be sent to Casual Company for immediate ELS.

"We're here to train men to be Marines," Capt. Ratliff says, concluding the proceedings. "That training demands total commitment, consistent effort, a willing spirit and strict obedience to orders. If you have these qualities, we can make you Marines. If you don't, we'll give you a walking chit— Burger King can always use a few more cooks."

In 1036 Series, morale rebounds. For the next few days, slackers tread the narrow path of righteousness. Recruit Hall snaps to on the parade deck and pays attention at lectures.

Four hours of this instruction are devoted to first aid. The section on the prevention and treatment of heat casualties is perhaps the most urgent, considering the imminent onset of the southern summer. Recruits are admonished to drink frequently from the two canteens they must carry everywhere, eat ample salt, and recognize and know how to treat heat victims. In both heat stroke and heat exhaustion, they're told, it is imperative to move the victim to a cool place and bring his body temperature down as rapidly as possible, giving him water to sip if he's conscious.

In the lecture on "Fracture and Transportation of the Injured," recruits learn to splint the two types of bone breaks, and five effective ways to transport casualties in order to avoid further injury. "Treatment of Burns," one of the most frequent traumas of combat, emphasizes the need to avoid shock and infection, and for fast, expert medical care. "Life-Saving Steps" teaches the basic techniques to cope with four common emergencies: clearing the airway for victims of choking, followed by mouth-to-mouth resuscitation; applying pressure dressings to wounds and tourniquets for arterial bleeding; improvising splints for fractures; and shock control methods.

These measures saved the lives of many Marines in the field during the conflicts discussed this week in three lectures dealing with World War II, the Korean War, and the Vietnam War. In all three wars the Marines fought with accustomed zeal, valor and success. Their victories at Guadalcanal, Tarawa, Iwo Jima, Okinawa, Inchon, Khe Sanh and Pleiku have the epic dimensions which confirm the boast that it is virtually impossible to stop Marines determined to vanquish the enemy.

Even the most successful actions, however, cost casualties, and in all three wars Marines have been taken prisoner. Lectures on the "Law of Land Warfare" and the "Code of Conduct" prepare recruits for this contingency. A prisoner-of-war must give the enemy neither aid nor comfort—only his name, date of birth, rank and service number. He must endeavor to escape, never accept favors or parole, and demonstrate the leadership he will develop at boot camp and in the Fleet. The more disciplined, knowledgeable, fit and aggressive he becomes, the less likely he is to suffer the disagreeable fate of captivity.

*　　*　　*

> . . . Frankly, I don't understand this "Code of
> Conduct" or "Law of Land Warfare." In war, it's
> okay to drop bombs on people—fathers and mothers
> and children—and wipe them out or maim them for
> life, right? But suddenly, when one of the bomb-
> droppers becomes a prisoner, all the rules change.
> You've got to feed him, give him TLC, ask only his
> name etc., treat him humanely. Fine, but what
> actually happened to Marines captured by the North
> Koreans, the Chinese, the Vietcong? I guess the best
> bet in war is to follow the 12th General Order. . . .

Aggression, in the Marine Corps, is synonymous with bayonet. Both are taught recruits of 1036 Series during their second week at boot camp by a large, hard-muscled dark-green
Marine. Standing on a high canvas-covered platform surrounded by rapt recruits in open ranks, he shows them how to
kill—quickly, silently and with the first thrust.

"There are five killing blows," the big sergeant tells them,
and he proceeds to demonstrate the vertical and horizontal
butt strokes and smash on his enemy Fred, a cami-clad
dummy held up at arms length by an apprehensive recruit.

"Deliver this," says the sergeant with a grunt and an evil
grimace, as he administers a vertical butt stroke, "and Fred'll
be singing soprano. I guarantee you he'll be breaking all the
glassware within a mile when you hit 'im in the groin.
You're going to hit the enemy in the gonads, and put 'em in
his throat—*right?*"

"*Right!*" chorus the recruits.

The instructor slashes at the dummy's neck with his rifle's
flash suppressor—for safety, neither his nor the recruits' rifles are equipped with the short, stiletto-like bayonet used on
the M-16-A1—and steps back to the ready position.

"Fred is a masochist. He loves to be tortured, and I'm
going to give him what he wants. So are you. Now, let's see
if you know how."

He drills the series in the preparatory moves, right and left turns, rest, turns about. They jab ferociously at the imaginary enemy, scowling and growling with each stab and thrust as the sergeant urges them to exercise their lungs as they exercise their arms.

"Volume is confidence!" he bellows.

"*Volume is confidence!*" they whoop, carving up the air with their attacks.

"We want to see his heart throbbing and beating at the end of this bayonet. Do it again!"

By now, it's beginning to dawn on the recruits that the fundamentals of bayonet drill resemble elements of boxing, especially balance, footwork and parries.

"Foot forward!"

The recruits plant their left feet one pace forward.

"Foot backward!"

The recruits stand fast.

"That's right," says the sergeant, flashing a rare smile. "Marines don't retreat."

"But in special cases," he goes on, "such as when you're surrounded by a dozen murderous maniacs, you are permitted to take some temporary defensive measures."

He proceeds to teach the series the "high block," the "low block" and the "parry." When they have executed these maneuvers to his grudging satisfaction, he goes on to more complicated evolutions, used in dealing with several enemies at the same time.

"Whirl!"

"Ninety degrees, sir!" they respond, ready to shift position.

"Right!"

They wheel ninety degrees to the right.

"Jab!"

They jab imaginary bayonets into the enemies' yielding flesh.

"Withdraw!"

"Twist and pull," they yell, yanking out their bayonets.

"Right about!"

"One hundred and eighty degrees, sir!"

"Being sadistic is realistic!" the D.I. exults.

"Being sadistic is realistic," thunder the recruits.

The big sergeant suddenly stops in the middle of a bayonet sequence. His rifle comes to the position of rest. "You know," he confides, "you people are lucky. Where else in the world can you kill people, chop them up into little pieces, and get paid for it?"

Under his guidance, the recruits prepare for their future good fortune during three hours of drill. Their mastery of bayonet techniques is then to be tested at the end of the week on a course consisting of twenty obstacles—high walls, shell holes, log balances, high dirt mounds, trenches and tunnels. Armed with "rifles" fashioned of iron pipe, recruits attack in teams of three. At each obstacle, recruits sound off with rebel yells—to stimulate their own adrenaline secretions and demoralize the foe—then jab, slash and uppercut an enemy concealed in foxholes and behind other defenses.

. . . Fine. I rip out the guy's guts and strangle him with them. Thinking about it, I guess that if it was him or me, I'd bayonet him, all right. But I guess we've got soft in the past couple of centuries. They used to whack off arms and heads with swords, and bash out brains with clubs, and then go out and eat beefsteak for dinner. Nowadays, I think Americans get queasy about that way of fighting. We don't mind killing with bullets from a thousand yards, where we can't see the poor b———— bleeding to death, but sticking a knife in him is something else, at least for me. Yet, it doesn't seem to bother a lot of other people fighting today's wars. I hate thinking about it. I mean really *thinking* about it. . . .

To critics who disparage the use of the bayonet at close quarters against an enemy who should be shot before he can close, the Marines counter with a riposte won from hard experience: they contend the bayonet is indispensable as a weapon of last resort, when ammunition is exhausted or the rifle jams; it is the weapon of choice in ambush and whenever stealth is imperative; and to those trained in its use, it imparts that ardent combative spirit which sets Marines apart from other military services.

That spirit is not easily acquired. In Platoon 1036, despite the example of Office Hours, despite the adrenalin-pumping exertions of bayonet practice, by week's end some recruits—Calvin Hall among them—have reverted to the sluggishness, slackness, sloppiness and shambling that characterized the first days of Forming. Hall entertains the delusion that, if he can walk that fine line between inferior performance and blatant insubordination, he may avoid court martial and yet be given a bus ticket home to wife and job by his disgusted D.I. He has not reckoned on S/Sgt. Dawson's powers of persuasion.

S.D.I. Dawson tries sarcasm mixed with a taste of the Pits:

"Thank you, Prayso," he says to a recruit who has just botched an evolution.

"Thank you, Prayso!" sings out the wrathful platoon in unison—the only harmony they've managed all day.

"We love you, Prayso," prompts S.D.I. Dawson.

"We love you, Prayso," growls the platoon, as it clumps down the ladder to the Pits for an agonizing session of leg-lifts. . . .

S.D.I. Dawson tries indifference. He musters the platoon outside the barracks and tells the recruits:

"Turn to the right. Now, take off! You're on autopilot."

He walks to one side, studiously ignoring the out-of-step recruits, disdaining to count cadence. He herds them across the access road onto the parade deck.

"In a second, you people, I'm going to tell you to stop. . . . All you little sensitive souls ready? Good, you can stop now. Please sit down."

"You don't want to drill," S/Sgt. Dawson goes on, with heavy contempt. "You don't want to work. Okay, we'll watch the other platoons. *They* want to learn. *They* want to work. You just sit here and see how real recruits train."

And he stalks off.

Returning ten minutes later, S.D.I. Dawson tries ridicule. He points to the other platoons.

"Look at them! They've got pride, haven't they?"

"Yes, sir!"

"They've got snap, haven't they?"

"Yes, sir!"

"You've got pride and snap, haven't you?"

"Yes, *sir!*"

S/Sgt. Dawson laughs nastily. "No, you haven't. You're sloppy. You're lazy and slow. I've seen more snap and pride in Girl Scouts selling cookies door-to-door."

Up till now, recruits have taken for granted that, so long as they commit no crimes or misdemeanors, they will get by. At the end of the week, on TD-11, Lt. Greenburg musters the series to set them straight.

"We don't want those who don't want to be here," he tells the throng seated on the squad bay deck. "We don't want those who lack the motivation to excel. Some of you are belligerent, hostile, and willfully disobedient. We've already got rid of four of you. We're ready to get rid of more. I see the *esprit* of this series going downhill, and I'm here to tell you it's going to stop."

S.S.D.I. Gy/Sgt. Lyons is even more brief and direct:

"We're tired of playing with you people. As of today, I'm instituting trial training. Those on trial training have five days to click to or click out."

From Platoon 1036, three recruits are summoned to Lt. Greenburg's office. They are Privates McClellan, Prayso and Hall. Between them, the three are a catalog of deficiencies the series commander is determined to correct. All have the qualities it takes to make Marines. None is coming close to his potential.

Lt. Greenburg interviews each man individually, reviewing his shortcomings. These are then presented to the recruit as a written indictment, along with the steps which he must take to correct them. His progress will be monitored each day by his drill instructors. If at the end of five days he isn't in step with the rest of the platoon, he will be dropped from 1036, to begin the recruit's life afresh from TD-1 in a new platoon.

Recruit Calvin Hall's performance, Lt. Greenburg notes, is conspicuously below his potential.

"According to your D.I.s' reports," he says, "you are inept at drill, slow to respond to orders, and you fidget in ranks. You have fallen asleep during lectures. You've been openly defiant. If you think this behavior is going to buy you a ticket back to civilian life, you're mistaken. You have the makings of a Marine. You signed up to become a Marine. A Marine is what we're going to make you. We can do it the easy way, or we can do it the Marine Corps way. The choice is yours. . . . Dismissed."

Recruit Hall salutes. He does an about face and marches from the office. His expression is no longer one of cool indifference. He swallows hard.

This bullet's got his name on it.

Following the Leader

To such recent civilians as Private Calvin Hall, "discipline" conjures up a vision of brutalized soldiery marching with leaden precision across a parade ground under the command of a monocled, jack-booted Prussian officer brandishing a riding crop.

To the U.S. Marine, by contrast, discipline is an amalgam of pride, honor, and a sense of fitness. It is the Marine's recognition that, in modern war, with its complicated machines and strategies, its lightning thrusts, its potential for catastrophic mistakes, no individual can fulfill his mission or even survive except as a member of a superbly organized and coordinated fighting force. Discipline is the glue that welds men of diverse backgrounds and capabilities into that fighting force, supple fingers formed into an iron fist.

Americans rightly cherish their constitutional right to do as they please, but on the battlefield the ultimate law is simple survival. Caesar's legions demonstrated the secret of battlefield survival two thousand years ago when they engaged the brave, aggressive, powerful and vastly more numerous Germans, who scorned Roman order and discipline as attributes unworthy of the warrior, and paid for their belief with their lives, liberty and nationhood.

If the ancient Germans lacked discipline, they had no shortage of leaders. In fact, that was their trouble: every warrior acted as though he were leader of an army—an army of one: himself.

Like discipline, leadership has not changed materially down through the ages. According to platoon leaders who engaged in America's most recent and most savage war, the principal ingredients of leadership are four:

CANDOR—telling one's troops what they need to know with an economy of speech, for time on the battlefield is too short to waste on empty words, and lies cause confusion punishable by death.

COMMITMENT—primarily to the buddies with whom one has shared suffering and terror. Men don't fall on enemy grenades to save the lives of strangers, nor do they leave a wounded buddy behind, to die in captivity.

COURAGE—a soldier never knows he has it until he needs it, when it comes unbidden. Courage in the face of certain disaster is stronger than reason, which is why men marvel at displays of reckless valor, and in war it finds so many imitators.

COMPETENCE—without it, there will be no survivors. Nor is competence related to rank, as stupid generals from Varro to Cardigan have demonstrated. In battle, men will ignore an ineffectual captain to follow a sergeant they trust.

Leadership and discipline are timeless virtues. They distinguish a military unit from an armed rabble. In battle, leadership directs most efficiently the energies and valor of a unit toward a key objective; discipline impels the soldier to do exactly what the leader expects of him, for both know that the man who fails in his duty becomes the weak point in the line through which the enemy will plunge, to slaughter the entire unit.

A military unit is formed of intricately assembled parts: one loose nut and everything falls apart. A classic demonstration of this truth came during the invasion of Sicily in World War II. Army paratroops took off from African bases for the first strike against the Germans, overflying the U. S. fleet with its huge landing forces waiting to follow up the airborne assault. Strict orders were issued in advance to fleet gunners to refrain from firing at the low-flying American aircraft. Nevertheless, a nervous gunner opened fire. A few other gunners, persuaded by the fusillade that the planes must be German after all—otherwise why would anybody be firing at them?—joined in the barrage. Soon the entire fleet's guns were blazing away. Every plane in the American air armada, each with crew and fourteen parachutists, was shot out of the sky.

Discipline is thus, in the largest sense, a matter of self-preservation. To instill discipline—the individual's consciousness that order, self-control, pride of unit, and perception that only teamwork can achieve common goals—is the drill instructor's main concern. He accomplishes this difficult task mainly by the force of his own example. The recruits want to be Marines, or they wouldn't be at Parris Island. To the degree that he embodies the qualities of the Marine ideal—pride, competence, endurance, military bearing, willingness to take responsibility and make decisions, confidence, fairness, toughness and fire—most recruits will strive to emulate him. They will be encouraged to do so, moreover, when they reflect that once he, too, was a muddleheaded, left-footed, rabbit-scared recruit, just like them. If he could become the model Marine he so obviously is, they reason, why can't they?

And half the battle is won. . . .

The good drill instructor strives to lead, not drive. Motivation is his crook, as he shepherds his platoon along the rocky path leading to military prowess. Marine history is, perhaps, the single most important factor in forming the recruit's attitudes. Two hundred years of a tradition of success through hard work, indifference to danger, group pride and sacrifice is a powerful inspiration to American youth in search of heroes. The drill instructor's love for the Corps and enthusiasm for his calling are similarly contagious; ideals he attempts to impart to his recruits, who may have encountered very little idealism in civilian life, are positive values that many yearn to believe in and to which those who do wholeheartedly respond.

Patriotism is a motivator especially evident during national crises. The Japanese attack on Pearl Harbor stimulated the enlistment of some 10,000 Marines within three weeks, and the bombing of the Marine barracks in Beirut in 1983 had a similar bracing effect on recruitment.

Sea stories celebrating Marine exploits, whether fact or fiction, are part of the Marine mystique, and serve as bench marks for the recruit's own expectations. They also define Marine standards and values. The protagonist of a barracks' yarn may be a catalog of human frailties, but still redeemed in the eyes of the storyteller and recruit alike when, for instance, he risks his life to save a shipmate in battle.

It is the senior drill instructor who sets the tone for a platoon's sense of order and discipline. Recruits learn fast, and some always test how far they can push the S.D.I. before lightning strikes. In such cases, the S.D.I. has a choice of lines of action.

He may be the patient "Big Dad," pretending to ignore the provocation of a recruit deliberately marching out of step. He treats the problem as if the recruit is merely slow of understanding, and drills him in slow-motion evolutions until the recruit is sick of his childish game. This approach comes naturally to the S.D.I., who by definition is *never* happy with a platoon's performance, which he feels can *always* be improved. On the other hand, he does recognize a platoon's all-out effort, which he may deign to acknowledge with a nod, as a milestone on the way to that unattainable goal, perfection.

To show his displeasure with a platoon's effort, one S.D.I. will take away privileges—causing the platoon guidon with its identifying number to be furled, thus cloaking the platoon in ignominious anonymity, or sweep clean the motivation table on the quarterdeck of the trophies won by the platoon in inter-series competition, to be stored in the gear locker until the platoon returns to his good graces, or clear the "hog board" of pictures of sweethearts and parents. Another D.I. will slow down training, suggesting to the shamed platoon that it is too backward to absorb instruction at a normal tempo. A third may combine military history with a scathing criticism of his platoon by telling his recruits the story of the Duke of Wellington at Waterloo who, when asked whether the appearance of his troops would alarm Napoleon's, replied, "I don't know if they'll scare the French, but by God, sir, they scare *me!*"

Recruits come to Parris Island fully expecting to be kicked and cursed for their smallest transgression. Most are rather disappointed when this doesn't happen—how, otherwise, can they boast later of the hardships they have surmounted? If they are treated with an impartial lenity, there is little to distinguish them from the soldiers who, in the opinion of Marines, are trained for summer maneuvers, not war. The good recruits, moreover, feel cheated when the slackers and incompetents—who number, by the recruits' own estimate, up to a third of an average platoon—cannot be summarily dropped, so the drill instructors can stop wasting time on them and devote their full efforts to training those who actually *want* to be Marines. Almost all drill instructors agree, but they are inhibited by an implicit 15 percent maximum drop rate which reflects Marine Corps policy. Once the worst 15 percent of a platoon's recruits are dropped (more often than not back to a following platoon, not out of the Marine Corps) the remaining malingerers and malcontents breathe easy, knowing that their graduation is virtually assured.

Today's philosophy of discipline in boot training has produced strange bedfellows.

In one bed are the vast majority of drill instructors and recruits, who advocate either mildly coercive measures for lazy, insolent or unmotivated recruits—such as more rigorous IPT, "motivation platoons" reminiscent of the road gang, the elimination of restrictions on the Marines' traditional salty language, and the corrective kick in the pants—or the S.D.I.'s option of unlimited drops. Either alternative, but preferably both, would straighten up or weed out those to whom the Marine Corps is merely a safe haven from the perils of job seeking in the civilian world. Either or both would allow drill instructors to spend their time and talents in training men to defend themselves and their country.

In the other bed are an odd couple. They are the timeservers—men with no burning desire to be Marines, but merely in out of the cold—and senior Marine officers who dictate training policy. The former can and should be dismissed, both from consideration and the Marine Corps. The latter are a more complicated case.

Senior Marine officers not only must scheme and conspire to attract good men to the Corps, a difficult business in this age of the all-volunteer armed services, but stroke the congressmen and senators who appropriate money to keep the Marine Corps operational. Congressmen and senators, in turn, live in fear of constituents who pay their handsome salaries and vote them into, and out of, offices top-heavy with power and perquisites. A considerable number of these constituents are mothers, some with sons at boot camp at Parris Island who construe every correction, punishment or lawful order as a violation of their civil rights. Phones begin to ring. Mothers call congressmen, who call the Recruit Depot commandant, who . . . In the end, the drill instructor is called on the carpet, and sometimes punished for brutality and misconduct—occasionally merited, to the predictable demoralization of the drill instructor corps of six hundred men.

The drill instructors' response is inevitable: to ease up on rigor in training, to "cover ass" with paperwork and pencil whipping, to develop a blind eye toward lapses in discipline and platoon morale which the system gives him no means to correct, and to graduate as Marines men whose attitude and indifferent training will constitute a positive menace to themselves, their shipmates and their units in combat.

The philosophy of those who seek to divorce the rugged realities of war from boot camp, which should train specifically for combat, is akin to the chess grandmaster preparing for a contest by playing Chinese checkers, or the midshipmen for the Navy-Army game with a session of touch football, or dear old Mom for the National Bake-Off by leafing through *The Joy of Cooking*.

Men and women do not run marathons because they're easy, but precisely because they are not. To *run* it takes guts, stamina, and training often involving pain and risk of injury. But the payoff is fitness, confidence, accomplishment and pride.

In the same way, men don't join the Marine Corps because it's easy, but because they expect it to be tough—"No pain, no gain," as the Marines themselves express it. Marine training is a rite of passage to manhood, one of the few left in a soft and flabby America.

The man who is unwilling to lie silent but alert for hours in the mud under pouring rain, go without sleep day after numbing day, march to the limit of his endurance and still plod on, suffer thirst, the bite of insects and blood-sucking leeches, scorching heat, scanty rations, the sergeant's ire and fate's injustice in all its myriad forms, should avoid the Marine Corps: when the shooting starts, he may expect all these things, and if he hasn't already been exposed to them, he will not know, until perhaps too late, whether he can endure them. He slaps at a mosquito; the enemy sniper hears and puts a bullet through his head. He falls out on the withdrawal from Chosin Reservoir—boot camp features no long sub-zero marches—and he spends six years in Chinese captivity where his jailors' proverb, "The more you sweat in peace, the less you bleed in war," is confirmed the hard way.

Tragedy is in the making in today's boot camp, where some men become Marines who shouldn't be, and no man is made nearly as good as he can be. Confusion between "civil rights" and the brutal exigencies of war, and the only slightly less brutal demands of training men to prepare for it, has made it so. Some of these men, as a consequence, will one day die, who, had they been trained to the limits of their endurance, would have lived. It will be instructive to hear what the gold-star mother and her meddlesome congressman have to say on this tragic occasion, and to observe in which direction they will point the finger of blame.

WEEK THREE

Grant, Keane and Townshend: The Invisible Men

"There are recruits who've been in this squad bay for three weeks whose names I don't even know yet," says S.D.I. S/Sgt. Dawson. "They do what they're told, and they do it now. You hardly know they're here."

S/Sgt. Dawson has in mind recruits like Dean Grant, Robert G. Keane III and Andrew Townshend, who to their good fortune have managed to remain all but invisible by staying in the middle of the pack, neither front-runners nor tail-end charlies. In boot camp, where the Pits yawn for the unwary, anonymity can be a virtue.

At PT all three men can do a creditable twelve to twenty pull-ups, more than sixty sit-ups in two minutes, and run three miles in under 23:40 minutes. Above average, but not conspicuously so.

On the evaluation reports the S.D.I. is required to write at least once a week on every recruit, the three jog along comfortably with the crowd. In rifle instruction, manual of arms, uniform, "knowledge," hygiene and inspections, they elicit such comments as "creates no problems," "well-adjusted to life in the military," "no difficulties with drill and rifle manual," and "tries hard."

Trying hard will be crucial this week, a watershed in the career of Platoon 1036. In addition to the S.D.I.'s periodic inspections of the squad bay, their persons, uniforms and gear, from TD-12 through TD-16 the recruits will be subjected to nearly five hours of tests and inspections to determine their progress during the First Phase in physical fitness, close order drill and academics.

Academic tests come first, on TD-14. To prepare his recruits, Sgt. Montgomery, the Heavy A, drills them with dry runs on previous examinations covering the same ground on the major subjects to be tested: the M16A1 rifle, Marine Corps history, first aid, the Unified Code of Military Justice, and interior guard. As always in boot camp, the incentive to excel transcends mere intellectual satisfaction and the thrill of accomplishment: those who fail the trial examinations get quarterdecked. Mountain climbing and push-ups, Sgt. Montgomery has found, exercise the powers of concentration fully as much as the triceps. He has, moreover, added a shrewd refinement to his pedagogy: those who excel on the exam must tutor those who fail; if the failure is repeated, then *both* recruits get quarterdecked.

After the rigors of their cram course, recruits find the actual examination relatively easy. Two hours are alloted to answer eighty multiple-choice questions, the passing grade being sixty correct answers.

Nine questions test their knowledge of the M16A1, e.g., "Which of the following may be used to clean the M16A1 service rifle: #600 sandpaper; WD-40, warm, soapy water; pipe cleaner?"

Seventeen questions bear on Marine history, e.g., "The U.S. Marine aviation tactics learned in Nicaragua is known as: (1) helicopter assault; (b) parachuting; (c) close air support; or (d) high-altitude bombing?"

Seventeen questions deal with first aid, such as: "When utilizing direct pressure in order to control bleeding, you should apply this pressure (a) for 4 to 25 minutes; (b) by squeezing just below the wound; (c) for 1 minute only; (d) for 5 to 10 minutes."

The Uniform Code of Military Justice, which in the naval service replaces Rocks and Shoals, the traditional Naval Regulations, reflects the recent national fixation on "human rights," and not surprisingly is the focus of more questions—

twenty—than traditional military subjects. A sample: "The purpose of the Uniform Code of Military Justice system is (a) to promote good conduct and discipline within the armed forces; (b) to help people in positions of authority; (c) to try someone that is innocent; or (d) to help you get promoted faster?"

Interior Guard accounts for seventeen questions, e.g., "The three purposes of Interior Guard are to (a) stop thieves, protect property, maintain security; (b) preserve order, teach discipline, stop thefts; (c) preserve order, maintain security, enforce regulations; or (d) enforce regulations, protect property, preserve order?"

Discontent among recruits who felt they were being pushed too hard during pre-examination cramming disappears when the results are announced: every recruit in Platoon 1036 passes the First Phase Academic Test. The average mark is 78, and 10 percent of the platoon score a perfect 100. (By contrast, among competing platoons of the series, from 1 to 14 recruits fail.)

Platoon 1036's reward is the first of several trophies honoring that platoon in 1036 Series excelling in various martial skills. The award for academic testing, a pedestal of burnished wood with a small golden eagle flanked by the American and Marine Corps flags, is presented by Series Commander Greenburg to S.D.I. Dawson at a ceremony in the 1036 squad bay, in the presence of the four platoons.

> . . . The platoon's starting off real well. Today we won the eagle for Academic Testing, and 1036's going to take the trophies for pugil sticks, marksmanship and final drill. Every time we go to the head and pass the Motivation Table seeing our awards gives us a lift. They're proof we're better than the other platoons in the series. At least the recruits think so. The D.I.s just laugh, nastylike, and say, "Just wait." I sure wish that was an order. I

heard that the Marine Corps was all "hurry up and wait." Up to now, it's all been hurry up. . . .

Having survived its first test on dry land, Platoon 1036 now faces the challenge of surviving in the water. As the nation's premier landing force, the Marines strive to put their men ashore dry of foot, but on occasion, as during the Battle of Tarawa, survival swimming techniques are the Marine's only hope of getting ashore at all.

The principles of water survival are summarized in the acronym FUSE: "F" stands for full-lung inflation; "U"—utilize the water for support by leaning forward, face down in the water, allowing water pressure to maintain one's buoyancy; "S"—slow, easy movements; "E"—extreme relaxation conserves energy, makes floating effortless. Recruits are warned of the danger of trying to swim in cold water. Movement dissipates heat, more quickly exposing one to chills and cramps; swimming should never be attempted in frigid water unless the swimmer is close to land or rescue.

Most astonishing to recruits is the demonstration of the combat-ready Marine stepping off the twenty-two-foot catwalk to plunge into deep water while fully equipped with utility uniform, boots, flak jacket, pack, helmet and rifle. Remarkably, he remains afloat. Buoyancy comes from the trapped air in successive envelopes in which his gear is wrapped: first his shelter half, then his poncho, a plastic bag, a WP or Wully Peter waterproof bag, and finally the pack itself. If assembled with care, the pack will float for at least five days. With his head protected from enemy flak by the helmet and his rifle resting upon the pack, the Marine who finds himself in deep water can push the pack ahead of him toward the enemy beach, ready to fire if necessary. This method of hitting the beach is used, obviously, only in extremity.

If immersion is unavoidable, and no pack available, the Marine resorts to flotation devices improvised from his camouflage jacket and trousers, with arms and legs knotted to trap air bubbles. Failing all else, the Marine employs the "drown-proof system" which permits the swimmer who has acquired the necessary discipline to resist panic and remain semi-submerged for twelve hours and more. This technique is demonstrated by a Marine who leaps into the water with his ankles roped together and his hands tied behind his back. He'll bob comfortably in the water, raising his submerged head at intervals to take an unhurried breath of air, as long as his audience cares to watch. By mastering such techniques, Marines learn that the sea can be friend as well as foe.

On the subject of survival, a Marine's pay is supposed to be more than a mere lifebelt in today's stormy financial seas. It seeks, in fact, to rival civilian pay scales, and thus attract good men to the service—and keep them. Left unspoken is the hard truth that the service may exact a sacrifice without price: the Marine's life. With that notable reservation, the services are now more generous than at any time in history, as the lecture on Military Pay and Allowances makes clear. Indeed, it sometimes even approaches what civilians would consider a living wage.

A private's base pay is $620.40 a month, which, unaugmented, would put him well below the civilian poverty level. It is also taxable. Various allowances ease the pain. Quarters are provided by the government. These range from one-man rooms for senior NCOs to squad bays holding up to sixty men in two-tier bunks, as at boot camp, for lower ranks. If government quarters are not provided, an unmarried private receives $122.70 monthly—$238.50 if married—toward supplying his own. Privates with more than six months service receive comparably handsome sums for rations—$5.21 daily; travel—$.15 per mile under orders, using his own vehicle (civil servants get $.20½); and uniforms—$9.30 a month.

Every year the Marine Corps Finance Center in Kansas City mails each Marine a "Personal Statement of Military Compensation." Besides basic pay and allowances, it lists the equivalent value of civilian benefits which the military receives as perquisites, such as retirement, medical care and Social Security coverage. For a typical gunnery sergeant with fourteen years service and a family of five, these amount to $3,878.51 in addition to direct compensation of $25,565.84, for a total of $29,444.35.

Low pay notwithstanding, the military life can have its material rewards. Commissaries and post exchanges, not required to operate at a profit, sell a large range of goods at near wholesale prices with no state or federal taxes. Special services provide free or subsidized facilities that include movie houses, golf courses, tennis courts, fitness centers, hobby shops and auto repair shops.

> . . . We had a lecture today on Military Pay and Allowances. The idea they promote is, we get a lot of pay and benefits. This may be true in peacetime. But when the shooting starts, no amount of pay will induce a guy to go out and get himself shot. The forces could save a lot of dough by paying less and going back to universal military service, for men *and* women. Why should us few have to carry the college students and divinity students and conscientious objectors on our backs? All citizens benefit from a strong defense, so all citizens should help provide it. But here we have poor and middle-class guys, willing to take their chances for three squares a day and $620.40 a month. We don't have a single rich boy, and only one college grad. That's democracy . . . ?

Educational opportunities offered enlisted men benefit them personally as well as the Marine Corps through enhanced professionalism. At the most elementary level are correspondence programs of the Marine Corps Institute leading to the equivalent of a high school diploma. The College Level Examination Program tests college-level achievement, for which colleges give commensurate credits. For Marines whose duties permit them to attend night school, often on base, tuition assistance programs help in obtaining a college degree; the Marine pays 25 percent of the cost, the Marine Corps the remainder.

Enlisted men ambitious for careers with the Marine Corps have a number of avenues for advancement. All are highly competitive, however, and meeting program requirements is no guarantee of selection. The Enlisted Commissioning Program (ECP) requires an SAT score of 1000, age between twenty and twenty-seven, and ASVAB of 115 on Electrical Composite. Under BOOST (Broadening Opportunity for Officer Selection and Training) Marines must have a minimum rank of lance corporal, be age nineteen to twenty-four, and have a minimum GCT of 110. MECEP (Marine Corps Enlisted Commissioning Education Program) leads to a college degree and a commission in the Marine Corps for lance corporals and above with one year active service after boot camp, for ages twenty to twenty-five, with a GCT of 120 or above. These requirements are in addition to a clean record, superior performance, and a lot of luck with selection boards.

The institution of choice for career Marines is the U.S. Naval Academy, whose bachelor of science degree in engineering is a traditional path toward a commission and professional preferment. High standards and statutory limitation restrict the total enrollment from the Navy and Marine Corps to eighty-five enlisted men annually.

Educational inducements figured largely in the decisions of Grant, Townshend and Keane to enlist in the Marine Corps.

Grant has been intent on a career with the Corps ever since the eighth grade, when he became a repeat customer for a Marine cinema saga, *The Boys in Company C*. After two years at a community college exhausted his savings, Grant, who has a GT of 121, joined the Corps with the intention of seeking a commission through MECEP. That ambition persists. While working toward the time-in-service prerequisites, he plans to study avionics when he finishes boot camp, in order to work on the HC-53-E *Super Stallion*, the services' biggest helicopter.

Two years in military school gave Townshend a taste of service life, and boot camp has fulfilled his expectations. Following seven weeks in Supply School, he will enter the University of Maryland, where his financial burdens will be lightened by his income as a reservist. On graduation, he may make the Marine Corps his career.

Restlessness, boredom and an appetite for adventure are the burr under the saddle of many civilians, and they spurred Keane to join the Corps. He felt that the self-discipline he sought and found there would help in his studies at Western Maryland College, where he hopes to get a liberal arts degree before going on to engineering studies. Native caution prompted him to join the Reserves, on the premise that, if he liked the training, when his current enlistment expired he could always transfer to the regular Marine Corps to specialize in motor transport. "More than likely I will," he comments, having found that, as tough as boot camp is, its terrors have been vastly exaggerated.

Drill instructors' periodic evaluation reports bear heavily on recruits' careers, including their opportunity for further study upon leaving Parris Island. Every deviation from the behavior norm expected of recruits is documented—which explains the sparse, terse comments on middle-of-the-roaders Grant, Keane and Townshend. The reports are expected to be factual. "Spare us the philosophy," company commander Capt. Ratliff counsels his drill instructors. "If the recruit can't master left face after half an hour of individual instruction, tell us. Also note positive aspects, such as the recruit's attempts to master the evolution on his own during evening free time." Every instance of dereliction of duty and exceptional performance, therefore, is written on the recruit's evaluation card, along with his vital statistics and test scores. They will all be used as evidence for special recognition, as in the award of the coveted blues on graduation day, and for dropping recruits who can't sustain the pace.

Recruit evaluation is more art than science. Most slow recruits can be coached to minimum performance standards, provided they're willing to live by that old Marine Corps maxim: "Nobody ever drowned in sweat." Recalcitrant and aggressive recruits, the D.I.s' despair, often make the best Marines in the Fleet Marine Force, once their combative tendencies can be directed against the environment and the enemy instead of their shipmates. This consideration underlies the policy of giving recruits every chance to develop, before the Marine Corps gives up and sends them home.

Nevertheless, remarkably few recruits favor retention of their insolent, unsanitary, lazy and undisciplined comrades. Their delinquencies visit frequent punishment on the whole platoon, involving not only unmerited pain but a loss of time devoted to training. D.I.s are unanimous in condemning the policy of kid-glove treatment of unmotivated recruits at the expense of the platoon as a whole. Whatever the official policy, the consensus of the squad bay is summarized by Recruit Joseph Weeks, whose father was once a Marine: "I expected—I *hoped*—it would be a lot tougher, both intellectually and physically. Frankly, I'm disappointed."

And a little apprehensive. The half-dozen recruits in 1036 who aren't pulling their weight could be the difference between being in the winner's circle or among the also-rans during the Initial Drill Competition on TD-16, one of the key events in the intraseries rivalry that will culminate on graduation day with the selection of the Honor Platoon.

The evening of Thursday, March 21, finds recruits Grant, Townshend and Keane and their mates spit-shining their boots, polishing their brass and striking while the iron is hot as they press their utility uniforms for the next day's competition. For ease of pressing, the uniforms—with their myriad pleats, ten pockets and twenty-nine buttons—could have been designed by an especially sadistic enemy. Their soft covers are ironed, too, a roll of toilet paper held in the crown for support. The recruits' task is complicated by the prohibition against using starch on the uniform, which was made for the bush, not the parade deck.

. . . Whoever thought up our uniforms should be court martialed and hung. The cami part makes sense. But the material—it's like wearing a plastic body bag. The socks have thick seams—instant blisters. And the boots . . . I won't say anything about the boots because "boots" aren't supposed to cuss. What I can't figure is, if the Corps can spend $20 or $30 million on a fighter plane one infantryman can knock down with a shoulder-fired missile, why can't the government provide that infantryman with decent boots? I figured it out. The cost of one plane is enough to buy 250,000 Marines the best boots ever made, and Marines spend more time walking than in all the planes they ever flew. Write your congressman, Mom. . . .

The next day, the four platoons of 1036 Series sit immobile at attention in the open bleachers of the parade deck, while officers and non-coms occupy the covered reviewing stand. It is a sunny, warm day, and the early-rising sand fleas are already taking their posts aboard forearms and under hatbands.

At 0800 the entire assembly rises to attention to observe Morning Colors. Immediately after, Series Chief Drill Instructor Lyon marches onto the parade deck, where D.I. S/Sgt. Gladden is waiting at Carry Sword. Gy/Sgt. Lyon gives the command for the platoon to be put through its paces. S/Sgt. Gladden orders Platoon 1036: "Fall in!"

The platoon flows from the stands and forms up in four ranks. S/Sgt. Gladden, at Carry Sword, now starts the platoon through the first of the thirty evolutions listed on the card just handed him by S.C.D.I. Lyon. Gladden has prepared the platoon for each of the evolutions, but their order of presentation is, until this moment, unknown.

Some movements, such as "Right, face!" will be simple. Others are far more complex. "Fall in!" for example, the first of the thirty orders, comprises "Report" (by the four

squad leaders who answer "All present!" at two-second intervals), "Inspection Arms!,", "Port Arms!", and "Order
Arms!" Then D.I. Gladden faces about to report to S.C.D.I.
Lyon, who in turn executes an about-face, and marches off
the field, leaving S/Sgt. Gladden in command.

D.I. Gladden commands "Right, face!" and "Forward,
march!" Platoon 1036 swings out across the parade ground,
Gladden calling out the cadence.

For the next twenty minutes, the platoon will be observed
at close range by clipboard-wielding S.D.I.s from the other
three platoons in 1036 Series. They will grade each evolution
as a whole, as well as the performance of individuals. Among
their written criticisms of the various platoons will be "Mis-
alignment of ranks and files on 'Extend, march!'" "Swinging
arms on 'Close ranks!'" "Skipping and hopping on 'Change
step, march!'" "Rifle not along trouser seams, palm not below flash suppressor, on 'Rifle salute!'" "Fingers not lightly
touching, at 'Form for Inspection!'" "Thumbs sticking out at
'Parade rest!'" and "Total confusion, at 'Dismiss the platoon!'"

The judges are merciless. Any deviation from the prescribed movement, however trivial, is noted, although the
grade for each movement will be on the basis of the performance of the platoon as a whole. The criterion is whether the
performance of the platoon reflects correct teaching. The
lowest grade is zero, the highest three, and at the conclusion
of the competition the results are tallied by company-grade
officers and the senior NCO.

The performance of the D.I., meanwhile, is also being
judged. The series chief drill instructor follows the platoon as
it marches and countermarches across the parade deck, grad-
ing S/Sgt. Gladden's command presence, confidence, crisp-
ness of command and military bearing. Criticisms of D.I.s
can be as severe as those meted out to recruits. D.I.s can be
penalized for bouncing the sword, failure to identify recruits
by name in dressing movements, moving the head un-
necessarily, failure to lock sword, and wrong command.

Recruits who were out of step, failed to maintain alignment or otherwise bungled an evolution wait with churning stomachs for the punishment which Argus-eyed S/Sgt. Gladden will inflict, should the platoon fail to emerge victorious. Grant, Keane and Townshend are tranquil. Being of moderate stature, they are inconspicuous in the middle of the platoon. Sometimes it pays not to be outstanding.

The issue is still in doubt when the four units fall in on the parade deck for the award of the trophy. Despite the bite of sand fleas and the searing sun, the recruits and their D.I.s stand as if carved from stone for the ten minutes it takes the judges to compute the scores.

Then Bravo Company commander Capt. Ratliff, followed by his First Sergeant bearing the trophy—two spit-shined field boots on a polished wooden pedestal—advance onto the field. Capt. Ratliff awards the trophy for the Initial Drill Evaluation to Platoon . . . 1037.

That they come in second is no consolation to 1036, especially as every recruit *knows* they should have won. But the slump in morale is only temporary, for the next day brings an event filled with unconscious humor—being taken by their leather-lunged D.I.s to a lecture on, of all things, "Hearing Conservation."

Despite their conviction to the contrary, the D.I.s' bellow is not the loudest sound the recruits will ever hear. Marines work around the world's most persistent makers of noise, not excluding themselves. Jet engines can reach one hundred fifty decibels in noise intensity, three times the threshold of pain (at about one hundred forty decibels; loudness doubles at about every three decibels), and thirty times as loud as normal—that, is *civilian*—conversation.

Marines are exposed to worse still. A rifle or pistol discharge produces from one hundred forty to one hundred sixty-five decibels, to which repeated exposure causes deafness in the unprotected ear. Some Marines neglect using the ear plugs or bulbous ear defenders provided range shooters, on the grounds that the noise causes no pain, until they learn that the level of noise that causes pain is far above that which impairs hearing. Once hearing loss occurs, moreover, it is forever.

The detonation of grenades, the firing of field artillery, the ear-piercing whine of helicopter engines, the explosion of irate D.I.s—all these will threaten the hearing of Platoon 1036's future Marines. But not, however, the voices of Dean Grant, Robert G. Keane III and Andrew Townshend, for in the world of the parade-ground bellow they were the quiet ones.

Gear

By the end of the third week, the invisible men Grant, Keane, and Townshend have broken in their heavy, and very visible, combat boots. In doing so, they have suffered but few blisters and no great discomfort, but in this they are definitely in the minority.

"Once wet, the boots take forever to dry," says a combat-seasoned gunnery sergeant. "When finally dry, they crack. They can't be spit-shined. They have no arch support. The soles wear out in two months of hard marching. Stitching of the sole to the upper quickly gives way. They're too flexible for mountain climbing, as the rubber sole buckles, and too stiff for a good kneeling position on the range. Also, they're ugly as hell."

"I've had my boots for years, on parade and in combat,"

says a lieutenant-colonel in public affairs. "I've never had a blister or any other complaint. They're superb footwear."

Remarkably, the two Marines are talking about the same boot, which has been Marine Corps (and Army) issue since 1961. They're both expressing candid opinions—and they're both right. The boots *are* as miserable for some as they are serviceable for others, which demonstrates the impossibility of two Marines—let alone 200,000—agreeing on anything.

Were military budgets unlimited, perhaps everyone could be made happy with tailor-made equipment. But budget constraints lump Marine Corps procurement with that of the Army, and seldom does the Marine tail wag the Army dog, whose kennel is the Department of Defense's Research and Development Command in Natick, Massachusetts. There, interservice equipment is designed, developed and tested, and commonality is king. Exceptions apply to equipment used exclusively by a single service, such as the LVT (Landing Vehicle, Tank), which the Marines designed, and specialized weapons of the SEALs, Rangers, Lurps, and Marine Force Recon, which each man selects for himself.

Despite interservice rivalries and differing missions, Marines and soldiers are working constantly, if at a glacial pace, to improve the gear with which the men must live and fight. Modifications of the generally—and privately—despised Vietnam era "McNamara boot," for instance, have been in progress since its introduction a quarter-century ago when, as now, its principal virtue was a low ($29.09 today) price tag. The new $52.57 boot has been exhaustively tested in a competition with five other candidates, by 2,400 soldiers and Marines who marched 280,000 miles through mud, water, sand, clay, dense underbrush, rotting vegetation and rock-strewn ravines. It has a softer and more comfortable upper, silicone-saturated leather for water resistance, a "mud-release" sole configured for a better grip with three times the abrasion resistance of the boot it replaces, improved arch support, a higher and padded counter, a firmer toe, speed lacing, and a replaceable heel. And it will last five times longer.

As with all equipment, the boot represents a compromise. The jungle boot with quick-drying canvas top and supple rubber sole is still considered much superior for tropical rain forests, and a cold-weather boot must be issued troops serving in arctic regions, but the new boot will have to suffice for all climatic conditions between these extremes.

Helping guard NATO's northern flank is a new Marine responsibility, and uniform and equipment designs are being perfected in the light of its accumulating experience. A four-layered camouflaged parka will replace the seven-layered parka dating back to the Korean War, and will protect from rain and wind as well as extreme cold, which the Korean-era parka did not. The ECWCS (Extreme Cold Weather Clothing System) parka's fiber-pile liner wicks sweat to a Gore-Tex jacket, allowing vapor to pass to the outer air, but doesn't permit rain droplets to enter. It is comfortable, a third less bulky and 28 percent lighter than former models, and fully protects the wearer in temperatures from forty degrees down to minus twenty-five degrees Fahrenheit. Its cost is approximately the same, but its materials and performance are a generation ahead of the NATO model. The 43,000 parkas needed will be bought at half the price of a single F-18.

Also being designed for cold regions is the shelter half, used to erect tents of variable geometry to house from two to a dozen men. Its advanced materials are lighter in weight, more water-resistant and vapor-permeable than the present canvas shelter halves, practically unchanged since World War I days. In the larger space of the new tents troops will stave off frostbite with an off-the-shelf civilian sleeping bag modified to accommodate a fully clothed, battle-ready Marine. So muddled and torpid is the Pentagon bureaucracy, however, that even this minor modification will take more than three years.

The Marine's weapons are undergoing a similar slow but steady evolution. The standard American infantry rifle, the M-16, is a relic of the early days in Vietnam, when it was adapted from an Air Force Military Police weapon. Millions of complaints later—of jamming, bore-fouling from slow-burning powder, flimsy plastic stock, ridiculous front sights that had to be set with a ten-penny nail, lack of ejector shield for left-handed shooters, a plethora of parts and difficulty in cleaning—led to the adoption of the M-16-A2 beginning in 1985. The A2 puts some grievances to rest. It is accurate to 800 yards, fires a standard NATO 5.56 mm, .223 caliber round that can penetrate half an inch of steel plate, has a solid feel, and is easier to maintain and more reliable. After a quarter-century of research and development, it had *better* be good.

The troops are less certain about the new high-strength kevlar helmet. After all, with its integral liner and cami cover, it can no longer be used to shave or wash socks or cook soup in or to scoop out a foxhole. Nor is it lighter than the old steel pot it replaced. But those responsible for its development argue that it fits better, has a better center of gravity—reducing neck and back aches, and tends to deflect rather than dimple on impact, preventing easy penetration of a rifle bullet or shell fragment. The 200,000-man jury is still out.

Few articles of Marine issue are so heartily reviled as the BDU (Battle Dress Uniform)—the "woodland" camouflage jacket, trousers, and cover. Marines complain that the combination cotton and synthetic material is hot, sticky, doesn't breathe, refuses to dry out, and doesn't hold a press for parades. However, it *does* have superior wear and rip-resistant qualities, features which designers of the new generation of BDUs hope to preserve while ironing out the present wrinkles. The Marine Corps' goal is to issue three distinct uniform styles, specifically for the desert, the arctic, and temperate/tropical climates. The experimental desert uniform, for example, is about half the weight of the present BDU.

Napoleon is supposed to have said (he actually didn't) that "An army marches on its stomach." He *did* say, "What makes the general's task so difficult is the necessity of feeding so many men. If he allows himself to be guided by the supply officers he will never move and his expedition will fail.'' Attempting to reconcile these contradictory observations is one of the dilemmas of warfare.

The Army and Marine solution is to shrink the ration's size and weight to minimum, while preserving its nutritional values. Presto! the MRE (Meal-Ready-to-Eat), field fare considered adequate by some, gall and wormwood by others, and delectable by none. To be fair, however, in variety, caloric content and taste the MRE is far superior to the garrison rations of most of the world's soldiery, and is designed to be fed to troops only under field conditions when serving hot meals is impracticable.

The unheated MREs possess virtues not immediately apparent: being dehydrated, they do not freeze, a weight savings of 20 percent; they can be eaten either dry or reconstituted by adding water; in the ALICE pack, they provide buoyancy for shore-bound assault troops; their tough plastic packaging resists weather's assaults; they have a long shelf life; and at approximately $50 for a case of twelve rations, they are cost effective when compared to the logistical headaches of transporting and supplying field kitchens, and safer than concentrating forward troops to be fed—with perhaps an enemy bombardment for dessert.

The MRE, a package about the size of a VHS videotape wrapped in dark brown plastic, comes in a variety of menus. Typical contents include packets of: (1) four crackers, (2) 10 ounces of meatballs with barbecue sauce, (3) dehydrated potatoes, (4) 1½ ounces of cocoa beverage powder (to be mixed with ¼ canteen cup of water), (5) 1 ounce of grape jelly, (6) a slice of chocolate-raisin cake, (7) ''accessory packet'' containing coffee, cream substitute, sugar, salt, chewing gum, matches and ''paper, toilet.'' Three such rations contain a substantial 3,600 calories (the arctic menu has 4,500 calories). Research is also in progress on an assault food packet.

Battalion commanders decide whether conditions permit setting up field kitchens which can serve hot food and coffee, or whether MREs are preferable. Soon they will have a third alternative: the Tray-Pack. A heavyweight cousin of the TV dinner with a shelf life of two to three years, the thermo-stabilized packs can be dunked in boiling water for immediate messing of twenty-five-men units with food comprising four main groups: meat, dairy products, starches and vegetables, incorporating a carefully calibrated quantity of sodium and other electrolytes to keep the troops in fighting trim. A special vehicle will transport and electrically heat a file-cabinet-sized rack of Tray-Packs en route to forward lines, feed seventy-five men, collect the debris and rattle to the rear, all in the space of half an hour.

That the U.S. Marines and other American forces are superbly supplied and equipped, especially when compared with such armies as the Russian, is beyond dispute. The danger is that perhaps *too much* emphasis and money is placed on creature comforts, which will attract recruits (no worry for the Russians, who compel universal military service), to the detriment of developing the tactics and implements of war and the hardihood of the men who will fight it.

Such considerations do not hasten the languid development of Marine gear and supplies. Nor is there a paucity of material deficiencies demanding attention—lumpy socks fathering blisters, gloves that court frostbite, ponchos that leak under an hour's drizzle, grenades that fail to explode, metal tent pegs to clang in the night and alert the enemy, medieval protection against gas attack, a pistol that has been in use since the decade before the Marine Corps' most senior general was born. But, snarled in red tape as luxuriant as the Amazonian rain forest, whose strangling tendrils stretch from the Pentagon to Massachusetts, progress is an endangered species. It is no exaggeration to say that the time from conception to adoption of a major weapon or piece of equipment can easily span a thirty-year Marine's entire career.

WEEK FOUR

Slaney:
Snap In or
Snap Out

Agreement is hard to achieve among a platoon of sixty-odd men and three drill instructors, but on one subject the members of Platoon 1036 are unanimous: Harris Slaney should be somewhere else, preferably far, far away. Transferred to 1036 on the eve of its departure for the Rifle Range on TD-17, Slaney has already been dropped from two other platoons, and for ample reason. According to nearly fifty evaluations during his month-long career as a recruit, he is a catalog of human frailties and failings.

Though physically fit, with a GT of 127, Slaney has been on the carpet repeatedly for insubordination, insolence, poor performance, belligerence, immaturity, lack of cooperation, disobedience of orders, argumentativeness, lack of motivation, poor hygiene and failure to respond to instruction. He is sly and self-pitying and believes that everyone is against him. In this, and this alone, he is in accord with his shipmates, for Slaney is a lightning rod, and when lightning strikes, the whole platoon is usually burned.

Why is Slaney hanging like an albatross around the neck of Platoon 1036? Because current Marine Corps policy gives every recruit the benefit of every doubt before he is judged hopeless and discharged, even though his presence severely impedes the progress of sixty men intent on training. In theory, drill instructors may recommend such misfits for discharge if counseling, IPT and their pitifully few other means of correction do not avail. In practice, however, they are limited to an implicit attrition rate of 15 percent. If they recommend a greater number for discharge, this is considered by senior officers to be proof, not of recruit stupidity, obduracy, self-indulgence, or plain swinishness, but of the drill instructors' inadequacy and want of effort. It is to protect themselves from such allegations that D.I.s must neglect precious training time to document recruits' deficiencies in painstaking detail.

In the cloistered world of the military, secrets are few and short-lived, and after a few weeks at Parris Island every recruit is fully aware of his "rights" and the limitations of his D.I.s' authority. Bad seeds like Slaney, perceiving that becoming a Marine actually involves effort and sacrifice, and realizing that because they are unwilling to bother their recruit days are numbered, sometimes with calculated malice try to destroy their D.I.s through allegation of abuse and brutality. Slaney boasts to fellow recruits, indeed, that he will goad S.D.I. S/Sgt. Dawson into striking him. Should this happen—should S/Sgt. Dawson even call Slaney what he so obviously is, viz., a contemptible, rotten little punk, the S.D.I.'s exemplary career of eleven years service, with two meritorious promotions, three overseas deployments plus duty at two diplomatic hardship posts, and numerous citations for excellence in his specialty, would come to an abrupt end. By a peculiar inversion of values, the Marine Corps today allows—some officers encourage—raw recruits to ruin the future of career Marines on a single, off-hand and not infrequently false allegation. The allegation may be, "He said 'Goddamit.'" It may be, "What kind of mob *are* you people, anyway?" Or, as recorded during 1036's training period, "[The DI] said, 'You move like a log.'"

Slaney wreaks more havoc than he knows: when other marginal recruits in Platoon 1036 observe his insolence, slack behavior and contempt for authority, and the D.I.s able to respond only with tongue-lashing and IPT, to which recruits become quickly inured, they follow Slaney's bad example, secure in the knowledge that no punishment they can't shrug off will befall them. The infection spreads and morale declines. Thanks to Slaney and a few like him, on TD-17 Platoon 1036 sets out on its route march to the Rifle Range a divided, disaffected platoon.

The ninety-minute conditioning march, along flat asphalt roads through stands of loblolly and slash pine standing eternally at attention, brings the platoon to the Weapons Battalion area, with a series of brick barracks and whitewashed wood temporaries on the left, and five rifle ranges, each half a mile deep, each with fifty firing points, on the right.

Each of the five ranges, with shooters in three fifty-man relays on line, and an equal number in the butts to manipulate the targets, can accommodate an entire series. Beyond the ranges is a vast tidal marsh, where spent rounds fall harmlessly. Between the ranges and the road are small wooden pavilions where individual platoons are taught the rudiments of marksmanship. Between the pavilions and the road is a large greensward where they practice "snapping-in," or dry fire, i.e., "shooting" at targets with empty rifles.

At the Rifle Range, recruits finally begin to appreciate the strict discipline their drill instructors have for the past four weeks striven to impart. In handling loaded weapons that can spit out enough copper-jacketed steel to annihilate a whole platoon in less than five seconds, a momentary lapse in concentration or careless procedure can be fatal. During the next two weeks, therefore, during which 1036 will fire a total of nearly twenty thousand rounds, safety and fire discipline are the recruit's main concern. To ensure the observance of proper precautions until they become habit, recruits are taught to handle their rifles at all times as if they were loaded, reinforcing the old hunter's adage: "The empty gun shoots the loudest."

Of safety measures honed by the experience of two hundred and more years, the Marine Corps emphasizes one above all others, the rigid application of which avoids most firearms accidents: "Never point your weapon at anyone unless you intend to kill him.'' Other basic precautions include the inspection of the weapon before firing, to ensure that the bore and chamber are unobstructed, and never greasing or oiling ammunition, which could result in dangerously high chamber pressures. On the range, the rifle must be carried with its muzzle always pointed toward the sky and down-range; it is loaded only on command from the range tower; except when actually on the firing line, its magazine must be removed, the bolt retracted and resting on a T block—a plastic plug blocking the chamber; and its safety must be engaged. Each of these measures alone ensures a safe weapon. But on the Rifle Range, where rank has no privileges, redundancy is a major concern, and only safety is general.

At first sight, known-distance (KD) marksmanship training with fixed, immobile targets seems an exercise in wishful thinking. In war, after all, troops cannot tape-measure the distance to the enemy, nor does he obligingly stand still, silhouetted against the sky, to be shot at. Nevertheless, long experience has shown that principles learned in known-distance range practice translate into better performance during field and combat firing. Army Rangers, who customarily fire under simulated battle conditions, have in recent years shot the regular Marine KD course after snapping-in instruction, and in every case have bettered their live-fire scores by as much as 30 percent.

Whatever the target, sound marksmanship depends on a few fixed factors: sighting and aiming, shooter's position, wind effects and trigger control. During Grass Week, when recruits spend some forty hours in class and snapping-in, in addition to PT, rifle maintenance and police details, the principles embodying these factors are planted so deep in the recruit's subconscious that, if he next picks up a rifle half a century thence, he will automatically observe them.

. . . I don't know what the other guys have been thinking about this week while snapping in, but when I see that black target on that white barrel, I was wishing it was the backside of the sergeant that recruited me. If I knew marksmanship was going to be like this, I'd have walked right back out the door. Well, maybe not, but this I can tell you: Grass Week is the most boring week of your favorite son's life. Necessary—maybe. But B-O-R-I-N-G. All day long, sighting in on a little black target, squeeze the trigger. Click! Sight in, squeeze. Click! Sight in, squeeze. Click! Get the picture? Well, that's what *we're* supposed to be doing, getting the picture—the *sight* picture. . . .

Sighting and aiming comprise several elements, of which the most important are *sight alignment* and *aiming point*, together making up the *sight picture*.

Sight alignment is the technique of looking through the round peepsight on the M-16 carrying handle close to the shooter's eye, and focussing that eye on the front sight blade, or post. The top of the pinlike post is ideally in the exact center of the peepsight. To hit the target consistently, the sight alignment must be the same for each shot. The aiming point is that point on the target which the shooter intends to hit. That point should be resting precisely atop the front sight blade.

The correct sight picture is thus formed by projecting an imaginary line from the eye through the center of the peepsight, across the top of the front sight, into the heart of the target. Given that miniscule deviations from this imaginary line by any of the four elements—eye, peepsight, front sight and target—can produce wild misses at several hundred yards, and that the KD course involves three targets on each of which the aiming point is different at the various ranges, the need for concentration and painstaking practice is obvious.

Marines must learn to shoot from four positions: prone,

sitting, kneeling and off-hand (standing), each successively affording a larger field of vision—and exposure to the enemy. A change of position, however, places the eye at a slightly different distance from the peepsight, causing the sight to appear larger the closer the eye comes to it. Despite the discrepancy in size, the peepsight must still frame the front sight in its exact center.

The front sight offers additional complications. Since the eye cannot focus on two objects at different distances at the same instant, to ensure accuracy of sight alignment, the eye must be focused on the front sight at the instant the rifle fires. Proper procedure calls for the shooter first to align his sights, focus his eye on the front sight blade, then shift his focus to the target to complete his sight picture. Finally, while squeezing the trigger, he shifts his focus back to the front sight—and prays.

For the increased visibility that comes with successively more elevated positions, the shooter pays the stiff price of exposure to the enemy and reduced stability. The ability of a shooter to maintain immobility depends on the area of his body in contact with the ground; the height of his body, or its center of gravity; the rigid support the arm gives the weapon; and the body area exposed to the wind.

The prone position is the most solid: the body is flat, the elbows planted on the ground, and the rifle steadied by the sling. In the sitting position, the ankles are crossed, and the shooter's triceps rest firmly on his upper shin. The kneeling position elevates the shooter by means of the right foot, resting on the ball, planted between his buttocks; his left arm is wedded to his left knee, but his free right arm no longer offers solid support. Least stable is the standing position. The left arm, resting on a far-from-steady rib cage with its thumping heart and respiring lungs, bears the weight of the rifle; the right, with elbow extended, is horizontal to the ground; and the front end oscillates in a lazy figure eight beneath the target, seemingly the size of a hummingbird's eye. The off-hand shooter must shoot that hummingbird—on the wing.

Wind affects shooting in two ways: it blows the bullet off course, and it buffets the shooter, spoiling his aim. At ranges shorter than two hundred yards, moderate wind has little appreciable effect on a bullet's flight. At longer ranges, the effect increases geometrically. At five hundred yards, it can be significant. The higher the rifle from the ground, similarly, the more pronounced the effect of the wind. Wind which may have negligible effect in the prone position will have *some* effect on the sitting shooter, more on the kneeling shooter, and may actually buffet the off-hand shooter completely off target.

Crucial though these elements are to good shooting, one remains that may be the most vital of all: trigger control. A straining grip on the trigger transmits muscular tension as a shot-spoiling tremor. Jerking on the trigger, the mark of a neophyte shooter anticipating the report of the shot and the weapon's kick, causes the shot to hit low. To avoid these two common symptoms of inexperience, recruits are taught to press slowly and steadily on the trigger so long as the sights are on the target. When they drift away—they will, however expert the marksman—the trigger pull is held, and resumed when the target drifts back into the sights. The shooter must concentrate on his steady squeeze and the sight picture, and the rifle discharge should, therefore, come as something of a surprise.

Full or empty lungs, like a tight trigger grip, tend to produce tremors that disturb the aim. Shooters are taught, therefore, to take a deep breath, expel half of it, then stop breathing while squeezing the trigger.

Theoretically, the precise application of these principles should produce an unbroken string of bull's-eyes. But not within memory has any rifleman shot a "possible"—a perfect score of two hundred fifty, for fifty shots—on the KD course, where combat ammunition with its uneven powder charge is used. Nevertheless, recruits properly trained can approach the scores of veterans after only one week on the grass, provided they listen carefully and apply their lessons in unremittingly serious practice.

For Platoon 1036, the instruction begins Monday, 25 March, on TD-18, at the grim hour of 0700, with a lecture on marksmanship principles and range safety. Other lectures and practice sessions deal with sight alignment and sight picture, the sitting position, trigger and breath control, and loading procedures. Even sling adjustment requires thirty minutes of instruction.

No one has ever called Grass Week fun. On the contrary, Marines of all eras regard the week of snapping-in during boot camp as the most boring of their lives. All the same, snapping-in is considered indispensable preparation for anyone shooting less than "Expert" (a score of 220 or better out of 250), and only those who qualify in this top marksmanship category can forego a period of snapping-in during requalification shooting the following year.

The PMIs (Primary Marksmanship Instructors) of Weapon Battalion have vast experience, high standards, infinite patience, and zero toleration for those who do not do exactly what they're told. They take no notice of individual variations in body build, endurance, temperament or susceptibility to the bites of sand fleas. S/Sgt. Walter Sansbury, the PMI assigned to teach Platoon 1036 to shoot, reiterates procedures with the regularity and precision of a jeweled watch movement, depending on repetition to make the procedures second nature. In describing the sequence of events in firing from the off-hand position, he accompanies each action as he demonstrates it with a terse litany the recruits must commit to memory:

"Snap in!"

"Load and lock!"

"Stand up!"

"Weapon in shoulder!"

"Unlock!"

"Sight alignment!"

"Sight picture!"

"Aim in—well-aimed round!"

"Breath control!"

"Fire!"

"Take weapon from shoulder!"

"Put weapon on safe!"

"Lock bolt to rear!"

"Sit down on ready box, rifle on lap, muzzle pointed down-range!"

"Call your shot! Mark it with a dot in the book!"

"Plot the shot, with number!"

"Reload! Let bolt go home! Tap bottom of magazine!"

"Push forward assist!"

"Stand up!"

"Put weapon in shoulder . . . !"

During snapping-in, S/Sgt. Sansbury repeats this blank verse endlessly, until recruits automatically perform the required movement when their turn comes to do it with live ammunition. The omission then of a single step can render the shooter a "temp fire," or safety violator, resulting in his banishment from the range for the rest of the day or, if the violation is flagrant, causing him to be dropped back to the next platoon to start afresh with Grass Week, a terrible punishment.

S/Sgt. Sansbury also officiates in the recruits' short course in body contortion. The prone position is relatively painless: the recruit lies face down, his body at a forty-five degree angle with respect to the target, rifle sling so tight above the left bicep (for right-handed shooters) as nearly to cut off circulation, cheek bone on rifle stock, nose barely touching charging handle, elbows planted firmly in the dirt—the left one directly under the rifle, heels inboard and flat against the ground to present the lowest possible silhouette, fingers of the left hand relaxed, forefinger caressing the trigger with the feathery touch of a pickpocket.

> . . . They say we practice this long enough, it becomes second nature. They ought to know. But in all the movies and TV I've seen, the four positions

we use are boiled down to two: a guy with a squirt gun shooting from the hip at twenty yards, and a sniper with a rifle and scope taking out a German general at 1,000 yards. The wars I read about these days are all taking place in city streets at 20 yards or at long range with artillery. That isn't the kind of shooting we're practicing. But they ought to know. I guess. . . .

The sitting position is simple in concept, muscle-wrenching in execution. The shooter crosses his ankles while standing and then lowers himself to the ground, his body again at a forty-five-degree angle from the line to the target. He now jack-knifes forward until his triceps nestle firmly against the bony surfaces of his upper shins. He straightens his left forearm to a vertical plane, and "welds" his cheek against the rifle stock. At this point, stomach cramps commonly seize the uninitiated, who straightens up to relieve them, and in the process loses the position that cost him so much pain to achieve.

Both kneeling and standing positions are at once less complicated and more frustrating, due to the loss of stability and, consequently, accuracy. Muzzle drift is marked in the kneeling position, while in the standing the muzzle of even the best marksman is in irrepressible motion. Where the prone shooter's platform is solid ground and that of the sitting and kneeling shooter the firmly planted leg, the off-hand marksman's arm and rifle form a triangle swinging on the shoulder and elbow like an unlatched gate in a stiff breeze. Only the concentration and discipline of constant practice dampens the figure-eight oscillation of the muzzle. Only breath control and gentle forefinger pressure when the target swings into view above the front sight enables the marksman to squeeze his shot into the black.

Platoon 1036's performance during snapping-in suffers from a lack of both concentration and discipline. These are chronic ailments of the snapping-in course, which involves interminable repetition of simple but many-faceted routines. Deployed at intervals in a circle fifty yards across, the recruits practice over and over the techniques they have learned in their lectures, under the unforgiving eye of the man who delivered them, S/Sgt. Sansbury.

They snap-in on miniature black targets painted on an empty white barrel placed in the center of the circle. The targets are scaled down to duplicate the Able, Baker and Dog targets as they will appear at distance of from 200 to 500 yards on the range. Each target has a specific aiming point, depending on the range. The aiming point on the Able target, a twelve-inch bulls-eye, e.g., at 200 yards, is six o'clock, at the lower edge of the black bull. At 300 yards, the aiming point should be a hairline higher, into the black, to compensate for the sag in the bullet's trajectory, which becomes evident at that range.

Practice perfects not only the various steps involved in firing each round, but the four firing positions. As the week drags by, the recruits' muscles stretch to accommodate the abnormal demands made upon them, until the positions become—if not natural—at least tolerable. It is important that the muscles achieve this flexibility, for if pain intrudes during firing, it will distract the shooter from the vital concerns of sight picture and breath and trigger control.

Hour after monotonous hour the recruits sit, kneel, stand or lie prone, peering through sights with sweat-blurred eyes at a bobbing black hummingbird's eye they find difficulty in imagining enemy heads and torsos. Repeating each step, accompanied by a monosyllabic mutter, they load and lock, cram the weapon into bruised and aching shoulders, align the sights, zero in on the hummingbird, breathe in, exhale half, and wait for the snap of the falling hammer.

Some, tiring of the tedium, aim at a passing car or the backside of a D.I. instructing a distant platoon. But S/Sgt. Sansbury and his fellow PMIs see everything, and vengeance is swift. This apparently innocent pointing of an empty rifle at a human target is more than an indiscretion: it is a violation of the first rule of range safety, and will result in banishment from the range for the day, hourly IPT, dropping back to another platoon, or all three.

Playing games is only one mark of the greenhorn of Grass Week. Another, more subtle sign, is the failure to take the Data Book seriously. The shooter is supposed to be looking at the target the instant the rifle fires (flinchers close their eyes, and invariably jerk the trigger and shoot low). Thus he should be able to tell approximately where on the target the bullet would have hit. This position he marks on a small "call" target in his four-by-six-inch spiral-bound Data Book, which is with him at all times on the range. When actual shooting begins, he will be able to tell from his "call" and the actual impact point of each bullet on the target whether his dope—sight adjustment—is correct.

If, for example, his calls at 200 yards are consistently in the black at six o'clock, i.e., dead center, and the shots were actually well-grouped in the four ring 12 inches below the bull's center, his front sights need to be lowered. Each "click" of the front sights moves the point of impact one inch for every 100 yards. Therefore by lowering the sights six clicks, he will move the point of impact *up* 12 inches, placing his succeeding shots—if his aim is consistent—in the center of the 12-inch Able target.

The same procedure applies to the rear peepsight (one click right or left changes the point of impact 1 inch per 100 yards of range), which compensates both for the characteristics of the rifle and the shooter's personal aiming idiosyncrasies, as well as the wind that happens to be blowing across the range during firing.

Reading the wind is an inexact science. Red flags mounted on poles at either end of the range indicate firing is in progress. They also serve as rule-of-thumb wind gauges. The flag blown eight to ten degrees from the vertical indicates wind at two to five miles per hour; this translates into zero clicks of windage at 200 yards, zero to one clicks at 300 yards, and one to two clicks at 500 yards. At the other end of the scale, when the flag whips out horizontally, the wind ranges from 15 to 25 miles or more per hour. At 200 yards, two to three clicks are set on the peepsight, while at 500 yards, five to eight clicks.

By TD-21, the lessons learned so far finally begin to sink in. On the 1000-inch Triangulization Course, recruits fire at diminutive targets simulating ranges of 200, 300 and 500 yards. These ranges preview the KD course they will shoot in a few days, during Qualification Week. If their firing technique is consistent, they will get a nicely grouped series of hits on the targets. By applying the proper number of clicks of elevation and windage at each range, they will move these groups into the black. "Kentucky windage," where sight adjustments are made by intuition rather than changes in the rifle's sights, is the mark of a novice, and its reward on the range is consistency of another sort: repeated poor scores.

Whatever he may compile on the range, Slaney's score has sunk to zero during Grass Week among his shipmates, to whom every day is Qualification Day in matters of teamwork and platoon pride. Slaney has been counseled by his D.I.s. He has climbed a dozen Everests. He has been cursed and shunned by other members of Platoon 1036. None of this has dented his obdurate contrariety. On the evening of TD-21, nature takes a hand. A freak tempest in the squad bay during the night saturates his field jacket with foul-smelling mud, and fills his boots—and, remarkably, his alone—with water. The hint is ignored. When TD-22 witnesses no improvement in Slaney's attitude, the evening brings a message he cannot fail to understand: in the darkness several of his shipmates entertain him at a blanket party. On the morrow, Slaney is sore-ribbed and puffy-faced.

. . . Had a little excitement last night. Couple of the guys beat up on Slaney, a real jerk who's been getting the whole platoon quarterdecked. We—I mean they—finally had enough. They tried a couple of hints. Slaney can't take a hint, so we gave him a hit. After lights out and the duty D.I. was asleep in the D.I. house, we punched him out a little. Not much, understand. Just enough to let him know how we felt. He squawked pretty loud, but not loud enough to wake up the D.I., who must be a very sound sleeper. I guess we were lucky, because Slaney could have alleged on us. But he didn't. . . .

As Platoon 1036 has had enough of Slaney, so has Slaney had enough of Platoon 1036. He refuses to train, refuses to fire the KD course the coming week.

S/Sgt. Dawson forthwith recommends Slaney for immediate ELS. That evening finds Slaney at Casual Company, awaiting discharge with fellow malcontents, malingerers and misfits.

Reminiscing on the eve of being sent home the following week, Slaney admits that "Maybe if somebody had kicked my ass good at the beginning of training, before I got into the habit of getting into trouble, everything would have turned out all right. Some people need that, you know, and maybe I'm one of them. It could have straightened me out."

His face is shadowed by misgivings, but only briefly.

"Anyhow," he says, "I won't have to sleep in a room anymore with sixty guys belching and farting and snoring. Two days from now I'll be sleeping with my Suzie. I'm going to go back home, smoke a lot of dope, drink a lot of booze. Then in about six months, when I've had a good rest, I'll join the Army or Coast Guard."

Good luck, Army. . . . *Semper paratus,* Coast Guard. . . .

Trojan Horse

That the short and dismal career of Private Harris Slaney as a recruit lasted as long as it did was thanks to the *Standard Operating Procedure for Male Recruit Training*, SOP for short, the drill instructor's bible. Like the United Nations Declaration of Human Rights, it is an attempt to dictate morality. Like that Declaration, it is windy, naive, and based on debatable principles. The Declaration fails to create virtuous governments and peoples; the SOP fails to create outstanding Marines.

The SOP found its genesis in tragedy, and tragedy may be its legacy.

An ill-considered night training exercise in 1956 at Parris Island by a Marine drill instructor caused the death of six recruits, when the marshland through which his platoon was marching was suddenly inundated by unexpected tides. Lengthy congressional hearings ensued. Impassioned pleas for human rights drowned out consideration of the need for the tough and realistic training that through history had made the U.S. Marines the nation's one and only force in readiness. Certain politicians suggested that Marine boot camp be abolished and replaced by an all-services recruit training program. Aware that this dismemberment would vitiate two centuries of fighting tradition and kill the Corps, alarmed Marine leaders hurriedly concocted policies designed to blunt congressional criticism. The SOP was born.

The new system, codifying every phase of recruit instruction, drastically reduced the drill instructor's role and authority. Over each four platoons, or series, a junior officer was assigned to ensure that such an incident as the Ribbon Creek disaster did not recur. Nevertheless, it did, in 1976, at the Recruit Depot in San Diego, when an apparently retarded recruit died as a result of pugil stick practice. Another outcry was heard from Congress, which weighed in with a 577-page report.

Strike two against the Marine Corps.

A revised and expanded SOP called for the assignment of a *second* officer to supervise training, still more restrictions on drill instructors, more watering down of recruit training. Today, a decade later, the Marine Corps—noting with frustration the absence of Congressional concern about the frequent deaths that occur during Army training, not to mention the dim prospects in battle of men trained to inferior standards—waits with resignation for a called strike three.

The 278-page SOP is a marvel of wrong priorities, bureaucratic nit-picking, triviality and outright nonsense. For the Russians, East Germans, Vietnamese and others for whom war is a nasty and brutal, but unavoidable, reality, the Marine SOP must provide comfort and a lot of laughs: a military organization that shackles itself with such sophomoric restraints, they cannot but conclude, need not be taken seriously.

In today's Marine Corps, a recruit who is "verbally or physically abused" by his drill instructor must report the incident to the Series officer, who will punish the offender and guarantee that the recruit suffer no retaliation. The SOP needs approximately 350 lines of text to say this. Yet it devotes to the vital subjects of interior guard, close combat, safety, health and *esprit de corps,* respectively, only 33, 14, 11, 15 and 5 lines.

Similarly, the policy on training in hot weather could be

summed up: "When recruits display the well-known signs of
heat stress, stop training." The SOP requires 13 pages, about
520 lines, quantifying the unquantifiable—for human toler-
ance of heat is widely variable—to tenths of a degree. It en-
joins the drill instructor not to trust his intelligence and
experience, but blindly follow a regulation that has little rele-
vance in daily life—America would starve were the SOP applied to its wheat farmers harvesting under the summer sun—
and none at all to the realities of battle.

The paperwork the SOP generates is awesome. Some 15
separate reports are required of each training platoon, ranging
from Recruit Abuse Report and Initial Hygiene Inspection
Report to Wet Bulb Globe Temperature Report. In the First
Phase, *each* recruit must be evaluated *daily* for discipline,
grooming, hygiene and *esprit*. By the Third Phase, he will be
the subject of periodic evaluation under *five* headings: Mental
Capability (the drill instructor chooses seven traits from precisely seven pairs, e.g., "smart/thick"); Emotional Maturity
(11 pairs, e.g., "poised/confused"); Personality/Character
(18 pairs, e.g., "humble/conceited"); Appearance (11 pairs,
e.g., "attractive/unattractive"); and Physical Attributes (9
pairs, e.g., "powerful/impotent"). *(Impotent?)* The senior
drill instructor, in addition to filling out Recruit Evaluation
Cards, must maintain the Platoon Log Book, Daily Platoon
Log Sheets, Platoon Roster, Sick Call Log, and Pick up/Drop
Log. This paperwork absorbs fully half of the one-hundred-
odd hours the S.D.I. spends weekly with the platoon.

The SOP takes nothing, however trivial or obvious, for
granted. In the case of accidents, "Casualties of all types will
receive immediate attention and take precedence over *all
other activities*." Also, "Duty houses will be neat and clean
at all times." And "When more than one platoon must cross
the Boulevard de France or Wake Boulevard in the vicinity of
the 3rd RTBn PT field, the first platoon will post road guards.
These road guards will remain in position until the last platoons of the formation or Series has crossed. Once the last

platoon has completed its crossing, road guards will be re-called. The road guards will double time and join the end of the last platoon."

Concerning PT, the SOP finds it necessary to recite twelve "do nots," such as "Do not have recruits lie on hot, cold, wet, hard or rocky surfaces." It outlines an eleven-step procedure for dealing with incoming telephone calls. *Thirteen* caveats apply to IPT, including "no PT in closets, heads, gear lockers, showers, D.I. houses, passageways, ware-houses, or behind racks." (By implication, therefore, PT is allowed on pitched roofs, under the commanding general's desk, and in the middle of Guadalcanal Street during full moon.) D.I.s are reminded that "ammunition, blackjacks, brass knuckles, knives, explosives and firearms, except those issued for training," are forbidden.

The drill instructor not trusted to lead his men safely across the street is the same non-commissioned officer who is ex-pected to lead his men safely through enemy fire. But of course, this apparent contradiction is not real. In battle, suc-cess—his men's survival and completing the mission—or failure will judge him. In battle he is alone.

In boot camp, though, generals and politicians conspic-uously absent from the front lines in time of war are watching him. Here he must "cover ass," writing reams of bilge to prove he did not violate the most piddling provision of SOP. If he even seems to—if, for example, a recruit who drops his rifle in the mud claims the D.I. said "That was stupid!"—and the recruit makes an allegation of verbal abuse, swift action follows. The drill instructor is summarily suspended from all duties and returned to quarters, pending an investiga-tion which may last anywhere from three days to two months. If "abuse" is proven—if, for example, he actually said, "That was stupid, stupid!"—then he will probably be fined, lose all opportunity for meritorious promotion, and per-haps even be deprived of his drill instructor's rank and priv-ileges.

Trying to make Marines of civilians while fighting a rear-guard action against childish and whimsical regulations devours drill instructors by the score. Offhand or malicious allegations by recruits have threatened or destroyed the careers of dozens of exemplary NCOs, often with outstanding combat records and years of unblemished service behind them. To cast aside such a Marine because of the accusation of an unproven recruit, who statistically stands barely a fifty-fifty chance of still being in the Marines nine months hence anyway,* is not only lethal for morale, but bad management. As a result of such harassments, perhaps unparalleled in the history of armed services, the enlisted ranks have become spoiled, undisciplined and demoralized, while invaluable NCOs, the backbone of any military service, are leaving the Marine Corps in ever-increasing numbers.

The SOP represents the official view that NCOs cannot be trusted to instruct the men with whom they will face the enemy. In today's Marine Corps, trust reposes, not in the hearts of men, but in a collection of fatuous regulations. An SOP mentality has taken command, and its ultimate effect cannot but be disaster on some future battlefield. Marines are being indoctrinated from boot camp, and Marine officers from The Basic School, that covering ass is the only way to survive and prosper. Where regulations cover every exigency, imagination and flair—the Marine's secret weapons—languish and atrophy. Dumb obedience to regulations becomes habit, eventually to emasculate the fighting man, leaving him little better than a rabbit-scared petty bureaucrat.

In Beirut in 1983, Marines were ordered by distant commanders to relax security precautions and customary vigilance so as not to annoy desperate men intent on taking their lives. The officers on the scene assented to this criminal dereliction of duty, reflexively protecting their rears and careers instead of their men. Everybody was happy. Everybody was covered, including 251 young Marines, covered by six feet of dirt.

---

*Attrition in boot camp averages 15 percent; of those who *do* graduate, 38 percent will not complete a year's service. Total first-year attrition: 47 percent.

WEEK FIVE

Charneski: Shooting for the Possible

Marine *esprit* is hard to kill and, despite the enervating effects of the SOP, it manages to survive, a fertile oasis of inspiration in a desert of puerile and sterile regulations and barren bureaucracy. For Marines, *esprit* is embodied in a single word, "motivation," which cascades ceaselessly from the lips of officers, D.I.s and recruits alike at Parris Island. It is the acme of Marine virtues. A recruit may be slow, uncoordinated and lack formal education, but so long as he is motivated, he may—and probably will—become an excellent Marine.

Albin Charneski is motivated. A D.I. will give the command "Attention!" and leave the squad bay. As the hatch closes behind him, eyes begin to wander, heads to turn, fingers to twitch. Whispers float down the long passageway between the twin ranks of racks. Coughs, belches and guarded laughter break the quiet. Shoulders slump. But Charneski doesn't stir. He stands at stiff attention, eyes front, just as if the S.D.I. stood before him, daring him to blink an eye.

Charneski, a tall, serious young man from Fort Lauderdale, Florida, who speaks with careful deliberation, is a pick-up from the Physical Conditioning Platoon, to which he was sent by Platoon 1025 for failure to do a minimum of forty sit-ups in two minutes on the IST. Married for a year-and-a-half, with a year at Ohio State and a two-year degree in photoscience from the Art Institute of Fort Lauderdale behind him, Charneski enlisted with the view of making the Marine Corps his career, preferably as an officer.

His prospects are bright. A GT of 122 and his academic background encourage Charneski to apply for the Marine Corps Enlisted Commissioning Education Program. If he succeeds, he will be able to enter one of twelve approved universities, receive 75 percent of all his college expenses plus his regular pay and allowances, and study either science or engineering. Charneski is serenely confident that, once admitted, he will excel in his studies and thus be eligible for meritorious promotion to NCO rank even before entering Officer Candidate School upon college graduation.

Charneski's first opportunity to show that he is officer caliber comes in Week Five, during rifle qualification, for it is axiomatic that Marine professionals be excellent marksmen. Should Charneski fail to qualify, or shoot a minimal qualifying score, his chances of becoming a commissioned officer would be virtually nil. This is not, surprisingly, because the Marine Corps demands that its officers be dead shots, but because failure to achieve a high score on the range is evidence of resistance to instruction. Marine marksmanship training has been so perfected over the years that any normal young man with good eyesight can be taught to shoot to Marine standards, provided he listens, thinks, and trains hard. Marines who won't listen, can't think, and are disinclined to work hard don't become officers.

Neither do those who don't have energy and endurance. Those qualities are especially essential during Qualification Week, when recruits are on their feet—when they aren't sitting, kneeling or prone—from 0330 until Taps.

Early Reveille permits recruits to finish their morning routine and be on the range by daybreak. By 0600, the first shooters are on the firing line. Of the five ranges—Able, Baker, Charley, Dog and Echo—1036 Series occupies the fourth, Dog Line. Half the series will shoot in the morning, the other half during the afternoon. The two nonshooting platoons work in the butts, raising and lowering, marking and pasting, the targets.

All five lines run parallel to the main road, Wake Boulevard. The 500-yard line, about 200 yards beyond the snapping-in sheds, is first. Then come the 300-yard line, the 200-yard line, and finally the butts, beyond which is Ribbon Creek and a deep stretch of estuarine marsh inhabited by alligators, moccasins and clouds of stinging insects. Down the center of each range runs an asphalt road, along which the rubber-tired two-story range tower, controlling all activity, is trundled from one line to another by six muscular recruits.

Not until the pit crew is in place, and the butts sealed off until firing is terminated for the morning, does the first relay of shooters advance to the firing line. Here each man takes his place at one of fifty numbered firing points, twenty-five on each side of the tower road; he will fire on the corresponding numbered target. That target will shortly come into view from behind the berm, a mound of earth shaped like a long loaf of French bread which protects the Pit crew, and is raised to the same ten-foot elevation of each of the three firing lines.

Every movement on the range is choreographed like a ballet in slow motion. The accent is on slow; events happening fast on the firing line are mostly accidents, generally avoidable. All shooters do the same thing at the same time, and only on specific orders that blare through the tower's loudspeakers at an amplitude that overpowers the drumbeat of rifle fire and pierces the ear plugs each shooter wears to protect himself from high-frequency sound. Deliberation governs every move, and a pith-helmeted coach is assigned to every four shooters to ensure strict observance of safety measures. Any deviation in routine will also be detected and corrected by monitors in the tower.

To provide base line data on his rifle, the shooter cranks in elevation of twelve clicks up, and windage of seventeen clicks to the right. This setting will put him somewhere on the Able target. He then fires ten well-aimed shots from the prone position. After the first three, for which he is allowed one minute to fire, the target is marked and scored. He repeats the string. Again the target is marked and scored, and similarly after a third string of four shots. These should comprise a tight group that, when corrections are made in elevation and windage, will put all succeeding shots from this range in the black. The corrections, once made, will constitute the setting on which all further sight changes, for wind and distance, are based.

Recruits from 1036, beginning their strings on the 200-yard line, have already blackened their front sights over a smoking smudge pot to minimize glare, and now tighten their slings around the upper arm for the first series of shots. These will be at the Able target with its 12-inch bull's-eye. Each recruit will fire from the sitting, kneeling and off-hand positions, and have twenty minutes to squeeze off five shots in each. By his side is his Data Book. After each shot, just as he practiced so tediously during Grass Week, he will mark his "call" target with a dot to indicate where he *thinks* the shot went. After the pit crew marks the shot on the target with a round spotter and scores it by means of a raised disk in front of the target, the shooter marks the *actual* point of impact on a large replica on the same Data Book page, with the number of that shot. A comparison between calls and actual hits, if each is consistent, allows the shooter to make fine adjustments to his sights that will, he fondly hopes, keep him in the black.

The M16A1 uses copper-jacketed .223-caliber ammunition, a high-velocity shell that is scarcely larger than the .22-caliber bullet often used in varmint guns, but can be lethal in battle. The instant the lightweight bullet hits a leaf, or even clothing, it tumbles, cutting like a buzz saw. The cost of the ammunition for the fifty rounds a recruit shoots each day on the range is between $15 and $20. Coaches are responsible to make sure each round they dispense is actually fired, and that no stray rounds leave the range.

As the shooters take their positions on the firing line, the second relay sits on a line of ready boxes ten yards behind them, and the third relay waits on the ready bench yet another ten yards to the rear. The recruits on the ready boxes mark the score of the shooter during slow fire. Slings adjusted on their arms, dope on their rifles cranked in, they are ready to move into place the moment the preceding relay has ceased fire. While waiting, they observe safety regulations by keeping the T-block in the rifle breech, and the rifle itself pointing down range.

After each relay has shot at 200 yards, the entire firing party—tower and all—moves to the rear to the 300-yard line and, when all relays have fired there, back to the last position 500 yards from the targets. Only when the tower announces "Cease fire," and all T-blocks are in place, ammunition secured and the line cleared, is the pit detail permitted to emerge from the butts and join the other platoons for the midday break.

> . . . Today we finally got to do what I came to P.I. to do—shoot! You aren't a Marine until you can shoot, and shoot straight, so I guess you can call me about three-quarters of a Marine: I shot 188 out of 250 possible. Didn't qualify, but I get other chances this week. It gives you a lot of confidence to lay there on your stomach, the length of five football fields away from your enemy, and know that you can kill him—seven times out of ten . . . if he stands up . . . and doesn't move . . . and isn't shooting back. . . .

In the afternoon, positions are reversed, the shooters of the morning descending to the butts to manipulate, mark and score the targets, while the morning's pit gang fires. The butts, protected by the ten-foot thick berm, is a tunnel of concrete open on the side facing away from the shooters. From its shelter, recruits operate the targets. The Baker and Dog targets are six feet square, while the Able target is six feet high by four feet wide. All are made of wooden frames covered with cheesecloth upon which is pasted the paper target, renewed each week on the morning of Qualification Day.

The targets are fixed to an inverted U-shaped mechanical hoist, so that as one target rises into view the other, counterbalancing it, sinks into the butts for marking.

In slow fire at 200 yards, e.g., the shooter fires on the Able target with its 12-inch bull's-eye. The moment the hit is observed by the target's two-man crew, they lower it, causing the Dog target—a solid black head-and-shoulders silhouette, to rise in its place. Its appearance tells the shooter that he has hit the target, and that his shot is now being marked and scored.

Within thirty seconds, if the target crew is alert, they will have marked the bullet hole with a 6-inch-round white spotter in the black bull's-eye (a round *black* spotter on any other hit), and raised the target again. The spotter shows the shooter exactly where his shot went. But he usually cannot tell what score he's made unless the white marker denoting *five* is in the bull.

The score is now indicated as the pit crew raises a disk mounted on a long wooden handle in front of the target. If the shot is a bull's-eye, the white side of the disk, indicating *five,* is displayed. If the hit went in the *four*-ring, the red side of the disk is placed over the bull's-eye; if a *three,* the red disk is high to the right; if a *two,* the red disk is high to the left. There is no *one,* and a miss of the target—*zero*—rates "Maggie's Drawers," the red disk (it used to be a red flag, hence its name) drawn slowly across the face of the target.

After marking, with the spotter still in place, the marksman shoots again. The target is then run down and the spotter removed from the old hole, which is pasted over. The appropriate spotter is now put in the new bullet hole, and the target run back up.

The sound of a bullet striking the paper target is like a sharp hand-clap, while the actual report of the rifle firing several hundred yards away resembles popping corn. But these faint sounds are almost unheard in the butts, a bedlam of purposeful, feverish activity.

The two recruits manning each target constantly shout encouragement to each other as they work, for the best crew that day, in the opinion of the pit boss, gets to make a phone call home that night. Hoists rattle up and down, and the pit boss bellows instructions in a continual stream over the bull horn to his fifty teams, which slap at face and arms in a futile attempt to ward off the legions of sand fleas, flies and mosquitos rising like a mist from the marsh just behind them. It's hot, nasty work, but not inherently dangerous. The only tragedy occurred when the son of Walter Winchell, the late radio commentator, as a recruit in the butts during the Korean War, was showing off by chinning himself on a target beam. Just as his head appeared above the beam, a bullet squeezed off on his target killed him instantly. The main complaints are more prosaic: fatigue, bug bites, stiff necks and aching eyeballs from squinting into the glare of the sun off the white target.

On the firing line Monday, 1 April, the recruits from 1036 are nervous.

S/Sgt. Dawson says, knowingly, "Today they'll forget everything they've learned during Grass Week. But by Wednesday, they'll settle down."

His prophecy is fulfilled. For the most part, scores are disappointing, and on more than a few occasions the shooters are treated to the spectacle of Maggie's Drawers. But as the week progresses, the recruits settle into a routine, learn that the kick of the M-16-A1 is gentle, that concentration on the principles they learned during Grass Week will put them in the black. Scores pick up. Charneski gets news that his wife has just delivered a baby girl, and makes it a perfect day by shooting 228, well above the minimum Rifle Expert score of 220.

This week the recruits shoot the KD course on three successive days, leading up to Prequalification Day on Thursday, and Qualification Day on Friday.

The KD course consists of fifty rounds fired at three targets from three positions, both slow and rapid fire. From 200 yards, shooters have twenty minutes to fire five shots from each of three positions—sitting, kneeling and standing—at the Able target, whose bull's-eye, *four-* and *three*-circles are, respectively, 12, 24 and 36 inches in diameter. From the same position, they then shoot ten rounds rapid fire in one minute, sitting from an initial standing position, at the Dog target, a head-and-shoulders silhouette 26 inches wide, with the *three*-circle 50 inches across.

Moving back to 300 yards, they have five minutes to shoot another five shots, sitting at the Able target, and ten shots at the Dog target rapid fire, from standing to prone, in one minute. On the last firing line, at 500 yards, they have ten minutes to fire ten shots at the Baker target, a silhouette of a head and torso 20 inches wide by 40 inches high, on which a direct hit scores the maximum five points.

Rapid fire requires a marksman to start in a standing position from which, on the command "Commence firing," he sinks either to the sitting (at 300 yards) or the prone position (at 500 yards), loads his rifle with a magazine of five rounds, and squeezes them off before ejecting the empty magazine, reloading, and shooting off the other five rounds. After allowance is made for getting into position and loading the piece, about four seconds remains for each aimed shot. For trained shooters, this is more than adequate, if they control their breathing. Time is lost by breathing between each round, because the rise and fall of the lungs causes a corresponding rise and fall of the rifle muzzle, requiring a new aim. To conserve precious seconds, the shooter is counseled to take a breath, release half of it, fire three rounds, then take another breath, release half of it, and fire off the remaining two rounds.

Rapid fire is scored after ten rounds have been fired, with ten spotters marking hits, and disking carried out in the usual way, beginning with the white *five* disk for the bull's-eyes. If the shooter has hit *all* bulls, the white disk is twirled in front of the target.

Because of the constant din of firing, communication be-

tween the coach of each four shooters and the tower is carried
on by signals. The variety of signals represents a catalog of
what can go wrong on the range. A coach's foot on the ready
box, his fist upheld, means "Redisk shot." His foot on the
box, hand waving, means "Disregard the last shot" (somebody shot by mistake on this target). His foot on the box, his
pith helmet raised in the air, tells the tower to have the butts
raise the target, as another shot must still be fired on it. A
coach's arms and legs spread-eagled is a call for a total score
from the butts, where a duplicate—and the official—score is
marked. Crossed arms summon an armorer—one is on hand
whenever firing is in progress—to repair a malfunctioning
rifle. Feet apart, arms spread diagonally, signals an "alibi"
due to a malfunctioning weapon, allowing the recruit to re-
shoot. Feet apart with folded arms tells the pit crew (via the
tower) to speed up its marking and scoring.

> . . . People think of Marines as fighters, and
> that's what they are, of course, or I wouldn't have
> joined, but they do a lot of coolie work too. Shine
> shoes, clean heads, swab decks, polish brightwork,
> work in the scullery, things like that. Like working
> butt detail. Constant noise of targets rattling up and
> down, the bark of the pit boss, the slap of shots
> hitting the paper target and recruits swatting sand
> fleas, sweat, aching muscles, thirst, quarterdecking
> for recruits who foul up, the burning sun—that's life
> in the pits. Ever see the pits in the recruiting
> brochures . . . ?

At 0600 Qualification Day, Platoon 1036 is on the firing
line. The firing of the previous four days won't count today,
but the habits of sling adjustment, picture sighting, breathing
and finger squeeze will. A superstition that good shooting all
week will be counterbalanced by failure to qualify today
gives many shooters jitters to add to their natural apprehen-

sions. Marines are expected to be riflemen before all else, and the expert shot has a distinct advantage over the Marine who merely qualifies. A high score today, therefore, will be a big step along every recruit's career path. Private Albin Charneski is confident he will take that step, for he has been firing well the past four days, and believes that experience provides a more reliable forecast than old wives' tales.

The weather is good—and bad. At this early morning hour it is cool and comfortable. Also, the raised red range flag, indicating firing in progress, hangs limp, a sign that wind will neither deflect the bullet nor buffet the shooter's body. On the other hand, the bright rays of the morning sun reflect off the rifle's flash suppressor, adding to the glare of the cloudless sky and the white target itself. And each shooter has his own private cloud of sand flies circling about his head, distracting him with painful bites as he concentrates on his sight picture.

The voice of the Tower NCO booms out across the 200-yard firing line:

"The first relay move up to the firing point and get yourself a good sitting position. Lock your bolt to the rear and remove your T-block. Aim in and make sure you're aiming at your *own* target, and check your position and sling. Get a natural point of aim.

"Second relay, move up to the ready box, then sit down on the ready box, and place the rifle butt between your feet. All shooters should have their loop sling on their arms.

"The first stage of fire is the 200-yard line slow fire. Fire five rounds in the sitting position with a time limit of five minutes, and a wind value of zero.

"On the firing point, with a magazine and one round—load!

"Is the line ready? Ready on the right? ready on the left? [Coaches indicate all shooters are ready.] All ready on the firing line.

"When the target appears, commence firing!"

The pit NCO waits three seconds, and orders all Able targets raised.

For the next three hundred seconds, the crash of ragged musketry resounds up and down the firing line from the muzzles of 50 M-16-A1s. As each target is holed, it is quickly lowered and spotted, raised and disked, and the shooter's back-up relay marks the score while the shooter himself adjusts his aim—if he has fired out of the black—for the next round.

When precisely five minutes have passed, the Tower NCO orders:

"Cease fire! *Cease fire!* Unload and lock. Insert T-blocks. . . . Coaches, check all weapons. Is the line clear? Clear on the right? Clear on the left?"

The coaches signal the line is clear, and the Tower NCO repeats his sequence of commands for the kneeling and off-hand positions.

During firing, the coaches are closely observing the recruits assigned to them. If a recruit has misfired due to a malfunctioning rifle, a misfeeding magazine or an imperfect round, the coach raises his cover to notify the Tower. After the malfunction has been corrected, the Tower allows the recruit to shoot compensatory "alibi" rounds beyond the time limit.

There are also "pit alibis," such as when, after rapid fire, a target is found with more than ten holes—indicating that somebody fired on it by mistake. In this event, the lucky shooter whose target it is receives credit for the ten *best* shots (the confused shooter whose target lacks the full ten bullet perforations gets only what can be scored).

The coach, meanwhile, corrects deviations from correct technique. A recruit may be counseled: "Touch the tip of your nose to the charging handle. That way you'll have the same eye relief and stock weld for each shot."

Another will warn: "Don't anticipate by leaning into the shot in off-hand. If you do, you'll shoot low and hit the berm every time. Remember, you can't afford to miss the target completely, because it'll take two bull's-eyes to make up for that Maggie's Drawers in order to maintain your qualification average," which calls for an average score of nearly four on every shot. A coach's frequent comment to a recruit who blames poor shooting on bad rifle dope: "Half the changes in point of impact are not the dope *on* the rifle, but the dope *behind* the rifle."

On Qualification Day it is too late to correct such bad shooting habits as jerking on the trigger, causing shots to go low, but the coach may do the next best thing to salvage that shooter's score by cranking in "jerking dope" on the sight to compensate for the recruit's failure to squeeze; this sometimes spares the recruit becoming an "unk"—unqualified.

In the butts, the target detail has been laboring to maintain the level of speed and efficiency set by the fastest team. The reward of a telephone call home tonight for the best crew is a positive incentive matched by another, less pleasant: those crews which cannot sustain the pace do push-ups and mountain climbs, in company with sand flies and mosquitos rising from the adjacent marsh, while the shooters move back from one line to the next.

Busier even than the pit recruits are their D.I.s, who act as verifiers. Each has to monitor five to seven targets, on which he must confirm every shot and every score. In their haste, recruits on the firing line often disk shots incorrectly, so that the score computed is wrong. The official score, therefore, is that marked and initialed by the verifiers in the pits.

Tension rises in exact proportion to the shooter's distance from the targets. Recruits take refuge in hope as they move back from the 200- to the 300-yard line, where well-aimed shots will retrieve a substandard score. Poor shooting often gets worse, though, as the shooter keeps mentally revising, ever upward, the number of bulls he must now make to reach the qualifying score of 190 out of a possible 250.

The morning brings many small dramas.

Tony Garcia, one of three ex-Army regulars, is shooting poorly, and the harder he tries, the worse it gets. The realization that he must relax only jangles his nerves, and robs him of concentration. He bites his lip, and tries to settle down.

The three men on trial training—Prayso, McClellan and Hall—are now back in good standing, and straining to stay there. All are shooting well and enjoying the taste of vindication. Hall is especially buoyant. Every time he scores a bull's-eye, he beams, and shouts "Hoo-rah!" in self-congratulation.

One inattentive recruit fails to revolve his rear sight the ninety degrees necessary to put it on "L" for long-range at the 500-yard line. He is baffled and frustrated at the sudden slump in his score, until he discovers the reason. Too late. He fails to qualify.

Charneski is shooting steadily, and better than on any other day this week. If he doesn't falter, he will be among the high finishers.

One of 1036's hopefuls is not firing—but fired. Recruit Hamblin has finally been dropped for repeated infractions of Rifle Range regulations. Told to tighten his sling during Grass Week, he surreptitiously loosened it, mistakenly believing he wouldn't be noticed. He paid little attention at classes, and was repaid with below-average scores during Qualification Week. Yesterday he committed a cardinal sin: he allowed his rifle to drift so it no longer broke the vertical plane through the firing line, and suddenly an irate coach found himself looking down the muzzle of Hamblin's rifle. Hamblin was forthwith relegated to the Marksmanship Training Platoon (MTP). During the ensuing week, the sobered and chastened Hamblin would retrain and shoot once more for qualification; this time he'd make it, permitting him to rejoin Platoon 1036 on TD-30. But because of safety violations, he receives no marksmanship badge; his only recognition is a notation in his Service Record Book.

Most recruits do better. Topping off the morning at 500 yards, firing ten rounds slow fire prone on the torso-silhouette Baker target, with a ten minute time limit, Platoon 1036 has made a creditable showing. Having steadily improved overall during the week, today eight men have bettered the 220 mark, achieving Rifle Expert status. Fifteen more have shot

210 or better, thus qualifying as Sharpshooters. Twenty-eight break the 190 barrier, becoming Marksmen.

Only seven fail to reach this standard. These men will go to MTP to fire the KD course up to five times more between next Monday and Wednesday. No matter what score they shoot at MTP, they cannot rank better than Marksman. In the event, Givlin and Graham qualify, leaving five "unks."

The final scoring gives the 230-man 1036 Series 181 qualifiers on this day, with another 13 qualifying later at MTP. Of the four platoons, 1036 shoots best, with a total of 91 percent qualifiers (85 percent is considered good). Their triumph is recognized at the end of the day. The 230 recruits are assembled, their faces and hands streaked with dirt, burned powder and oil, and patches of red-on-red from insect bites atop peeling sunburned skin.

Series Commander First Lieutenant Greenburg marches onto the field, while behind him walks S.S.D.I. Lyon bearing the Marksmanship Trophy. To the cheers of the troops, the SC presents it to 1036. It will adorn their Motivation Table on the quarterdeck of the squad bay, along with their trophy for First Phase Academic Testing, and medals and citations of their drill instructors.

Kudos for Platoon 1036 are individual as well as collective. The highest scores in the Series were shot by Platoon 1036 recruits Bail and Charneski, tied at 231. It is an excellent score for first-time qualification on the KD course. In fact, it is an excellent score at *any* time, and only 11 points below the all-time Parris Island recruit record of 246.

With a newborn daughter and series-high score, both in a single week, Charneski feels like breaking into song. He wisely refrains. Recruits aren't home on the range.

Dago

"Hollywood Marines," graduates of Parris Island boot camp derisively term those produced in the more civilized surroundings of the Marine Corps Recruit Depot, San Diego. West Coast recruits shrug off the slur good-naturedly. They are well aware that their training is equally thorough, usually more intense—outdoor exercises at San Diego are but rarely halted because of inclement weather—and that for both the reward is the same: the title U.S. Marine.

All the same, conspicuous differences as well as the breadth of the American continent separate the two recruit depots. One is purely demographic: recruits from west of the Mississippi are customarily assigned to San Diego, while those from the East usually go to Parris Island. Until recently, approximately 25,000 enlistees per year (men only at San Diego, which has no women's training) reported for boot camp at each installation. But as the population shifts westward, San Diego is receiving an ever greater share of the 50,000-odd recruits trained annually.

Environmentally, too, the bases are at opposite poles. The city nearest sprawling Parris Island is Savannah, Georgia, seventy miles away in another state. The one-half square mile San Diego Recruit Depot, by contrast, is locked in the urban embrace of the burgeoning city on the north and the San Diego International Airport on the south. Recruits here are reminded of the civilian life they've forsaken every few minutes as wide-bodied jets hurtle down the runway a few hundred yards distant, and into the sky with a roar that smothers conversations and commands alike.

Perhaps the main difference, at least for D.I.s and other permanent personnel, is cultural. At Parris Island, the intense isolation imposes stresses on men and families largely dependent on their own resources for social life, entertainment and education. On the other hand, as the eighth largest city in the land, San Diego has more than enough allurements to absorb all the restless energies of San Diego Marines. In consequence, their marital and alcohol problems are few, and the retention of D.I.s for second tours is higher than at Parris Island.

Recruits fare better, too. The better weather and more pleasant surroundings may have contributed to somewhat higher scores in swimming, final physical fitness levels and rifle qualification than at P.I. The introduction of the M16A2 has raised the latter even higher, so that up to 99 percent of San Diego recruits graduating each month wear one of the three marksmanship badges.

Rifle qualification as well as Individual Combat Training is reserved for Camp Pendleton, a huge hilly expanse on the California coast an hour's drive north from the recruit depot. In some respects, it has advantages that the corresponding areas in Parris Island lack. On the Pendleton Rifle Range, the weather is mild, the wind off the sea constant, and there are no sand fleas. The precipitous hills on which physical training exercises and maneuvers are held build leg muscles seldom taxed on Parris Island's flatlands. The rugged terrain, with its lively population of poisonous snakes (protected by law), is a realistic introduction to the unpleasant conditions under which Marines have traditionally fought. Moreover, because the Infantry Training School as well as the First Marine Division are both quartered at Camp Pendleton, recruits on ICT can profit from the observations and experience of seasoned comrades-in-arms with whom they will soon serve.

The advantages San Diego recruits enjoy are of relatively

recent vintage. Marines first saw the area back in July 1846 when members of a ship's detachment landed to raise the American flag on the plaza of the old town; the site of the recruit depot-to-be was, like much of Parris Island today, a flat tidal marsh. It remained so for nearly seventy years, until in July, 1914, Colonel Joseph H. Pendleton established the Marine Barracks, San Diego, on Dutch Flats, a soggy area swarming with insects.

By 1921, much of the marsh was drained, and was augmented by the purchase of 232 acres of fairly dry land plus another 500 acres that required dredging and filling. Under Pendleton, now a major-general fresh from command of Marine Barracks, Parris Island, long, low arcaded buildings built in the Spanish colonial style were erected facing a spacious parade ground. But it was not until 1923 that recruit training for the West Coast, carried out at Mare Island Navy Yard and Puget Sound Naval Shipyard in Washington state, was consolidated in San Diego.

In 1932, recruit training lasted a bare eight weeks, with a concentration in Marine history and combat skills followed by four weeks of Sea School, to prepare recruits for service aboard ship in Marine detachments. The Rifle Range was located at Camp Matthews, a few miles north of the Recruit Depot, but by 1964 the pressure of the encroaching city forced a move to Camp Pendleton.

The framework of the depot has, like the American populace itself, put on some weight over the years. Barracks have been erected across the parade deck from the original structures, enclosing the drill area in a large quadrangle. Behind the barracks are open wash racks, where recruits still launder their clothes as in bygone days (Parris Island boots enjoy the services of a base laundry). Between the barracks and the roaring jets lie the obstacle, circuit and confidence courses and rappelling tower, as well as a runner's path that skirts the entire installation. Near the center of the barracks area stands the depot's mess hall, the largest in the Marine Corps.

The Marine Corps' Sea School and Recruiters' School, located on base, respectively provide men for duty aboard men-of-war, and men and women for duty at its recruiting stations. The base's Drill Instructors' School, on the other hand, trains men only for D.I. duty in San Diego. Among the innovations in its curriculum is the use of computers and lifelike models to train future D.I.s in effective cardiopulmonary resuscitation. The students also learn to administer the Heimlich Maneuver. Both techniques have been used to resuscitate recruits in distress.

In one respect, the "Hollywood Marine" image fits the San Diego Recruit Depot: graduation ceremonies, in which nearly one thousand recruits (equivalent to four complete Parris Island series) pass in review, is a production of which any producer of a movie spectacular could be proud.

The ceremony begins in the base auditorium, before an audience of some one thousand family and friends. Officers and drill instructors, drawn up in military ranks on stage, repeat the Oath of Enlistment, echoed by the assembled recruits. Then the officers call up, one by one, those recruits who have distinguished themselves during training. With each award, on cue, the recruits of the honored man's platoon burst forth with a thunderous "*Hoo*-rah!" Following the benediction, the recruits file out to take up their positions for the graduation parade, which their guests observe from the reviewing stand.

The band marches on, the bandmaster twirling his baton. The adjutant presents the command to the commanding officer. Orders of the Day are published. Officers advance front and center. The command is presented to the reviewing officer, then proceeds to pass in review to the roll of drums and the blare of martial music. After the march-past, the platoon guidons are retired for the year, and the troops dismissed. Proud parents pour onto the parade deck, and for a few euphoric moments recruits put aside military bearing to receive congratulatory bear hugs and kisses.

It's quite a performance. If the same planning and precision can be translated to the battlefield, the nation can rest easy.

WEEK SIX

Santiago:
The Sweet Taste
of
Command

On 6 April at 0700, Platoon 1036 marches back from the Parris Island Rifle Range to B Company barracks, First Recruit Training Battalion, at the main base. The day is cool and breezy, and the men are in buoyant spirits. Not only has the platoon won the series Marksmanship Trophy, but two of their number—Recruits Charneski and Bail—have posted the series-high scores shot on Qualification Day: 231. Furthermore, they are moving down to the *second* deck of the barracks whose top deck they left two weeks earlier, another sign of being "over the hump," at TD-29 more than halfway through boot camp. From here on, it's all downhill. Best of all, they are breaking the ceaseless daily grind of training with a week's Mess and Maintenance (M&M), as they turn into mess cooks—cooks' helpers—in the mess hall.

A seventeen-hour working day in steamy scullery or sub-zero reefer is not a civilian's conception of a welcome change of routine, but recruits view it differently. They fondly believe that, for once, they will get to gorge on steak, pie and ice cream, that they can move at a more leisurely pace than usual, that their D.I.s won't be around to bellow at them. Disillusion awaits them: they will not be allowed to eat a bite between meals, and the meals themselves will be the same as all other recruit's —ample but not lavish; their days will be a blur of constant motion except twenty-minute breathers at mealtime; and they will find that cooks can bellow quite as loud, and as often, as D.I.s.

Yet, Mess and Maintenance has its rewards. The recruits of Platoon 1036 will learn to work together as they never have before, experience the euphoria of a D.I.-free existence for seven days, discover the limits of their endurance when, toward the end of the week, they begin to shuffle like sleepwalkers, and enjoy the exhilarating sensation of yelling at someone else—First Phase recruits.

The yeller-in-chief will be Edward Santiago, the tall, slim young recruit from Staten Island, N.Y., who has been Platoon Guide since the first week of boot camp. The guide, chosen by the S.D.I. for discipline, intelligence, quick response to orders, hygiene and leadership, is the senior recruit, and assumes command of the platoon in the absence of the D.I. The job is fiercely competitive, for the best-all-around recruit, in the opinion of the S.D.I., will be awarded the coveted Blues on graduation day. The guide, frequently the front-runner, must therefore not only see that the platoon performs smoothly and efficiently at all times, but demonstrate his leadership. No recruit works harder, sleeps less or worries more than the guide, who hurries through his own duties in order to help slower recruits with theirs.

In the mess hall, Santiago will have his first modest taste of independent command. He will be held responsible for the efforts of the platoon as a whole, and of every man in it.

Platoon 1036's long days on Mess and Maintenance begin in the grim darkness well before dawn on Sunday, 7 April. Turned out of their bunks at 0300 by the duty D.I., they shave and make their ablutions in haste, don their camis and boots, and are marched by their D.I. through silent streets to the Second Battalion mess hall half a mile away. They are due on deck one hour before chow call. On arrival, the D.I. turns them over to the mess sergeant and departs.

The recruits already know what is expected of them, hav-

ing worked for three hours the previous afternoon alongside
the recruits whose jobs they now occupy. In the galley they
greet every superior—everybody else wearing boots—with a
formal "Good morning, sir!" But this will be done only on
first meeting. The traffic between galley and mess hall is too
frenetic for further salutations until a final weary "Good
night, sir!" at the end of a long, long day.

They doff their camis and put them in steel lockers. They
don starched white duck trousers and white skivvy shirts, and
paper fore-and-aft caps on which they inscribe their function:
Pastry, Linebacker, Guide, Right [chow] line, Coffee, and so
on. Twenty-two caps are unfilled; the table of organization
calls for a minimum of fifty-five recruits, but only thirty-three
are available, the other members of 1036 being either on duty
at the First Battalion mess hall, on sick call or on fire watch.
The manpower shortage will test Santiago's organizational
ability, and his capacity to squeeze one and two-thirds days'
work out of each recruit.

Before they are allowed to touch either food or utensil,
however, recruits are subjected to a hygiene inspection. Lined
up in facing rows, they stand at attention as a mess sergeant
walks slowly down the ranks. He stops before each man to
examine his uniform, hands and fingernails for cleanliness.
He also looks carefully at both sides of the hands and forearms, as well as the face and neck. Any skin eruptions, abrasions or cuts disqualify a recruit not only from food handling,
but even from working in the scullery or on the garbage detail. Since sand fleas invade even the mess hall, recruits are
warned not to scratch bites, which can lead to dangerous infections. The inspection finished, they take their places behind the steam table, in the galley and scullery, and slip on
new rubber surgical gloves, which regulations require food
servers to wear.

Morning routine calls for the recruits to set up the chow
lines for the other series which will shortly appear for breakfast. They must make fresh coffee in the big stainless steel
urns, fill the juice machines and set in their slots in the steam

tables trays heavy with scrambled eggs, bacon, French toast, grits and home-fried potatoes. The food has been freshly prepared by the cooks, who reported for work at 0230. Two chow lines serve the recruits, another the officers and NCOs, who dine in their own section at the center of the mess hall.

Promptly at 0430, the first recruits arrive for breakfast. They march through swinging doors at each end of the mess hall in four compact columns. The platoons stop at their guide's command at a tall wheeled rack of steel trays. Trays are passed across the ranks, and the first column steps smartly forward. While awaiting their turn, recruits are edified by watchwords and slogans placed at strategic intervals on the mess hall bulkheads:

READY TO FIGHT, READY TO KILL/READY TO DO THE DEVIL'S WILL, reads one. Another: EITHER LEAD, FOLLOW, OR GET THE HELL OUT OF THE WAY! A third: "TO ERR IS HUMAN, TO FORGIVE DIVINE—NEITHER OF WHICH IS MARINE CORPS POLICY."

After contemplating this wisdom-for-the-day, each recruit makes a quarter-turn as he comes up to the chow line, and side-steps along as his tray is filled.

In relation to the recruits on Mess and Maintenance duty, all others are either ahead or behind one phase. Their behavior in chow lines leaves no doubt as to which phase they belong. Those in the First Phase are diffident and apprehensive: those the M&M recruits in the surgeon's gloves feel are *theirs* to cut up with sharp remarks. "Move along there, recruit!" one orders. "Empty that tray!" commands another. A third, loudly and somewhat cryptically, urges "Motivation!" while a fourth shouts "Hurrah!" for no other reason, apparently, than that he can get away with it. First Phase recruits take what they're given, including exhoration, in cowed silence.

Third Phase recruits, on the other hand, are identifiable by their dignity, stern demeanor, and approximately two more millimeters of hair atop the head than the M&M recruits possess. They pass briskly down the line, thrust their trays beneath the glass louver, and declare their desires in a tone that admits of no dispute: "Roast beef . . . spuds . . . corn . . . no broccoli . . . pie—a *big* piece, recruit!"

> . . . You wouldn't think a few weeks of training could make such a difference in the way men feel and act. First Phase recruits coming through the mess hall are scared rabbits. You can see it. You can feel it. Sort of furtive. Third Phase recruits carry themselves differently. They act older and wiser, and I suppose they are. But it's more than just training. Third Phasers seem to be better aware of how far they can go—marching, talking up to D.I.s, pounding "knowledge" into their skulls, doing PT, gold-bricking—before hitting the wall. It makes them more relaxed, more comfortable. You see it in their eyes. . . .

At the far end of the steam table stands a D.I. inspecting the recruits and their trays. As they approach the D.I., the recruits snap to attention, elbows in, thumbs on the flat edge of the tray, eyes straight ahead.

"Good morning, sir!" the recruit bawls. "Recruit Stefanowski!"

It is the D.I.'s responsibility to see that each recruit has the ration corresponding to his dietary requirements. On the steam tray shelf, sample trays, wrapped in plastic, serve as a guide for the obese and for the underweight. The meals for the normal recruit will supply a total of 3,500 calories a day. The obese are restricted to 1,500, while the underweight are stuffed with 5,000 calories a day. When the D.I. confirms that the recruit has received his designated ration, that his uniform and hands are clean, that his pockets are buttoned, his collar smoothed down, and his position of attention impeccable, he signifies his approval.

"Go!" orders the D.I., and the recruit steps off on his left foot toward that section of the mess hall assigned to his platoon. He will have twenty minutes to eat, but will typically spend much of that time jawing with his messmates. Mealtime is the only period, save the hour's free time each night before Taps, when a recruit is allowed to speak unless spoken to by a D.I. When the platoon guide rises, signalling the end of the brief respite, all rise. They empty the remains of their meals in a GI can, hand their trays and plastic glasses to the scullery crew, and form up in ranks outside the mess hall to await their D.I.

In earlier times, the mess halls of all services were emblazoned with a cautionary message over the entrance: TAKE ALL YOU WANT, BUT EAT ALL YOU TAKE. These signs no longer exist, and the last clause has become a victim of times of plenty. Recruits still take all they want—but frequently dump half of it in the garbage on their way out. Their D.I.s deplore the flagrant waste, but cannot order a recruit to eat what he has taken. Mealtimes are sacred, and D.I.s are not allowed to talk with them except to enforce order and discipline.

As the cans are filled, the refuse is trundled away by a two-man GI-can detail, who also remove waste from the scullery, galley and pot shack. In a GI-can shed behind the mess hall they first drain the contents of the forty-gallon containers through a steel strainer to recover lost silver, then cart the soggy mass to a dumpster. They then machine-wash and scald the cans with steam before returning them to the mess hall. The quantity of waste thus processed is prodigious. During Platoon 1036's stay in the Second Battalion mess hall, an average of one hundred full cans pass daily through the shed—approximately four thousand gallons of leavings divided about equally between discarded food, parings and bones, and plastic, paper and metal containers, about four gallons for each of the one thousand men being fed in the mess hall daily. Though much of the waste is edible, by farm animals at least, only grease is reclaimed by a civilian contractor for recycling.

. . . I watched Romania today while we worked in the mess hall. Every time some recruit dumped half a tray of chow into the GI can, Romania would wince. He doesn't talk a lot about life back in the old country, but it must have been different. He shakes his head when recruits gripe about the chow. Sure, like they say, it's a Marine's constitutional duty to gripe about everything. But when people are going hungry even in *this* country, you have to wonder why the D.I.s aren't allowed to make recruits eat what they take. It may not be gourmet cooking, and no health-food nut would touch the white bread or drink the sugar-water that passes for juice, but that's no reason to take it and then throw half of it away. If the Marine Corps throws food away that easy, what about men . . . ?

The GI-can-shed recruits comprise one of the thirteen divisions of labor called for by the T/O (Table of Organization) to keep the mess hall running smoothly. Each chow line requires seven men, and an equal number work in the chill of the salad room. The scullery has eight, the pot shack five, and the storeroom and galley two each. Five recruits fill the juice machines, two the coffee machines and bins for sauces and condiments. Four recruits do nothing but clean the tables and sweep and swab the decks. One does the paperwork, among other things logging in the first and last men of each platoon to ensure that everyone has twenty minutes to eat.

The denizens of the pot shack work with strong soap and corrosive disinfectants which seep into their heavy rubber gloves and cause rashes and fissures. For this reason, a pot shack tour is limited to two days. Yet, their duty is so free of supervision that, when relief fails to appear, they don't complain.

The banging of the heavy steel trays, kettles and caldrons

as they are scraped and washed, and the hiss of steam as they are sterilized, overwhelm all other noises in the pot shack. The five pot wallopers, clad in long yellow rubber aprons and elbow-length rubber gloves, take advantage of the cover by singing marching songs, joking, shouting, splashing hot water on each other, and dancing on the wet deck, all of which are expressly forbidden.

The same light spirits possess the scullery recruits. The clash of steel trays, the clatter of silver and the throaty rumble of dishwashers drown out every other sound. In this inferno of sound, suds and steam, fun and games escape the vigilance of the mess sergeant, who sensibly keeps his distance.

All M&M recruits, in fact, enjoy the novelty of their work, except perhaps the shivering toilers of the salad room. There, all the vegetables are stripped and washed in warm water and mild soap and thoroughly rinsed. Then, because four recruits are doing the work of seven, says weary Recruit Thomas Young, "Our knives never stop moving." With his mates, he pares and cuts up two hundred fifty pounds of carrots, two fifty-pound boxes of lettuce and an equal amount of cabbage each watch. They also cut up peppers, celery and tomatoes and, because of the room's low temperature, are charged with making huge tureens of jello, served practically daily. No fun and games here, for the recruits work in the chilling presence of permanent personnel, who must be present in any area where kitchen knives are used.

The juice recruits tend the six mechanical cows ranged around the periphery of the mess hall, dispensing milk and juice through stainless steel nipples. Each machine holds three six-gallon plastic containers—two of milk and one of juice at breakfast, two of juice and one of milk at other meals. The "juice" tastes as if concocted wholly of sugared water and artificial flavoring and coloring, but at least the milk is real.

In the galley, two recruits assist the cooks in such chores as dipping chicken legs in flour preparatory to deep frying, but no recruit is permitted to do any of the actual cooking or baking. Two others man the supply room, a dank retreat with wooden shelves piled high with fuel for ten thousand PT sessions; they also form the nucleus of working parties to unload trucks arriving with provisions.

After each meal, the four-man tables that cover the large hall in rows of four are washed from top to bottom with sponges and hot soapy water. They are then disinfected and stacked so the sweepers can clean the deck. Decks are swept and swabbed after each meal, and after breakfast they are cleaned with a mechanical scrubber as well. While cleaning, sweepers take care that neither swab nor broom is raised to table-top level. The tools of their trade are stowed in large open racks behind the mess hall after each use. There they will be dried and aired by wind and sun.

With scarcely more than half the needed work force on hand, Guide Santiago is a man in motion, shuttling recruits from one detail to another, filling in himself when no one else is available. He plainly enjoys his first experience in independent leadership, but tries not to let it show. Nor does he use his position to avoid the dirty jobs: when a recruit accidentally dumps his full tray into the ice cream freezer, it is Santiago who, bare-handed, pitches in to clean up the sticky, congealed mess. Santiago's eyes are on the stars—he aspires to a career in computer technology—but for now, his feet are firmly on the ground.

The mess cooks of Platoon 1036 have been working steadily for more than three hours before the last recruit platoon leaves the mess hall shortly after breakfast each morning. Only then do they sit down for their own breakfast and their first cup of coffee of the day. Two months earlier, a leisurely cigarette would have been for some a part of the morning ritual. No more: not only are they, as recruits, forbidden to smoke, but no one, officer or man, is *ever* permitted to smoke in the mess hall except in a small area set aside for permanent personnel. Nor do they get a full twenty minutes for morning chow; they are already running behind schedule, and must begin at once to prepare for lunch which, like dinner, they will eat before their hungry shipmates descend upon them.

Immediately after breakfast, clean whites are issued to all hands; if they become conspicuously soiled during the day, they will be changed again. Then all hands turn to at their assigned tasks, which will take them up to their own lunch time in mid-morning. In cleaning up after that repast, they will be assisted by ten "chow guards" from other platoons messing here, who sweep, swab, wipe tables and generally assist their seniors on M&M.

The pace is swift and admits few liberties with the schedule. Mess sergeants know from experience that it should take a First or Second Phase platoon eight minutes to pass through chow line. With two lines running, therefore, a two-hundred-forty-man series can be served in sixteen minutes. A Third Phase platoon—lean, keen and hungry—can sweep a chow line clean in three to four minutes. Thus a thousand men can be fed three times a day at the rate of an hour per meal, each of which, however, requires nearly six hours of preparation and clean-up.

Recruits soon discover that, in the mess hall, an unfilled minute does not exist. Even when every utensil gleams, the deck shines, steam tables are wiped clean of water spots and brasswork glows like gold, a little art may make chow more closely resemble food, perhaps even cuisine. Recruits will then learn to ripple a pan of mashed potatoes with a spatula and fancy wrist action, sprinkle it with patterns of paprika, and garnish it with sprigs of parsley. They embellish steam-tray counters with tasteful and tasty arrangements of grapes, bananas, oranges, pineapple and grapefruit atop a bed of greens. It still isn't home cooking, but it helps.

The recruits of 1036 get an emotional lift out of their first three days of mess duty. Not only do their responsibilities have the attraction of novelty, but having to cooperate closely to get the work done builds trust and mutual confidence. Friendships begun that first far-off February night in Process-

ing ripen in the mess hall's warmth. By graduation, they will
be solid enough to last a lifetime.

But after the lift comes the let-down. The seventeen-hour
days begin to tell.

"They're pretty frisky the first few days, singing and hors-
ing around," comments a mess sergeant who sees a new crop
of recruits every Sunday, "but just wait till tomorrow—
Thursday. That's zombie day. They'll be dragging around,
haggard and hollow-eyed, like sleepwalkers. Their legs are
aching and swelling from long hours on their feet. A couple
of them will fall asleep standing up behind the steam
table.

"Parents sometimes wonder, you know, what their boy is
doing working in the mess hall—what kind of military training *is* this, anyway? Well, surprisingly, it is a very important
part of boot camp. They'll have a lot worse in the Fleet,
where on patrol they can be without sleep for days at a
time—and in the mud and freezing rain to boot. In combat,
of course, it'll be worse than that. Here they begin to learn
that civilian standards of stamina and cooperation don't come
close to what the Marine Corps demands. Believe it or not,
they'll leave here with considerable more self-confidence than
they had last week."

Perhaps, but by 1930 each night, when the last half-acre of
deck is swabbed, they can feel only bone-numbing fatigue.
They change into their camis in silence, march back across
the parade deck to Bravo Company barracks, and trudge
heavily up the ladder to the second deck.

"As soon as we get out of the shower," says an exhausted, hollow-eyed Santiago, "we hit the rack. And as
soon as we hit the rack, we're out. There's no talking—just
snoring."

Instead of the usual eight hours of sleep, recruits on M&M
get six to seven. Even so, this is more than four of their
mates who remain in the squad bay on fire watch get: they
average about four hours. "Fire watch" is deceptive. The
men on duty indeed "give the alarm in case of fire or disor-

der,'' and guard the platoon's rifles and personal effects. But the four recruits also do all the household chores for those absent on M&M—make racks, hold field day in squad bay and heads, collect laundry, iron uniforms, design range flags and clean rifles, so that those on M&M have no responsibilities outside the mess hall. In these duties they are assisted by men on light duty, such as the two returning from the Naval Hospital at Charleston, where they spent one night under observation, a routine precaution after the removal of wisdom teeth.

Also present in the squad bay are left-handed, bespectacled look-alike recruits David L. Wright and Clarence L. Sharpe, Jr. Nicknamed by their fellow recruits ''The Wright Brothers,'' Wright and Sharp act as company clerks, or scribes. They make up the platoon rosters, walking- and sick-bay chits, fire watch lists and training cards with the daily schedules for the three D.I.s. It is not always the cushy job some suppose, for in addition to their clerical duties, they must keep up with drill and all other platoon activities. Also, working at a desk next to the D.I. house, the Wright Brothers are highly visible, so that any transgression is instantly detected. ''We get quarterdecked a lot,'' says Wright, ruefully.

At 1400 on Saturday, 13 April, Platoon 1036's reliefs file into the Second Battalion mess hall and take seats. The Number Ones of the 1036's thirteen mess hall details stand in a line at stiff parade rest, intent upon showing the new boys proper military bearing. As their names are called, the new mess cooks rise and fall in behind a Number One. For the next three hours, 1036 will show the new men how the jobs are done. They themselves leave immediately after evening chow.

The luck of the draw put Platoon 1036 in the mess hall. Other platoons in the series were assigned to the other half of Mess & Maintenance, laboring for the police sergeant in inspecting plumbing, unplugging drains, painting, cutting grass or raking leaves in the great outdoors. Platoon 1036 will have its own crack at the great outdoors next week, however, when it marches out to the tall pines for Individual Combat Training. It's about time, the recruits agree: combat is what Marines are made for.

Chow Down

"Three things keep a Marine happy," says an old adage— "pay call, liberty and good chow." To which Guide Edward Santiago, coming off Mess and Maintenance, would have added—"and a good night's sleep."

But even with that qualification, when compared with soldiers of other lands, Marines have every reason to be content. They receive high pay, generous liberty and leave, and food of quality and quantity available to few men in uniform anywhere. Moreover, the hygienic standards of Marine mess halls are far more stringent than those of all but a few civilian restaurants, and they can even boast a variety in their cuisine rare in military messes.

The variety is assured by a forty-two-day master menu cycle, revised annually, and formulated by dieticians and medical personnel on the basis of "nutritional adequacy, patron acceptability, and availability."

Nutritional adequacy for the normal recruit calls for an intake of from 3500 to 4400 calories per day. But fewer than half the recruits are considered "normal" according to weight/height tables, and for these men special diets are devised. For example, overweight recruits with a physical problem precluding heavy exercise assigned to the Physical Conditioning Platoon (PCP) receive 1750 calories per day (overweight females get 1200 calories). The obese undergoing rigorous physical conditioning at PCP receive 3000 calories, while the underweight are fed 5000.

Marine preferences dictate some food selections. Ham, chicken, roast beef, ground beef, hamburgers, hot dogs, corn, peas and green beans are favorite foods, and they appear frequently on recruits' trays; okra, squash, tuna-noodle casserole, liver and corned beef, on the other hand, are scorned by most troops, and consequently are rarely served. Mess sergeants serve illusions, too: to lend diversity to ground beef, often scheduled every three or four days, they disguise it successively as meat loaf, ground beef in white sauce on toast, spaghetti sauce, salisbury steak and hamburger.

Menus vary according to season, as well, with high carbohydrate items predominating in cold, wet months, and dishes with a high liquid content—jello, melons, spaghetti, soups, milk and juice—during HOT/SOP from mid-April until mid-October. In all seasons, however, the emphasis is on greens and fresh vegetables, with that elusive "balanced diet" the objective.

A typical COLD/SOP meal served at Parris Island's seven mess halls on Platoon 1036's Training Day Five consisted of lettuce, jello, macaroni salad, cole slaw, pickles, cranberry sauce, cucumbers, celery, carrots, peppers, apple sauce, jelly donuts (one to a recruit), hamburgers and hamburger buns, chili, fish, french fries, onion rings, spinach, red beans, bread and butter.

Confronted with such variety, the average recruit heaps his tray with as much as it will bear. As a result, prodigious quantities of wholesome food are thrown in the garbage at the end of each meal. South Carolina law forbids the use of waste food for any purpose (the government receives from private contractors one cent for each ten pounds of grease) so the waste is total.

To this waste must be added many left-overs. Gallon containers of pre-mixed food such as macaroni and potato salad, once opened, must be thrown out by the end of the next meal. Display food trays, made up as models for recruits on special diets, are also thrown in the garbage. Hygienic standards require that no leftovers be served more than thirty-six hours after preparation. Leftovers from lunch may thus be served at dinner the same day, and leftovers from dinner, refrigerated during the interim, may be served for lunch the next day, but whatever then remains must be consigned to the garbage. To ensure that leftovers are readily identified as such, they are entered in red ink on inventory records; successive red-ink entries, therefore, are prohibited by regulations. These strict standards contrast sharply with those of most civilian restaurants, which serve leftovers repeatedly for up to five days.

Leftovers do not, of course, appear on the bill of fare for the six days of the year when special meals are served. The most elaborate celebrates the Marine Corps birthday on 10 November each year. A typical birthday lunch: French onion soup with crackers and Parmesan croutons, chilled fruit cup supreme, grilled strip loin steak, baked potatoes, sauteed mushrooms and onions, buttered whole grain corn, polonaise broccoli, hot dinner rolls, anniversary cake with butter cream frosting, assorted pies and beverages.

For this and other festive meals—served on Thanksgiving, Christmas, New Year's Day, Independence Day and Easter—place mats are used and nuts and candy served but not, any longer, the cigars traditionally dispensed.

Four large mess halls feeding more than 500 Marines and recruits per meal accommodate the three recruit training battalions and the support battalion at the Rifle Range. Three smaller mess halls provide for the Women Marines, the Weapons Battalion and Headquarters Battalion. The larger installations require the services of more than 30 cooks and bakers, divided into two watches—from 0300 to 0900 and from 0700 to 1830, assisted by 35 to 40 recruits. A large mess hall typically feeds 1200 recruits a meal, but in the heavy summer training season, with the help of 60 recruits on Mess and Maintenance, they can mess as many as 2500 at a sitting.

A mess hall galley imparts a welter of conflicting sensations—the enticing aroma of fresh-baked pastry, an ear-splitting racket from the pot shack, the orderly frenzy of cooks stirring simmering vegetables in ranks of waist-high caldrons, slippery decks, clouds of vapor shrieking from leaky steam pipes. A cook removes meat loaves from revolving oven shelves, deftly carves each into 13 slices, and slips the tray onto a 15-shelf steel dolly; it takes 77 such loaves to feed 1,000 men. At a long stainless steel table a baker spreads 18-by 26-inch cakes with icing; each will make 50 portions. One cook does nothing but fry chicken legs in deep fat, another supervises the shivering reefer crew chopping up greens for salad, a third stirs corn in a giant tureen with a ladle the size of a cricket bat.

The men and women who prepare these meals all learn the fundamentals of their craft at an eight-week Basic Food Course. To be promoted, candidates must later attend the eleven-week NCO School and, after some years of service, the twelve-week Staff NCO School. Bakers, on the other hand, are a disappearing breed. Their school lasts for twelve weeks, but their trade is slated for extinction due to competition from the civilian sector. Already, the baking of bread has ceased (the civilian dollar-loaf costs the government $.51, less than base-baked bread), and soon Marine bakers will produce only pastries and sea stories about a more flavorful past.

One item in no danger of short supply is paperwork, which has multiplied in recent years to the point where fully half the sixty to eighty hours a week mess sergeants work is occupied in filling forms. More than thirty long, detailed forms, many of them inventories, must be completed every day—some every meal—in order to prove that the troops are receiving authorized rations and that no food is being misappropriated. Occasional thefts do occur: in a recent case, a cook detected stealing a tray of beef patties found himself the meat in the sandwich when he received "six, six and a kick"—six months loss of pay, six months in the brig, and a bad-conduct discharge.

The Marine's Basic Daily Food Allowance (BFDA) is approximately $3.60 for three meals, a sum that changes monthly due to fluctuations in the cost of fifty-two food items as computed by the Department of Defense. Twenty percent of the BFDA is allocated for breakfast, with 40 percent each for lunch and dinner. Thus it costs the government approximately $250 to feed a recruit during his seventy-odd days at Parris Island, a small fraction of the estimated $11,000 total cost of boot training.

The spectre of food poisoning is the mess sergeant's recurring nightmare. Since a single tainted dish could infect upwards of two thousand men, extraordinary precautions are observed to maintain the highest standards of hygiene in the mess hall.

Water and ice are periodically analyzed by the base preventive medicine laboratory, the noise levels are tested monthly in various locations in the galley—especially the pot shack, insect-control teams spray the premises on a regular basis, and garbage is removed as it accumulates in the galley and scullery. Bug lights are currently being installed to eliminate flying insects, and the replacement of steel mess trays with hard-plastic trays will significantly reduce noise in mess halls.

Food handlers undergo comprehensive physical exams every year, as well as after three day's absence for illness, thirty day's leave, or return from overseas. All get a PPD (Purified Protein Derivative) shot against tuberculosis, and each year they attend a three-hour refresher course in hygiene. Rubber surgical gloves (at $1.80 for a box of fifty) are required for all food handlers, and are especially necessary for recruits on M&M, whose hands frequently bear cuts and abrasions after returning from the Rifle Range.

As a result of strict hygienic precautions—Parris Island mess halls average 90 percent to 92 percent on periodic sanitary inspections versus the 70 percent rating of the average civilian restaurant—it may actually be safer to be a Marine recruit than a civilian.

WEEK SEVEN

Garcia:
No More Jokes

"No more jokes, no more cokes, no more smokes," is Tony Garcia's succinct assessment of life as a Marine Corps recruit, as compared with the Army, in which he served as a medic for three years. The Army was too easy, too lacking in the challenge and discipline that are the essence of the military life he intends to make a career.

A native of the Bronx, N.Y., Garcia is a physical fitness fanatic, and has literally outstanding weightlifter's muscles to prove it. His only regret so far in joining the Marine Corps is that he wasn't able to bring his bar bells with him; his consolation is that there is a set in the gear locker, and he pumps iron during his nightly free time instead of cramming for his exams, as many of his more forethoughtful shipmates do.

Employment in industrial park maintenance was a let down for Garcia, who had been junior and senior class president of his high school, and he soon quit to join the Army. When that service fell short of his expectations, he decided that the Marine Corps was the only reasonable alternative.

By Training Week Seven, Garcia has had no reason to change his mind. Though he complains bitterly about the chow, he is a human vacuum sweeper in the mess hall, and generously volunteers to help out fellow recruits with overfilled trays. He piously claims to avoid fights, but is generally believed to be the chef responsible for Slaney's dish of unspared ribs during Grass Week. In short, Garcia already possesses, fully developed, two traits which all recruits must demonstrate to become real Marines: a locustlike appetite, and the love of a good fight. This week he hopes to have the opportunity to indulge both proclivities to the fullest during Individual Combat Training.

The first day of this week, 15 April, marks the beginning of Hot Weather Standard Operating Procedure or HOT/SOP, which extends until 15 October. Precautions are taken during this period to ensure that recruits do not succumb to heat exhaustion, heat stroke or other heat-related ailments. Activities of overweight recruits, and those having recent inoculations or suffering from sunburn, are closely monitored. Frequent drinking of water from the two canteens recruits customarily carry during HOT/SOP is encouraged, as is the use of salt with meals—though not in the form of salt tablets.

Four temperature/humidity indices, signaled by flags displayed throughout the base, regulate all activities. A Wet Bulb Globe Temperature Index (WBGTI) of 80 to 84.9 degrees is denoted by a green flag flown throughout Parris Island. It is primarily a temperature alert. A yellow flag indicates a WBGTI of 85 to 87.9 degrees, and restricts strenuous outdoor effort, while a red flag (88 to 89.9 degrees) further narrows the range of permissible drills. The black flag (90 degrees and above) applies to *all* Marines, and effectively cancels outdoor activity.

Emergency vehicles must be present at all training such as PT and conditioning marches. On HOT/SOP, moreover, recruits perform PT in the cool morning hours, wear aluminum-coated "chrome dome" helmets to reflect the sun's heat, and drill with rolled sleeves or, more frequently, in skivvy shirts. Complementary measures ensure the safety of Marines in COLD/SOP from 15 October to 15 April, in cold, rainy or very windy conditions.

> . . . Mind you, I'm not kicking about air-conditioned barracks. And I'm not kicking about knocking off training whenever the temperature

reaches 90 degrees and the black flag goes up. In
fact, there ought to be a law prohibiting *all* military
activity when the temperature exceeds 90 degrees. If
that had been law, there never would have been a
Guadalcanal, Bougainville, or Khe Sanh; no North
African campaign; no Arab-Israeli wars. And if there
weren't any hot-weather wars, we wouldn't have to
train for them. Simple. . . .

If it's hot outside today, and it is—very near 90 degrees—
it is even hotter under the collars of the D.I.s of 1036, who
view the platoon returning from mess duty as relaxed, undisciplined, and more smug than recruits have any right to
be. Remedial measures are instituted at once on the quarterdeck, a dozen recruits at a time climbing mountains and
doing side-straddle hops and push-ups to exhaustion—they're
out of shape for want of PT during the past three weeks—at
which they're replaced by a fresh group of alpinists.

"Faster!" urges the D.I. "Speed it up, girls, or you're
fixing to go down to the Pits for some *real* fun. Up! Down!
Up! Oh, you're tired, you poor dears. All right, then—rest:
halfway!"

The recruits allow their bodies to droop to the excruciating
half-push-up position, at which the D.I. seems to lose all further interest in the proceedings. Sweat streams from brows
empurpled by the exertion. Limbs tremble and twitch. Arms
seem too thin and frail to contain so much agony. Bodies sag.
The D.I. rounds on them with a roar: "You're touching my
deck, son!" he says warningly to Recruit Weeks, whose body
is wilting like steamed spaghetti. The D.I. is unhappy with
Weeks who, as gear locker custodian, has committed the hor-
rible crime of allowing two scut rags to go astray.

"Diamonds!"

The recruits groan. Diamonds is, predictably, prohibited by
the SOP. It is an especially diabolical variation of push-ups,
in which the forefingers and thumbs of the two hands form a

diamond pattern on the deck just beneath the chin, wrenching muscles recruits never suspected they had, as they alternately extend and retract their arms.

At last, surcease. All return to their preparations for the coming week sobered and attentive. Spaulding, whose plaint that he wanted to go home helped visit punishment on the entire platoon, is having second thoughts. Only after having qualified as Sharpshooter, and First Class on PT, and scored one hundred on the First Phase Academic test, did he discover that, at his present age of eighteen, he will have to wait two years to be eligible for officer training. Those heavy minutes on the quarterdeck have persuaded him that he has more immediate concerns than visions of gold bars on his collar tabs.

On Monday, TD-30, the platoon is issued ALICE (All-purpose Lightweight Individual Carrying Equipment) packs. Introduced for the first time a few years ago to replace the pack Marines carried since 1941, the ALICE is made of water-resistant lightweight nylon, and has padded shoulder straps and a metal frame. Three big pockets on the outside give access to frequently needed gear. The recruits are also issued shovels, shelter halves, aluminum tent pegs and wooden poles, and other equipment they'll need in the bivouac area for the next week. While being taught how to stow it, inevitably the attention of some recruits wanders. It is brought back again into focus when they are encouraged to take their time re-stowing their packs. Meanwhile, however, all the other recruits are made to hold their fully packed ALICE gear at arm's length. Since this punishment is forbidden, the D.I. ordering it leaves the squad bay so he will not witness this shocking breach of regulations. When he returns a minute or two later, all packs are shipshape.

Since the purpose of ICT is to simulate battlefield conditions, the recruits of 1036 are instructed in techniques of fire. Most of today's youth, educated in war by preposterous television fantasies, regard these techniques as one: wait until the German (or Japanese or Russian) strolls across the skyline, and blast him, preferably at the range of twenty-five feet. It's as easy as shooting squirrels.

In real life, though, the squirrels shoot back, and usually in company strength. Safety can be bought only with rigorous fire discipline, where each unit's fire is controlled and directed toward specific targets. The Marine fire team's mission is based on a command which will include the direction of fire, description of the target and its range, who fires what weapons, and the order to commence firing. The fusillade may be concentrated against a single target such as a machine-gun emplacement, or distributed over a wide front, such as an advancing line of infantry. The character of the fire may be frontal, flanking, oblique, or enfilade, depending on the deployment or angle of approach of enemy troops. With respect to the ground, the fire may be grazing (not rising above the height of a standing man), plunging (striking the ground at a high angle), or over the heads of friendly forces. In many situations, if not most, fire will be directed against an enemy only dimly seen, if at all.

Often more deadly than enemy fire are conditions in the field where men breathe dust, drink foul water, slog through mud, shiver in snowstorms, and suffer insect infestations and the "jungle rot" of fungus infections. Until recent times typhus, pneumonia, gangrene, malaria, dysentery and a catalog of other ills killed more men than the declared enemy. Marine training in field sanitation emphasizes bodily cleanliness, prophylaxis against disease, the proper disposal of bodily wastes, and how to conduct a rear-guard action against those perennial companions of the fighting man—flies, fleas, mosquitos, ticks, and half a dozen varieties of body lice.

Thus forewarned of what the week in ICT will bring, at dawn on Wednesday, TD-32, 1036 Series marches off to the Rifle Range. There, indoctrination firing of the .45-caliber automatic pistol and field firing of the M16A1 will occupy the day, prior to the movement to the ICT encampment area. Platoon 1036's guidon is tightly furled—it has been ever since the platoon's return from Mess and Maintenance. "It's for your own protection," S/Sgt. Dawson explains as they move out. "I don't want anybody to know who you are. After all, we can't have everybody throwing rocks at you."

The attitude of their D.I.s, and a consciousness that they really *haven't* been performing up to par, puts Platoon 1036 in a murderous mood during the two-mile route march to A-Line at Weapons Battalion. This is the proper frame of mind for TD-32, when they shall fire the two basic weapons in the infantry inventory.

The .45-caliber Colt automatic, the U.S. service pistol developed for its massive stopping power during the Philippine Insurrection in the early years of this century, is carried only by officers and senior NCOs, but even Marine privates must be familiar with its operation and capabilities. These they learn in a three-hour session dealing with the characteristics, disassembly and technique of fire and, axiomatically, safety. Each recruit then has the opportunity to fire the pistol course for familiarization; recruits do not fire the service .45 for record.

Neither does the field-firing exercise count in the recruit's official record, even though this is the type of fire most closely approximating actual combat. Slow-fire consists of aimed shots at pop-up targets (controlled by battery-operated mechanisms) at ranges varying between 115 and 425 yards. Sights are set at battlesight zero, and the weight-bearing arm is steadied by the hasty sling, in which the sling, fully opened, is wrapped around hand and forearm.

The rifleman shoots at the targets from behind seven firing positions similar to those he is most likely to encounter in actual combat: the Fighting Hole, Window, Kneeling-Supported, Log, Bunker Fighting Position, Roof-Top and Wall Barricade. At each position he may support the weapon as he sees fit, but always so as to present the smallest possible silhouette to the enemy. Under the watchful eye of a coach, he fires five shots from each position. The shooter must estimate the range of his targets and the aiming point, although he is counseled to shoot low rather than high. Thus, even if he misses, the puff of dust or rustle of foliage may tell him where his shot went or, with luck, score a hit with a ricochet.

Aimed single shots are only one of the rifleman's options. He practices another on the rapid-fire line. Again he fires at pop-up targets, this time two ten-round clips, in bursts of two or three rounds, with the M-16-A1 selector switch set on automatic. In a subsidiary exercise, he ceases fire on command, rolls over on his back, dons his gas mask, and rolls back into firing position to resume firing. The interval between the two strings of fire must be less than nine seconds. He completes his rapid fire by loosing two 10-round magazines with the rifle muzzle supported by the clip-on bipod.

> . . . Realistic rifle shooting yesterday, sort of. We fired under simulated combat conditions, from behind various types of concealment. We were supposed to remember all the stuff about sight picture and breath control, but mostly I just took quick aim and let fly. I learned one thing: when you're shooting like that, having a couple of bandoliers of ammo is a plus. . . .

In combat, instead of the single glint of light that appears as a spent shell is ejected, a golden stream of yellow brass will spill from the ejection port, for the objectives on the range and in combat are very different. In the latter, where most targets will be in the one-to-fifty yard range, pinpoint accuracy is seldom necessary: any Marine can consistently hit exposed targets at such a short range. But more commonly encountered than sitting ducks are dug-in troops over whose heads Marines will send a drum-rolling suppression fire to keep enemy heads down as friendly forces advance under the steel umbrella. Harassing fire, on the other hand, keeps the enemy awake, jumpy, and wishing he were far behind the lines. Those who *are* provide targets for Marines with sniper rifles and telescopic sights who can kill at one thousand yards.

According to those who have had to subsist on them, MREs (Meals-Ready-to-Eat) can be equally deadly, although allowance must be made for the compulsion—it's practically a General Order—of Marines to gripe about everything. In fact, during an interval in the six hours spent on A-line, 1036 Series downs its first MRE without visible complaint. Garcia actually enjoys his. Consuming an MRE demands instruction as well as a keen hunger. Twelve rations, each different in composition, come in a heavy cardboard box. Individual rations are packed in a thick dirt-brown plastic envelope about the size of a gothic horror paperback, which could well have been its inspiration.

S/Sgt. Gladden, an NCO of considerable field experience, explains to the troops how to cope with the MRE:

"You'll find crackers in there someplace. You don't like crackers? Eat 'em anyway—they've got salt in them. Don't eat pork patties and trash like that dry. It'll just swell up in your stomach. You pour water on it and give it time to be absorbed. There's coffee, cream and sugar, but you're out of luck unless you like to drink it cold, because we have no way to heat water. Pass the matches and chewing gum to your squad leader—you won't be needing them. One more thing—drink a canteen of water with each MRE. And two are better than one."

The typical MRE contains half a dozen individual plastic envelopes and wrappers, constituting on the company level an appalling amount of litter. The food, eaten with a plastic spoon, is largely an homogeneous, unidentifiable mass. Its consistency is that of pulverized phonograph records suspended in library paste. Though varied, filling and containing sufficient calories, it is not fighting man's fare. It cannot compare with simple but well-cooked food and *hot* coffee from a field kitchen. The MREs are an assault on the senses and sensibility of the man in the field, but do little to combat his hunger. Perhaps they are supplied to make him fighting mad.

Thus provisioned, in late afternoon of TD-32, 1036 Series moves out in route march toward the bivouac area three miles away among the remains of Page Field, a World War II air station long since abandoned to the wilderness and field training.

The Individual Combat Training area eases the recruit into the field environment painlessly. The bivouac stands on perfectly flat ground covered with a soft bed of scented needles from towering white pines which give a cathedral air to the surroundings. Ten paces away is a concrete taxiway, on the far side of which stands a row of portable toilets; they are emptied and cleaned daily. No washing of mud-caked clothes in mosquito-infested pools in ICT, either: regular laundry runs provide the recruits clean clothing just as in barracks. Fresh, pure drinking water is available in abundance from faucets connected to the base supply. During their week in the tamed wilds of Page Field, the recruits will eat three meals—or, rather, three MREs—shave, brush their teeth, polish their boots, and listen to lectures in covered bleachers, every day. They will, it is true, be allowed only one shower during that period, and will sleep on the ground, atop a one-inch layer of foam rubber, two to a small tent illuminated only by the stars . . . and their flashlights. Boot camp's ICT area is *not* to be confused with the environment of *real* combat.

The first night in the field, little can be done besides setting up tents formed by mating two shelter halves, having evening chow, and performing the limited ablutions permitted. After humping with full pack, helmet, rifle and two water-filled canteens for two hours, plus six hours frying on the front burners of the Rifle Range, the recruits are ready for the rack. Except for the fire watch, which rotates among the recruits at two-hour intervals, 1036 Series sacks in for the night, lulled to sleep by the murmur of a myriad mosquitos rising like an aerial armada from the nearby marshes.

Classwork, in the field as in barracks, occupies a considerable portion of each day. Eighteen hours will be devoted to combat-related subjects in the three remaining days of this training week.

TD-33 leads off with two hours of lectures. Tony Garcia's eyes glaze over, as do those of a goodly number of his mates. They share the conviction that, if they wanted to attend class, they'd have gone to college. The realization that a Marine's training, even in the field, comprises more—a great deal more—than marching and drilling and firing guns from the hip is depressing. They're bored, and that's the dilemma: land navigation, the subject of the lecture, would teach them how to get from here to somewhere else, if they could only stay awake and listen.

Theoretically, land navigation is fairly straightforward. Following the same principle as using a road map, the navigator lines up his map with visual reference points, notes his objective, and moves toward it by the most convenient means. The distance to and relative bearing from observed landmarks—hills, streams, valleys and structures—allow the navigator to plot his course with the aid of a compass: so many steps northeast will bring him to the abandoned barn, a ninety degree right turn puts him in line with the lone oak tree, and 340 paces towards the southeast takes him there, and so on to his objective.

In practice, land navigation can be a nightmare. Compass readings are anything but precise, irregularities in terrain cause deviations in direction, and estimating distance is at best a rough guess. Stumbling among brambles and bushes, seeking inconspicuous markers that must be there but never are, is an essay in frustration. After the very first exercise, Tony Garcia confesses he soon became lost, and never did discover the path he was to take.

Sandwiched between two dry periods on land navigation is a long session on hand grenades. Contrary to popular belief, hand grenades do not merely blow people up. In fact, they are designed for a variety of purposes, some humanitarian. The egg-shaped MK-1 illumination grenade is not among these. Thrown behind an advancing enemy, it burns for twenty-five seconds with an intensity of 50,000 foot-candles, silhouetting the attackers like so many Baker targets. The AN-M18 is a grenade that emits yellow, green, red or violet smoke for signalling helicopters, e.g., being guided in to lift out troops or casualties. Another grenade, the AN-M18HC, spews a cloud of thick smoke for more than two minutes, to screen troop movements. Three varieties of grenades are used for riot control: CN is a macelike disabling agent, DM induces vomiting, and CS is a lung, eye and skin irritant.

The MK3A2 fragmentation grenade, though shaped like a can of beer, carries considerably more punch. Its certain-casualty radius is two meters, but it can be deadly up to two hundred meters. The M34WP contains white phosphorus, spreading acrid smoke and casualties to a radius of thirty-five meters. Its five thousand degree F. flame can reduce abandoned vehicles and weapons to scrap within minutes.

Two hours of lectures lay the groundwork for throwing real grenades. Recruits are instructed in the proper way to hold, carry and remove the pin from grenades. Then, wearing flak jackets and helmets, they throw dummy grenades, containing only the explosive primer, at realistic bunkers and firing holes from the prone, kneeling and standing positions. Finally, on the range, each recruit throws a live fragmentation grenade from behind a concrete wall and earthen berm, with an instructor standing beside him to monitor each move, while range officers and NCOs observe from a raised platform behind double thicknesses of bulletproof glass. Safety precautions are more stringent here than even on the rifle range. Every phase of the exercise is endlessly rehearsed, experienced NCOs oversee the recruit's every move, and twenty-eight detailed safety procedures encompass every conceivable situation.

The second night in bivouac is more eventful than the first. Safe from the eyes of their D.I.s, sitting around a fire at the other end of the neat rows of tents, a few recruits put on an impromptu show featuring imitations of, among others, S/Sgt. Gladden, a compact man with an oversize voice, unaware that the veteran of countless FMF patrols is observing every move from the darkness. Retribution is swift: he inducts the guilty recruits Barker and Daugette into his "Every-Hour Group," which the D.I. blandly promises will do PT every hour from now until graduation.

> . . . We're finally in the field, if you can call it that. More like a city kid's Boy Scout camp. Tents in straight rows between lines of tall trees, the smell of pine needles, drinking water piped in, MREs, a campfire at night, and *Portajohns!* Everything but Muzak. S/Sgt. Gladden barking at Barker and yelling at Daugette is the only music we've had so far. . . .

The next day brings classes on weapons that may decide future wars—NBC (Nuclear, Biological and Chemical). These horrors are not always or totally without a defense, however. Heat, blast and radiation effects of atomic explosives are, to be sure, deadly except for those very distant. Biological agents—viruses, bacteria and toxins—are slower and more insidious, but quite as lethal. But against chemical attack—nerve, blood, blister and choking agents—there is some chance of survival, if immediate measures are used. Men trained in NBC techniques will, ironically, be better equipped to survive future wars than the civilian populations whom they are fighting to protect.

NBC instruction ends as do many protest demonstrations— in a cloud of CS riot gas. Recruits are led into the gas chamber and don their masks. They make sure their masks are tight and the airways clear. The integrity of the mask is tested when the instructor pulls the ring on a canister of CS, filling the room with almost impenetrable fumes. Recruits are then ordered to remove their masks. They are made to stand fast for fifteen seconds, choking and weeping and itching, before being given the signal to grope their way to the hatch.

"That was the longest fifteen seconds of my life," gasps Recruit Garcia as he stumbles out the hatch into the sunlight, his face streaming tears, his eyes red and puffy, his skin blotched from the stinging gas.

If the gas clears the nasal passages, it also stimulates the appetite. That night after Taps, Garcia slips out of his tent. The only lawful excuse to be out of one's rack after Taps is a head call. But Garcia is heading in the other direction. As stealthy as a Commanche, he flits through the shadows toward Platoon 1038. He waits, barely breathing, as the fire watch approaches. The two watchstanders fail to spot him in the darkness. As they do an about face and walk toward the opposite ends of the row of tents, Garcia quickly abstracts a pair of MREs from a box of rations, and glides back the way he came. If he learned nothing else, the Army taught Garcia how to conduct a successful food reconn. . . .

The last two days of the week are stiff with lectures and demonstrations. Recruits study the deployment of troops in fire teams—the smallest tactical units, and squads, and the hand and arm signals by which their leaders silently control their movements. The signals number more than a dozen, and may be supplemented by whistles, pyrotechnics and even taps on the helmet to convey information in the heat of battle or at night.

Mines and booby traps are such large and diffuse subjects that only a hint of their complexities and dangers can be given in boot camp. Recruits learn the major components of mines, the four ways they may be detonated, the six actions that may cause a mine to explode, and the four types of mines likely to be encountered and how to avoid detonating them. The ingenuity displayed by the enemy in rigging mines and booby traps is a main consideration in the slow deliberation with which seasoned troops advance through unknown territory. The Marine Corps, of course, has its own arsenal of concealed explosives, including the M-18-A1 anti-personnel (Claymore) mine which, scattering a fan-shaped pattern of seven hundred steel pellets lethal at one hundred meters, can wipe out a large enemy patrol when properly deployed.

In war, surprise has always been among man's most effective weapons. Camouflage, cover and concealment have been means to achieve surprise. The components of camouflage, cover and concealment are practically without number, and include the six "factors of recognition"—position, shape, shadow, texture, color, and movement—along with the techniques of hiding, blending, deceiving and disguising, and the methods and materials used to put these techniques into practice. Familiar to the movie-going public is the use of burnt cork, dirt, charcoal or face paint to help the Marine blend with his surroundings.

The account of an actual battlefield situation in Vietnam is used to impress upon recruits the importance of accurate Observing and Reporting. In 1967, the 3rd Battalion, 5th Marine Regiment, launched an attack against what were believed to be Vietcong numbering only three hundred troops. The true number was about four thousand five hundred. The Marines killed most of them, but at the cost of jeopardizing the regiment as the result of misinformation.

Observing and Reporting involves identification of noises such as the opening of field rations, the snapping of twigs, the gurgle of water in a canteen, and the rattle of a rifle bolt. It also encompasses techniques for visual search of terrain, and the contents of a worthwhile report. Embodied in the acronym SALUTE, the report should make known the enemy's Size (number), Activity, Location, Unit (artillery, motor transport, etc.), Time of observation and Equipment with which the enemy is supplied.

Effective observation often depends on good night vision. After one minute of darkness, the eyes' sensitivity to light increases 10 times; after 20 minutes 6,000 times, and after 40 minutes it achieves the maximum sensitivity, 25,000 times. Human eyesight is so sensitive that it is possible, from a mountaintop at night, to detect the flare of a match 50 miles away. On the other hand, if that match is used to light a cigarette, the smoker's night vision is cut by 50 percent after just a few puffs. Off-center vision and scanning also enhance the sensitivity of the eye in detecting faint objects. When these methods fail, Marines have recourse to trip flares, illumination grenades and star shells, which can light up large areas with their 40,000 to 55,000 candle-power glare.

In their first four days in the field, Garcia and his fellow recruits of 1036 Series have spent considerably more time in the bleachers listening to lectures than in field exercises applying them. Next week the ratios are reversed. The recruits will finally get a hint—no more than that—of the Marine grunt's daily destiny: muddle, misery and mud—face first.

Shaping Up

Getting shot was a hazard Tony Garcia felt prepared to face, but he didn't expect it would happen in his first week at Parris Island, when boots receive a veritable fusillade—shots for measles, tetanus, typhoid, yellow fever, smallpox, bicillin (a long-acting antibiotic against throat and blister infections), diphtheria, polio, PPD, meningococcal vaccine and adenovirus four and seven. Partly because of these shots, but more importantly today's recruiting standards, Marine enlistees are the healthiest in history. It is the responsibility of the Branch Medical Clinic (or Recruit Depot sick bay) of the Beaufort Naval Hospital to keep them that way.

The sick bay is halfway house between the five battalion aid stations where routine complaints are processed and Beaufort Naval Hospital, five miles away, where approximately

1,000 Marines are sent annually for treatment or observation. The aid stations treat the 80 percent of recruits who appear with minor muscle aches and strains, blisters and colds. All others, as well as emergencies, are sent immediately to the sick bay.

There a full-time Navy medical staff—six physicians, four physician assistants (warrant officers with specialized training), two optometrists, two podiatrists, a physiotherapist, a psychologist and four Nurse Corps officers, assisted by nearly a hundred enlisted hospital corpsmen—examine and treat outpatients whose visits total 140,000 a year.

Of this number, 105,000 recruit visits are for general medicine consultations, 9,500 are referrals to the optometry department, 8,000 see podiatrists, and 4,000 undergo neuropsychiatric examinations, to which all D.I. candidates, incidentally, must submit.

During HOT/SOP, around two hundred fifty recruits may be expected to experience symptoms of heat cramps, heat exhaustion or, rarely, heat stroke. SOP ensures that recruits drink frequently from the two canteens they carry at all times on the field, and dictates training within temperature limits denoted by flags of various colors. Even so, recruits sometimes betray symptoms of heat stress—staggering, weaving, or falling behind in runs—whereupon an aid truck, always standing by, is summoned to rush the boot to the sick bay. There, though rarely needed, ice-water baths and IVs are kept in constant readiness. Salt tablets, incidentally, are *not* recommended by the medical staff, for the recruit receives an adequate salt intake from his regular diet.

For safety reasons, recruits are not allowed to wear contact lenses or retain their own prescription glasses. Instead, they are fitted with shatterproof government-issue glasses in utilitarian black frames. Ground on the premises, the new glasses are fitted and issued, along with a spare pair, in approximately two hours.

Of the complaints registered by the six thousand-odd recruits on the base at any one time, foot ailments predominate.

The two staff podiatrists examine up to seventy recruits a day, and can fit and prescribe corrective orthotics, which take two weeks to be fabricated. Sorbothane, a soft, foot-conforming synthetic, is being issued to some recruits in an attempt to eliminate shock and stress fractures, traditional disabilities among foot soldiers.

The generally robust health of future Marines is reflected in the better condition of recruits' teeth in recent years, the result, according to base dental officers, of the emphasis on dental hygiene in advertisements, the proliferation of community water fluoridation and peer pressure.

On TD-1, a busy day during which they get their shots, glasses, and rifles, each recruit also spends several busy hours at the Dental Clinic. There the recruit's complete dental history, pulse rate and blood pressure are recorded, after which he views a twenty-minute videotape on oral hygiene and maintenance. Next a team of eight technicians instructs each platoon on the proper way to brush and floss teeth—which drill instructors are charged with enforcing. A bite-wing x-ray for crown portions of the teeth and a panorex x-ray precede a fifteen-minute individual examination, during which a chart is made of the recruit's teeth and fillings.

In a typical year, twenty-five thousand Parris Island recruits will be examined and treated by Navy dentists. Of these, only 9 percent of the males will be classified as having perfect teeth on entry, 15 percent will need plaque removal and minor restorative work, and 76 percent will require major restoration. By the time the recruits graduate, after having spent an average twenty-four hours on dental recall (mostly during TD-1, TD-16 and TD-30), 19 percent will have moved into Class I with perfect teeth, 27 percent will be in Class II, still requiring minor work, and only 44 percent will still need major restoration, which they will receive at their next station. Some two dozen will have refused any treatment at all, most of them recruits with second thoughts about becoming Marines. The Marines Corps, having second thoughts as well, will send them home.

The Dental Clinic is staffed by fifty-two dental officers and eighty-six technicians in a brick building across from the parade deck. It houses the most modern dental equipment available, including state-of-the-art optical-fiber illumination and composite restoration techniques. New staff dentists are all graduates of recognized dental schools, have passed their state boards, and during their first three years at Parris Island make a complete rotation of the departments of oral surgery, periodontics, endodontics, prosthodontics, oral diagnosis and recruit-in-processing.

The Dental Clinic copes with 185,000 patient-visits a year, including 10,000 from personnel of the nearby Marine Corps Air Station, 8,000 dependents, and 25,000 military and naval retirees living within thirty miles of Parris Island. Staff orthodontists and pedodontists treat dependent children who, along with everyone else on the base, receive an annual exam, cleaning and fluoride treatment.

The quality of health care at Parris Island, especially for recruits, is implicit in its mortality statistics. During the last fifteen years, thirty-five deaths have occurred among a total of 425,000 recruits in training. Sixteen died from chronic conditions that escaped detection on pre-enlistment medical examinations—pneumonia, meningitis, brain tumor, renal failure and cancer. Heart trouble and cardiac arrest, mostly from pre-existing ailments, caused the death of thirteen. Four recruits drowned while trying to desert. In 1976 a recruit committed suicide, and another died in a training accident when he dropped a live grenade. Statistically, Marine boot camp is about the safest place a young man can be.

WEEK EIGHT

Johnson:
Goin' Grunt

Just after dawn, eight columns of men crouch in a dense copse at the edge of the dirt road, waiting for the signal to advance. The early morning quiet is broken only by forest sounds—the buzz of insects, the croak of frogs, the flutter of wings.

The platoon commander extends his palm toward the men in battle garb, signaling "Are you ready?"

The leader of each squad, in turn, extends his own palm, signifying "I am ready."

The platoon commander raises his hand above his head and brings it down parallel to the ground, pointing ahead, signifying "Forward!"

The squad leaders drop to the earth and, holding their rifles at arm's length ahead of them, squirm across the dirt road toward the barbed wire on the other side, where the enemy's defenses begin. Almost immediately they are spotted, and defensive fire erupts from mortars and heavy machine guns. Clouds of sand and dust envelope the attackers. They shake it off and wriggle under four successive lines of barbed wire. The shell fire bursts get closer.

Seventy-five yards from the road, their lines still unbroken, the men reach the rampart which marks the position over which the enemy is firing. With a rebel yell and a rush, the attackers scale the breastwork, drop to the ground on the other side, and commence fire at the disconcerted enemy, unprepared for such a determined attack.

The machine-gun fire intensifies, and the explosions of artillery at lethal range rend the air. Through a curtain of dust and thudding detonations the skirmishers press forward. Snaking beneath seven more barbed wire entanglements over a 125-yard stretch of no-man's-land, they occupy the abandoned position of the enemy, who has finally broken and fled.

Make-believe battle? Yes, but the barbed wire, the dirt, the noise, the confusion, the exhaustion of the victorious troops—all these are real enough, and so is the surge of adrenalin that courses through the veins of recruits in their first encounter with the ''enemy.''

The drumbeat of automatic fire comes from a heavy machine-gun simulator ''fired'' by an instructor pressing a pickle-switch, and the ground-shaking thunder of artillery fire from quarter-pound charges of TNT in sand-bagged positions along the line of the attackers' advance. The TNT is detonated from the tower overlooking the infiltration course which 1036 Series runs—or crawls—on the morning of TD-36.

Recruits whose limbs the deafening noise turned to jelly, or who failed to demonstrate the proper aggressive spirit, are summarily quarterdecked by their D.I.s on completion of the course. The rest, their bodies and hard-rubber exercise rifles encrusted with a thick layer of grime, are sent off to wash both under showers near the infiltration course. The water is ice-cold but welcome, especially since this is the only bath they'll get during their week-long sojourn in the boondocks.

One of the battling bathers is Darrel E. Johnson, who, somewhat to his surprise, has discovered that life in the field is not only tolerable, but actually agreeable. The eighteen-year-old high school graduate from Annapolis, Maryland, joined the Marine Corps neither for three-squares-a-day nor a career, but for those old-fashioned goals of challenge and adventure. Boot camp, he says, has already taught him the discipline he found wanting in civilian life. He wishes there were more of it.

"Nothing makes me madder," he says, "than seeing the platoon marching like a mob. A Marine's survival depends on discipline, and close-order drill is the best teacher. Recruits who can't work together on the parade deck won't be able to work together in combat, and you can kiss them good-bye."

This week in the comparative wilds of South Carolina has made up his mind. "I *love* this part of the training. It makes me feel like a *real* Marine. Even so, I realize this is only a taste, a beginning. I like night maneuvers best. At night you can take the initiative, take more chances, penetrate into enemy territory easier than you can during the day.

"Funny thing is," he goes on reflectively, "a couple of weeks ago I wasn't sure I'd get *this* far. I went 'unk' on the range, and had to shoot in the requalification round. The second time, I made it, and it was like throwing a switch: I became a different man. Motivated."

Johnson has no doubt now that he'll get through boot camp and graduate. When he does, he is guaranteed further training in Operations and Communications in accordance with a pre-enlistment contract. But he's still seeking challenge and adventure; he's sure he'll find them pursuing his specialty as a grunt.

Later in the day, Johnson and his fellow recruits of 1036 Series will discover that a grunt needs to know a great deal more than simply how to crawl through fields of barbed wire entanglements under fire. Infantry in modern war is no longer the refuge of those who cannot absorb technical knowledge, but a specialty in its own right, demanding a combination of theoretical and practical skills.

Offensive operations, for example, even at the small-unit level, must be based on explicit information in order successfully to engage the enemy. That information is summarized in the Five-Paragraph Order, which can be as complex as a Shakespearean sonnet. Like many service procedures, the Five-Paragraph Order resounds with mnemonic acronyms. The five paragraphs themselves are embodied in the acronym SMEAS, for Situation, Mission, Execution, Administration and logistics, and command and Signals.

Paragraph One sets the stage for the operation by presenting the disposition of enemy and friendly forces. The mission—the who, what, when, where and why of the operation—are summed up in Paragraph Two. The next paragraph considers *how* the mission will be achieved, listing the responsibilities of each of the component units engaged. Paragraph Four, commonly referred to as the "Four B's—Beans, Bullets, Bandages and Bad Guys—deals with supply and rations, ammunition, evacuation and POWs. Command and signals, the last paragraph, stipulates communications procedures such as passwords, smoke signals, and radio frequencies.

. . . Acronyms—the Marines have got them for everything. SMEAS, AWOL, EST, FTU, NCO, PX, T/O, RIS, RAM, radar, ALICE, BDR, DI, sonar, PFT, Pfc, SOP—the list goes on forever. At first I thought the idea was to communicate in a sort of secret language, which an eavesdropping enemy would have difficulty in interpreting. I was wrong. It's just that a Marines's life centers around weapons, equipment and situations not encountered by civilians, and the terminology with usage gets stripped down to essentials, like "scuba" for "self-contained underwater breathing apparatus." A smart boot learns the jargon ASAP. . . .

Marine doctrine dictates attack whenever possible. But even in the heat of an offensive physical defenses cannot be neglected, both as jumping-off points for attack, and as fallback positions in the event of enemy breakthrough or flanking movements.

Field fortifications, recruits are taught, offer good observation, good cover and concealment, and good fields of fire.

Hasty emplacements—rocks, shallow pits, shell craters, logs—can be used when enemy contact is imminent. If he has time, the savvy Marine digs a fighting hole—called the foxhole in wars past—or more defensible positions. Marine fortifications tend to the simple and make-shift: they don't intend to be back there long, but somewhere up front. If they're *already* up front, such as when they've penetrated the enemy's supply lines and dug in, the enemy must attack or die.

In such situations, Marine Corps tactics are designed to assure that the enemy attacks *and* dies. At the squad level, the Marine may then be part of either a linear defense or a perimeter defense, a circular disposition of troops when all-around security is required. The individual Marine will commonly occupy a fighting hole on the FEBA (Forward Edge of the Battle Area) from which he can direct fire to overlap the fire zones of positions on either side. Security against impending attack is assured by forward listening and observation posts and security patrols probing to determine enemy dispositions, strength and intentions. Combat patrols seek to throw the enemy off balance and disrupt well-laid plans by destroying his lines of communication, supply and command.

Enemy beaches have always been the Marines' prime targets. After Marines secured a beachhead, traditional practice called for the Army to follow up by storming inland toward the enemy's heartland. Beginning with World War II, however, the Marines have pushed ever farther into the interior, being used as shock troops wherever the enemy has proved obdurate and hard to dislodge. In addition to amphibious principles pioneered by the Marine Corps in that war, therefore, the Marines have added a new method of attack to their battle repertoire: vertical envelopment by helicopter.

Helicopter and Amphibious Indoctrination gives recruits their first acquaintance with the machines and techniques used today to capture beachheads and cut off enemy units far inland by means of vertical envelopment.

Modern landing craft can carry up to 400 combat-equipped troops (each, with full gear, weighing 240 pounds) from transport ships to the beach at 8 miles an hour through heavy seas. The LVTP, carrying 25 troops, can then speed inland at up to 40 miles an hour, and disgorge its troops, ready for action, from a rear ramp.

Four principal types comprise the Marine helicopter fleet: the *UH-1N Huey,* used for command, medical evacuation and reconnaissance; the *CH-46 Sea Knight,* carrying twenty-one fully equipped Marines; the *CH-53E Super Stallion,* basically a cargo helicopter, can also accommodate fifty-two combat-equipped Marines; and the *AH-1J/T Sea Cobra,* which provides close-in fire support with Gatling-type twenty-mm. armament as well as pod-mounted rockets.

Recruits are schooled in the basics of emplaning on and deplaning from helicopters, and similar procedure for amphibious craft, as well as the responsibilities of each craft's fighting teams and their commanders. They are briefed on safety, and emergency measures to be taken in case of crash landing and ditching at sea.

On the evening of TD-36, 1036 Series is divided into aggressors and defenders to practice their lessons in the art of squad defense. Their faces darkened with dirt and green greasepaint, their helmets sprouting sprigs of green, the defenders take their positions in a line of shallow fighting holes in the pine forest and await attack. Their rifles are loaded—with blanks. But since even blanks can burn at close range, each M-16's muzzle is covered by a box-like metal shield—the BFA, or blank-firing apparatus—which traps the hot gases and diverts them to the rear to operate the rifle's bolt.

They wait. The shadows lengthen, and the mosquitoes swarm out of the marshes to relieve the flies and sand fleas which go off duty at dusk. The recruits, bored with straining their eyes into the growing gloom, begin to talk in guarded tones among themselves. An occasional slap is heard, as they counterattack the only aggressors who have yet appeared. A sharp crack disturbs the silence; it is not a sniper's bullet, but the snapping of a twig in the darkness as a recruit shifts his position to ease a leg cramp.

From his observation post twenty yards to the rear, a drill instructor shakes his head in disgust.

"No discipline," he whispers, in a voice as soft as a lover's caress. "They haven't learned that war is a matter of hurry-up-and-wait, and it's the waiting that's the hardest. And all the racket they're making—they might as well send up flares."

Minutes later he points into the darkness. Nothing. He keeps pointing. Gradually, a shadow slowly splits in two. One half stands still, the other moves. The phantoms multiply, and grow larger. Suddenly they are upon the defenders like a wave breaking on the beach, flames spouting from their rifles as the defenders are taken totally by surprise.

The D.I. stands up and shouts above the din of tardy defensive fire: "Save your ammunition, you sleeping beauties—you're all dead!"

At a dark, distant outpost, Recruit Darrell Johnson is on watch for the enemy. He is joined by two recruits from an adjacent platoon, who slip into his firing position from the next bunker for a little conversation to break the tedium. The talk, in barely audible whispers, inevitably turns to a discussion of the virtues and vices of their respective D.I.s—with the emphasis on the vices. Only later do Johnson and his mates discover that their congenial recruit neighbors were actually D.I.s in boot disguise.

"I learned something," says Johnson. "Never—*never*—trust strangers, especially in the dark. If they'd been the real enemy, we'd have been slaughtered." As for the punishment that inevitably follows, he's philosophical: "The experience was worth the quarterdecking. Made it stick in my mind. Who knows, it might save my life someday. This is the kind of training there should be more of."

The same night, Tony Garcia is on his third night patrol. Like Johnson, he enjoys field operations, and already has demonstrated some aptitude for it, eluding the fire watch guarding a neighboring platoon's provisions and making off with two extra rations. When the next day's count shows a shortage and explanations are solicited, Garcia honors the Marines' so-called wisest maxim: "Keep your eyes open, your mouth shut, and don't volunteer."

Last night he did even better. Snaking through the underbrush in enemy territory, he stole the guidon of rival platoon 1037 and, to the plaudits of his shipmates, brought the trophy safely home.

Tonight Garcia will stretch his luck too far. On patrol—an authorized patrol for a change—he blunders into an enemy position and is captured. The D.I. of the enemy platoon asks, not unreasonably, since this is only an exercise, from which platoon he comes.

Garcia, invoking the Geneva Convention, gives his name, rank, serial number and date of birth. And, despite the D.I.'s threats, that is all this prisoner-of-war gives. No question about it, Garcia has the right temperament for his chosen line of work. . . .

On TD-37 begins the offensive exercise to practice the maneuvers they've studied in class. Squad-strength units of Platoon 1036, armed with blank-loaded magazines, form a ready circle near a helicopter mock-up. With the squad leader counting them off as they enter, the men board the helicopter, muzzles of their rifles pointing downward, magazines extracted.

As the make-believe helo wings inland and crosses into imaginary enemy country, the squad leader orders: "Magazine, lock and load."

The D.I., acting as an observer, announces: "Helo is down. Ramp is down."

"Move out!" cries the squad leader.

The two firing teams pour out of the helo and form a semicircular "hasty defense" in front of the helo, then consolidate their position.

. . . Today we practiced an enveloping movement from a "helicopter." It was pathetic. Up to then a lot of us, barging around in the boondocks with rifles at the ready, were beginning to feel like old combat veterans. But this exercise cured all that. We stumbled around, shooting blanks in all directions, running into each other, making ourselves targets like German generals on TV, and generally being confused. But it was a good lesson, at that: it taught us that when it comes to combat, we still don't have a clue. . . .

Re-forming on the D.I.'s command, the recruits board a dummy landing craft. Hitting the beach, they advance as fire-team skirmishers. Both individuals and fire teams make coordinated rushes forward in a frontal attack on an enemy emplacement, firing as they go.

The objective taken, the squad makes a final assault from a helo. While one fire team pins down the enemy with concentrated fire the other, taking advantage of the dense underbrush cover, launches an envelopment to the right. Coordinating their attack, the two fire teams storm the redoubt from two directions, putting the enemy to rout—in theory.

In fact, the operation is a shambles of confused orders, fire teams gone astray, men tripping over logs and twisting ankles, poor ammunition discipline, men getting lost in the woods, men walking in tight groups into a whirlwind of enemy fire like so many movie German soldiers. The recruits are disappointed. It didn't go this way in the neat diagrams and scenarios outlined on the blackboard by their instructors. Nevertheless, the real lesson slowly sinks in: the Marine grunt is no mere hack with a pack; he must be thoroughly disciplined, well-versed in the infantryman's myriad arts, self-confident, determined and a member of a smoothly functioning team. The morning's exercise brutally demonstrates how far he is from that goal, which will be fully realized only after months of arduous training in the Fleet Marine Force.

Back in the bivouac area after a grueling day in the field, the recruits of 1036 are formed into ranks and marched onto the abandoned taxiway next to the tent area. Here, seated in rows and stripped to the waist, they shave and wash off a few layers of sweat-caked dust using metal ammunition boxes as basins. While choking down the homogenized MREs an hour later, a recruit passes down the ranks distributing copies of *Today's English Version of the New Testament and Psalms* in an edition that fits neatly in a blouse pocket, and has a cami cover embossed with the Marine Corps emblem.

The Series will have little time to study it, however. After evening chow, preparations get underway to break camp and move out before daylight. The recruits clean rifles and stow their gear in their packs, leaving out only the clothing they will wear on the morrow.

Reveille is at 0400. The fire watch noiselessly shakes the men into wakefulness. No voice is heard, no light shown, for the Series is deep in enemy territory, from which it will now make a forced march to friendly lines. In total silence the tents are struck, and the shelter halves and bedding rolls are strapped to packs. In a matter of minutes the recruits are saddled up, wearing pack, rifle, helmet and two full canteens. In the darkness, each man has a hand firmly gripping the pack of the man ahead. Leading the march is First Lieutenant Herrera, the assistant series commander, while at the rear, to see that no stragglers are left behind, comes Series Commander Greenburg.

The series moves out. Lt. Herrera sets a swift pace in the darkness, following a circuitous route with many twists and turns through the pine forest. The line of march leads through heavy thicket and stagnant pools, across mud pans and the weed-grown pavement of old taxiways. It threads through the trees for the first hour in near-total darkness. In the false dawn around 0530 visibility improves, and the recruits can now see to dodge or step over the broken branches and mud

holes in their path. The pace picks up, broken only by a brief
halt for breakfast, and a pause every hour to ease the strain of
the back-chafing load. The sun's rise brings out the sand
fleas, and the sweat begins to flow freely as the temperature
begins its inexorable climb into the nineties.

In mid-morning, 1036 Series approaches the barracks area
of the First Recruit Training Battalion, swinging—some
limping—along at route march. Striding along beside them,
S/Sgt. Dawson begins calling cadence, and the platoon falls
into step. Dirty, winded, sweat-stained, bone-tired, and with
shoulders numb from the bite of ALICE's shoulder straps, the
recruits look suspiciously like real Marines returning to base
from a patrol. They feel the gratification of having completed
the ten-mile march in good time and order, with no stragglers
impairing the unit's integrity.

S/Sgt. Dawson halts the platoon before the barracks, and
falls the platoon out. They crowd through the hatch of the
squad bay on the first deck, which is their billet as senior
series in the barracks. When they finally leave here, they will
be Marines.

Eighteen training days still stand between 1036 and that
goal. Week Eight of their training program, indeed, is not yet
half over. The rest of this day will be devoted to rifle maintenance, field day and getting their 782 gear in order for turn-in
on Friday.

The first, and certainly most welcome duty of the day, is a
hot shower to rid themselves of the accumulated grime of the
past three days. A Navy hospital corpsman is on hand for a
hygiene inspection when they emerge. He inspects most carefully for rashes and bites that might become infected and, of
course, blisters. Despite having drilled and marched in their
boots for a full two months, so shoddy is the fabrication of
their footwear that twelve of the sixty recruits have blisters,
most of them ruptured, and some bleeding. The corpsman
issues sick bay chits to the dozen "blister bandits." They
will be spared heavy marching duties until their wounds of
battle heal.

As the recruits wearily square away their gear, S/Sgt. Dawson rewards a respectable march by favoring them with a D.I. chant, which the recruits enthusiastically parrot, line by line:

> Twenty days and I'll be home, baby . . .
> Twenty days and I'll be home—maybe . . .
> Twenty days and I'll be home, drinking foam . . .
> Twenty days and I'll be home, baby.

"Yeah!" says S/Sgt. Dawson wryly, as the squad bay resounds with their chant, proving that 1036 still possesses its fair share of energy. "We're slimy, we're dirty, we're disgusting—but we're motivated."

And he sets them to work to expend some of that energy cleaning their M-16's, a process which will occupy all their free time for the rest of the week, so many fiendishly inaccessible nooks and crannies, notches and recesses the rifle has to harbor dirt. Marines in former times needed only oil and patches to clean their weapons. After firing an M16A1, an expert can clean the rifle satisfactorily in from three to six hours; a recruit may spend his spare time for two weeks to achieve the same result. To clean the M16A1, moreover, requires patches and oil *plus* a two-headed brush, a scuz rag, pipe cleaners, several dozen Q-tips, and several applications of boiling water, conveniences not likely to be available under battle conditions.

. . . People who talk about American know-how ought to have to carry and clean an M-16. Vietnam vets tell horror stories about how they'd throw their M-16s away if they could find a captured Russian Kalashnikov. I thought that was bull until I got my own M-16. It takes minutes to field strip its many parts, and hours to clean properly, feels flimsy, is a

lousy drill weapon, and—I could go on. Of course, I
haven't been in combat, but now I believe the vets
when they say it's a piece of junk. If we Americans
can't make a good basic infantry weapon ourselves,
maybe we should get Honda to do it for us. . . .

Only battle conditions would induce recruits to forego the
haircut they get on TD-40. The haircut is not really necessary—they had their last one on TD-30. But this haircut is
different: it's a "high-and-tight." For the first time, only the
hair on the side of the head is shorn to the scalp; the hair on
the crown is left intact, giving a rakish Mohawk Indian effect
(the real Mohawk leaves only a short one-inch-wide swath
down the center of the crown; it is reserved for Marines, not
recruits). The "high-and-tight" symbolizes the senior status
of Third Phase recruits, and is a coveted hallmark which,
unfortunately, is usually concealed from jealous juniors by
the cami cover or chrome dome.

Another rite of passage is "03 Clothing," the penultimate
clothing/fitting issue. The 01 issue of basic items and utility
uniforms came their first night at Parris Island. The 02 issue,
immediately after the Rifle Range, was of the uniforms they
will wear after they become Marines. The 03 fitting is to
readjust measurements of uniforms already fitted during
02, to compensate for weight gained or lost during the
interim.

The issue includes six shirts, three wool trousers and two
trousers of synthetic material, an all-weather coat, and other
items costing the recruit $305 of his clothing allowance,
added to his initial hygiene issue valued at $265. The Marine
Corps hopes to supplement the basic issue with a camouflage
field jacket and a British-design olive-drab wool sweater, or
"wooly pully," but the addition of either will require a compensatory subtraction of present items. This is because the
Congress, which always finds funds for a congressional pay
hike, imposes a ceiling on the cost of the contents of the
seabag issue. It is these "economies" which condemn Ma-

rine infantry to march in uncomfortable, unserviceable boots at great cost in efficiency and health. Over the years the Marine Corps tested and wanted to order superior boots, but congressional budget cutters prohibited their adoption to save a few dollars a pair.

The 02 initial fitting takes the Series five hours, and the 03 nearly as long. The fitting is meticulous, done by tailors of long experience (one has been fitting uniforms at Parris Island for thirty-four years). Most items that can be tailored *are* tailored, including all-weather coats and belts, with alterations made by a crew of seamstresses in an adjoining loft. The S.D.I. must concur with the fit of each item before it goes into a recruit's seabag. Before anything is worn, it is sent to the base laundry for cleaning and pressing. When the recruit finally gets to try on his uniform for the first time in his tenth week of training, he is not yet a Marine, but he very much looks and feels like one.

The recruit this week receives another indication that his boot training is finally drawing to a close: he is given his first pay. His first check is for $300 (in Receiving he has already received $100 in chits for post exchange purchases). The recruit is encouraged to mail the check home for deposit, or open a bank account in the base bank. In any case, he will not have a chance to cash the check or spend any money until his first brief liberty on the eve of graduation.

If the Marine Corps has its way—and it usually does—his pay won't be spent on drugs. During the last lecture of the week, on drug abuse, the D.I. asks the assembled Series:

"Imagine yourself a member of a platoon responsible for the defense of a strategic hilltop. It is 2300 and a heavy fog has set in. Listening posts have been established one hundred meters down the slope. The two Marines assigned to the LP in front of your position are lighting up their third joint. How would you feel entrusting your life to these two 'squared-away' Marines?"

The question is rhetorical these days, thanks to a policy which has all but eliminated the use of drugs among Marines.

Marine Corps officers and senior NCOs found to be using cocaine, heroin, amphetamines, or taking so much as a puff of marijuana or hashish, are summarily discharged from the service, and incur other heavy penalties, usually including imprisonment. Other ranks *may* get a second chance to stay in the Corps, but had better not count on it. They receive judicial punishment, in any case. There are no third chances. Nor are the chances of escaping detection very bright. Random urinalysis of all Marines occurs on a regular basis. The test is conclusive for use within the previous sixty days, and it's getting better all the time.

The recruits of Platoon 1036 don't need drugs: with TD-57 fast approaching, they're already high on the prospect of imminent graduation.

In a sense, Darrel Johnson feels that he has *already* graduated. He feared that he, a city boy, would not be able to take the grueling marches in intense heat, hours of enforced immobility and silence on outpost, crawling on his belly through mud and thornbush. Now fear has been replaced by confidence that he can take anything the Marine Corps can dish out. It's a good feeling: he didn't know he had it in him.

Esprit de Corps

The intense *esprit de corps* that exists among grunts is one of the main appeals of the Fleet Marine Force to recruits like Darrel E. Johnson. A cement which binds together men facing a common danger, it is often stronger than that most primeval of human drives, the instinct for self-preservation.

Esprit de corps, the consciousness of and pride in belonging to a particular group, the sense of shared purpose and fellowship, ideally should apply to every military unit. To the degree that it does, that unit will distinguish itself, especially in combat, from others not similarly animated.

That conclusion, demonstrated with monotonous regularity during millennia of combat, stems from the objectives for which men fight. Contradicting the popular view, men fight first—not for flag or fatherland, but for the sake and respect of buddies in their squad. The next tier of loyalty is to their company (or ship), the third to their branch of service, and only then come the more nebulous considerations of flag and nation.

The British have profited from an understanding of this reality at least as far back as the sixteenth century, when Shakespeare spoke of the solidarity of "We few, we happy few, we band of brothers." Officers and men do not join the army as such, but individual regiments in which men serve their entire careers, promoting the strongest bonds of mutual loyalty. The Coldstream Guards, Honorable Artillery Company, Gurkhas, and the Black Watch are but a few of the units made famous by fighters fierce in fidelity to their fellows. At the other end of the scale are many infantry units of the U.S. Army, in which men are replaced like spare parts on an automobile, with consequent lackluster performance in battle. After all, who willingly and habitually risks his life for *strangers*?

The Marine Corps' characteristic *esprit* was born in the crucible of combat, in which for its first two centuries it seldom lost a battle, and never a war. The habit of success stimulated a feeling of pride: Marines, Marines told themselves—and anybody else who would listen, are America's first line of defense, the force in readiness that can be thrown into the breech in an emergency, while the nation cranks up its industrial machine, and fills the ranks of soldiers and sailors to steamroller the enemy into submission. *Esprit* was honed in an almost continuous series of campaigns and wars—the Marines have fought during more than half of the nation's two hundred years of existence—by a Corps which until recent years numbered only in the thousands. The Marine Corps was a physically extended but spiritually tight little family, with its Lou Diamonds, Dan Dalys, "Chesty" Pullers, Greg Boyingtons, Smedley "Old Gimlet-Eye" Butlers, John Basilones, "Red Mike" Edsons and Evans Carlsons the familiar subject of mess hall conversation. In those distant days, when Marines weren't campaigning in Nicaragua or China or Fiji, they maintained their fighting edge by breaking up bars and bloodying noses because somebody had said an unkind word about the Corps.

They had *esprit*.

They still have it, but these days it is harder to come by. *Esprit* is created most swiftly and surely in the white heat of battle, and will course like hot blood through their veins so long as the participants in that battle shall live. The aging veteran of Iwo Jima may be getting hazy about the details, but he will remember until his dying breath that it was with C Company, 3rd Battalion, 26th Marines, the best outfit that fought in World War II, that he stormed ashore.

But the last Marine battles were fought some two decades ago, and their veterans have mostly left the service. The wellsprings of reminiscence that would inspire the new generation of Marines have dried up. Furthermore, since Vietnam, careerism has filtered down from the commissioned to the noncommissioned ranks, and further undermined the basis for unit solidarity and *esprit de corps*.

Since World War II, a breadth of experience has been considered the path of advancement to general and flag rank. Very early in their careers ambitious officers can chart a path—a nicely balanced combination of specialist service schools, unit command, staff duties, an M.A. or Ph.D. in international relations, command and staff college is typical—which leads to the stars . . . on the shoulders. Transfers are so frequent that not only is the officer seldom thoroughly grounded in any particular military skill, but his associations are too brief for him to develop the close personal relationships which are the basis of *esprit de corps*. Except for the uniform, the rising young peacetime officer could be a rising young executive in IBM.

This baneful philosophy has finally infected the Marine Corps, and percolated down through the ranks to enlisted men in the technical specialties, who can plot their advancement with the same passionless precision. They, too, become itinerants, with fleeting personal associations. They live in two-man rooms instead of squad bays, or go home at night to the wife, attend schools, sign up for carefully calibrated tours of foreign duty, keep out of trouble, and periodically add a stripe to the collection on their sleeves. First loyalty is accorded their career because it offers the only semblance of permanence in the Marine NCO's life.

With the grunts, who spend months at a time in the boondocks and on floats under conditions of great stress, discomfort, fatigue and enforced intimacy, the situation is different. They are more aggressive, boastful, confident, fit, competent in the arts of war, and loyal to their shipmates. They have *esprit* to spare.

Unfortunately, *esprit* is not transferable. The diffuse structure of today's Marine Corps with its multiplicity of arms and missions, and the mobility of its men, makes its development difficult. Still, the Marines do what they can to preserve and promote that single most important ingredient of any fighting unit. If they cannot produce living examples of the men whose exploits have inspired generations, they do the next best thing: they relate their legendary exploits, and impress on every recruit that, if he works like a dog and runs like a deer and fights like a wildcat, he too may one day find a place in the Marine pantheon.

That pantheon is embodied in the list of Congressional Medal of Honor winners. Established on 21 December 1861 by the Congress on President Lincoln's recommendation, as an "act to further promote the efficiency of the Navy," the medal was later bestowed for "deeds of gallantry and heroism in times of Peace and War." In 1878 Secretary of the Navy Thompson commended the Medal of Honor (MOH) "in order that the rising generation of American Seamen may be incited to emulate these deeds of their predecessors, and thus perpetuate in the Navy that devotion to each other in time of peril, and to honor the flag in time of storms and battle, which has hitherto characterized the Naval Service."

The Medal of Honor has been earned by, and awarded to, Marines from private to general, but cynics can detect a pattern in which the act of valor that wins the private a Bronze Star, and the captain a Silver Star, and the colonel a Navy Cross, will earn the general a Medal of Honor. Dozens of privates have died to protect their shipmates by smothering with their bodies the blast of enemy hand grenades, posthumously winning the MOH; to date no general has fallen on a grenade. The citation of a general, who probably didn't fire a shot, is likely to read: "his tenacity, courage and resourcefulness prevailed against a strong, experienced and determined enemy, and the gallant fighting spirit of his men under his inspiring leadership enabled them to surmount all obstacles. . . ."

No such vaporous generalities embroider an enlisted man's citation:

> During the assault on Iwo Jima, assailed by a tremendous volume of small-arms, mortar and artillery fire . . . Sergeant [Darrell Samuel] Cole boldly led his men [through a barrage] of flying shrapnel and personally destroyed with hand grenades two hostile emplacements. . . . [When halted by three Japanese pillboxes] he delivered a shattering fusillade and succeeded in silencing the nearest . . . before his weapon jammed. Sgt. Cole, armed solely with a pistol and one grenade, coolly

advanced alone. Hurling his one grenade . . . he quickly withdrew, [returned to his own lines for grenades], again advanced, attacked and withdrew. He ran the gantlet of slashing fire a third time to complete the total destruction of the Japanese strongpoint. Although instantly killed by an enemy grenade as he returned to his squad, Sgt. Cole had eliminated a formidable Japanese position, enabling his company to continue the advance and seize the objective. . . . He gallantly gave his life for his country.

Or this:

. . . Private First Class Lucas and three other men were suddenly ambushed by a hostile patrol which savagely attacked with rifle-fire and grenades. Quick to act when the lives of the small group were endangered by two grenades which landed directly in front of them, Lucas unhesitatingly hurled himself over his comrades upon one grenade and pulled the other under him, absorbing the whole blasting forces of the explosions in his own body. . . .

Miraculously, Pfc Jacklyn Harrell Lucas lived to collect his Medal of Honor from President Truman, as did Hospital Apprentice First Class Robert Eugene Bush, in action with the Fifth Marines on Okinawa in May 1945.

. . . Fearlessly braving the fury of artillery, mortar and machine-gun fire from strongly entrenched hostile positions, Bush constantly and unhesitatingly moved from one casualty to another to attend the wounded falling under the enemy's murderous barrages. As the attack passed over a ridge top, Bush was advancing to administer blood plasma to a Marine officer lying wounded on the skyline when the Japanese launched a savage counterattack. In this perilously exposed position, he resolutely maintained the flow of life-giving plasma. With the bottle held high in one hand, Bush drew his pistol with the other and fired into the enemy's ranks until his ammunition was exhausted. Quickly seizing a discarded carbine, he trained his fire on the Japanese charging point-blank over the hill, accounting for six of the enemy despite his own serious wounds and the loss of one eye suffered during his desperate battle in defense of the helpless man. With the hostile force finally routed, he calmly disregarded his own critical condition to complete his mission, valiantly refusing medical treatment for himself until his officer patient had been evacuated, and collapsing only after attempting to walk to the battle aid station.

The machines of war change, but valor is immutable. In Korea, Marines won forty-two Medals of Honor, in Vietnam, fifty-seven, under such conditions that just being there warranted a medal for bravery. It is the memory of these heroic acts of these shipmates of another era, and the conviction that when the occasion arrives they will emulate them, which arms Marines with that most enduring and deadly—and noblest—of weapons: *esprit de corps*.

WEEK NINE

Petrović: Bouncing Boot from Bucharest

Platoon 1036 boasts sprinters who run as if their lives depend on it, but only Velezar Petrović's life once actually *did*.

Luckily for him, Petrović's early school years were unconscious preparation for his eventual dash to freedom. In his native Romania, he was wrestling champion at his high school in a suburb of Bucharest. He also participated in running, football, gymnastics and water sports from an early age. The training he received in these sports earned him the stamina and will to flee Romania when thwarted in his ambition to study civil engineering. He displayed talents that would be useful, two years later at Individual Combat Training, when he stole past Romanian border sentries, snaked through mine fields and masses of accordion wire, to reach the Danube. He swam the frigid waters to find refuge and freedom in Yugoslavia.

After eight months in a United Nations camp, he immigrated to the United States, where he has relatives. For a year, he worked at odd jobs to support himself while he studied English on his own. When he received his "green card" as a permanent resident alien, and had acquired a fluent if imperfect English, he joined the Marine Corps. Petrović and Guerra, both possessing first-hand knowledge of the nature and threat of the communist regimes they escaped, are under no illusions that their adopted country can survive without the active involvement of young men like themselves in the national defense.

At first Velezar Petrović, a small, wiry, intense young man, suffered in Platoon 1036. His D.I.s and shipmates had difficulty in even approximating his name—which, by the way, is not Petrović; by unanimous and implicit agreement, they called him "Romania." Romania was confused by orders given in the distinct and unfamiliar dialects of upper New York State, Georgia and Tennessee. When he was chewed out and quarterdecked for not responding to orders he failed to understand, his face turned sunset red from rage and frustration. He had trouble with examinations. The detailed nomenclature of the rifle, the endless acronyms and the unfamiliar Marine jargon, puzzled and frightened him—with the prospect that he might be dropped. The first days and weeks were dark and cheerless, but Petrović hung on, and gradually the sky began to clear.

The obstacle course was an early test of Petrović's gymnastic prowess. The barriers bear names nearly as intimidating as the obstacles themselves: rib cracker, the wall, hand-over-hand bar, high single bar (negotiated with the "college boy roll"), log walk, low hurdle, rope climb and belly-buster. Romania came through scarcely breathing hard.

With his uncertain command of English, however, academics were something else. But when he finally faced, and passed, the First Phase Academic Test, Petrović, in the words of S.D.I. Dawson, "gained an immense degree of self-confidence." The taut bow string unwound a few turns, the cheeks no longer suffused with boiling blood, and Petrović's all-around performance so improved that even he became guardedly optimistic about his chances of graduating. Optimism became certainty during Week Nine, when recruits of 1036 faced the most grueling tests yet of their physical capabilities and, for once, Petrović was running near the head of the pack.

Remedial swimming, on TD-43, tests the thirty-odd recruits of Platoon 1036 who either failed the minimum requirements on TD-15, or wish to upgrade their rating from S-3,
with the ability to survive in the water for five minutes, to
S-2, requiring them to stay afloat for ten minutes. Petrović,
an S-2 swimmer, does not participate. That he knows how to
survive in the water has already been demonstrated: he is
here.

In water survival, relaxation is imperative. Pugil sticks demand survival tactics of the opposite sort: maximum aggression. The use of pugil sticks is a modern adaptation of an
ancient fighting instrument with many incarnations: the Irish
blackthorn shillelagh, the African knobkerrie, the bamboo
staff of Japan's kendo cult. Today's version is a twelve-
pound hickory staff four feet long with padded extremities
and hand guards. Wielded like a medieval British cross-staff,
in man-to-man combat it simulates bayonet attack and defense.

The contestants are protected by a football helmet and
mask, rubber neck roll and crotch cup, and by the rule that
only two kinds of blows are permitted: the slash and the horizontal butt stroke, both to the well-protected head and neck.
Only a clean blow to the head or neck counts; whoever
strikes the first such blow wins, ending the bout. The aim of
the contest is to breed fighting spirit, and little emphasis is
put on art or technique.

"Do not, repeat not, run from your opponent," the instructor cautions. "Because if you do, your head is exposed and
you're defenseless. Don't duck—if you do, you lose sight of
the enemy's stick, and when you next see it, it'll be coming
at you out of left field. Keep your eyes on your enemy, and
attack, attack, attack—always attack. Remember, you're a
vampire, and you're out for blood. . . ."

The battleground is on the Third Recruit Training Battalion's combat course. The pugil stick arena is a big circle of
soft sand, ringed by old yellow-painted automobile tires and,
on either side, the warriors of each platoon suiting up, bel-

lowing "Kill 'em!" "I hate them!" "I'm going to make them pay!" and similar slogans of the "peace" paraders of the sixties.

The referee blows his whistle and the fighters dash to the center of the ring, pugil sticks held high overhead, with shouts calculated to unnerve their opponents. Another whistle blast and, as both platoons shout encouragement, the battle of slash and parry begins. Because of the weight of the sticks and their protective gear, the recruits seem to be performing a waltz under water. The referee dances just beyond the range of the sticks, whistle between lips, ready to stop the fight as soon as a killing blow is struck.

It's not long in coming. Pugil stick fights rarely last so long as a minute, when exhaustion inevitably overtakes the contestants. The one who first drops his arms and his guard also drops the fight. But the typical encounter lasts no more than ten seconds, and sometimes it's over with the first blow.

All three types of victories are won in the first round of fights, with Platoon 1036 paired with Platoon 1037. Recruit Hall, who has long since rebounded from trial training, wins in a hard, quick assault, and leaves the battlefield with arms upraised in a gesture of victory. Garcia wears down a faster opponent in a shoving match in which his iron-pumping muscles are finally exercised to the limit. Calley, whose muscles are quite as prominent, dispatches his opponent in a heartbeat on his second quick slash. Petrović's gymnastic talents temporarily desert him as he stands, rooted to one spot, parrying for dear life until fatigue and a quick horizontal butt stroke defeat his opponent.

Midway through the competition, a recruit pops an ankle in the soft sand, and is hauled away to the sick bay by the emergency vehicle. Until it returns, all hostilities cease, for SOP demands that the vehicle be on hand during all such training events.

Platoon 1036 ekes out a meager victory in this encounter, winning by a margin of one. In the playoffs, 1036 faces Platoon 1039, fired up by an overwhelming win against its opponent. Platoon 1036 starts out well. Taking S.D.I. Dawson's exhortation ''Wear 'em out!'' to heart, they take the first three fights. They then lose the next nine straight. One 1036 recruit gets knocked on his backside four times before his opponent lands a killing blow.

Recruit Hamblin, self-appointed coach and cheerleader, shrieks, ''Quit back-pedaling—you're going to *lose*. Attack! Attack!''

To no avail. Platoon 1036 continues its losing ways.

With the score 11 to 4 against his men, a disgusted S/Sgt. Dawson makes the humiliated platoon sit down, facing away from the action.

''I'm ashamed of you people,'' he tells them. ''You've forgotten everything you've been taught. The rest of you—when it's your turn, go in there and drop your sticks and get it over with.''

The order is, of course, disobeyed, but not with the desired resurgence of fighting spirit. Platoon 1036 keeps on losing, by a final score which the next day they've conveniently forgotten.

Of the three pugil stick competitions, the third, on TD-47, is the one that counts. In this contest, two men of one platoon fight a recruit from the other side, with the odds alternating after each bout. This time 1036 acquits itself honorably, but the outcome is the same: Platoon 1039 wins the fight, and its S.D.I. S/Sgt. Colson is awarded the cami-covered miniature pugil stick which will adorn the Motivation Table on his quarterdeck for the remainder of the training schedule.

> . . . Pugil sticks sounds brutal, but with all the protection it's about as hard to get hurt as in a pillow fight. You'd be amazed how much guys in our platoon—and I'll have to admit I was one of them—were afraid of getting hurt. Yet when you *really*

fight, somebody *does* get hurt, and fighting is why
we're here. Pugil sticks, though, teaches you that
even if you do take a few good licks and pick up
some bruises, they won't kill you. They only make
you mad enough to fight back. It's been great for
morale and building the fighting spirit that sets
Marines apart. Recruits should have more pugil stick
competition—maybe every day. . . ?

In the same way pugil stick training builds the combative
spirit, the Confidence Course presents recruits with daunting
physical challenges which, once overcome, convince them
they can triumph over any obstacle. Moreover, to get recruits
in the habit of tackling formidable obstacles as a matter of
course, they are required to run the Confidence Course three
times during the Third Phase of training. Running the course
demands speed, agility, upper-body strength, endurance, and
a disregard of heights. A fear of water, paradoxically, may be
an asset.

The Confidence Course embodies eleven obstacles, carefully graded so that each is more demanding than the
one before. A platoon can run the course in forty-five minutes.

The first obstacle is called the Dirty Name. It is simply a
pair of upright timber posts with log crossbeams, resembling
a mammoth croquet wicket. The nearest is about seven feet
off the ground, the farthest is parallel to it, about four feet
beyond and three feet higher. The recruit runs, leaps upward,
grabs the first crossbeam, and hoists himself to the top. There
he stands, balancing himself on the round log, then flings
himself upward to the second crossbeam. He scales this and
drops to the ground on the other side.

Run, Jump and Swing is made-to-order for would-be Tar-
zans. Ropes are suspended midway over a shallow sand pit
about 12 feet across. The running recruit launches himself at
the rope, catches it, and swings to the other side. That is, he

does so if he grabs the rope at the right height: too low and he drags his feet in the sand, too high and he falls short of his goal.

The Inclining Wall is about eight feet high, sloping toward the runner. With no foot support, he must leap up and grab the top of the wall and lever himself to the top by arm power alone, scrambling over and sliding down on the other side.

The Confidence Climb is nothing but an oversized ladder, with ten big rungs spaced unevenly two and a half to three feet apart. The recruit simply scrambles up one side and down the other. This is the first in a series of events for which the best advice is, "Never look down!"

The fifth obstacle is the Monkey Bridge. The recruit must climb a twelve-foot rope to a platform, and then cross a shallow thirty-foot stretch of water, sliding along a foot-rope while balancing himself by means of a head-high rope parallel to it. It is not obligatory to hang onto the upper rope, but everybody does.

The Tough One is an understatement: it is *double* tough, testing both body and nerves. Recruits first climb an 18-foot cargo net, such as is used by Marines debarking at sea into landing craft. At the top is a series of a dozen crosswise logs with man-sized gaps between them, like the ties on a railroad trestle bridge. Walking gingerly, recruits come to another of the Confidence Course's oversize ladders, consisting of five rungs more than a yard apart. Climbing these, they find a long, long rope down which, usually after some hesitation, they slide swiftly, and more often than not with rope-burned hands, to the ground.

Beyond the Tough One is the Reverse Climb, similar to the Inclining Wall, but higher, and made of widely spaced iron bars instead of solid wood. Using only his hands, the recruit must hoist himself one rung at a time to the top, and there cross over and climb down. At last, recruits discover why they've spent so much time in physical training doing pull-ups.

Though not the most difficult, the Slide for Life is easily the most dramatic of the course's obstacles, and generates more anxiety than any other, despite the safety net of a pool of shoulder-deep water in case of a fall. The recruit climbs a cargo net, this time to a platform the height of a three-story house. On instructions from a D.I., who has previously nego-tiated each obstacle to ensure the serviceability of the appara-tus, the recruit faces the opposite end of the pool and straddles the rope down which he will slide to reach it. Grav-ity will help him get there.

He pushes off—or rather, *pulls*. Hand over hand, he drags his body forward until, one-third of the way along, he is or-dered to turn upside down. He must invert his body so that he now faces the sky, holding on to the rope by his hands and crossed ankles. Further along, he must change position again, reversing his hands, releasing his feet, and executing a half turn toward the now-near end of the pool. Here both strength and agility are required. He must flex his arms to raise his body, and at the same moment swing his feet up to engage the rope. If he manages to do so, all is well. He simply shin-nies the rest of the way feet first toward the dry bank of the pool. If he doesn't, the determined but weakening recruit twists and turns, struggling like a fish on a gaff, trying to swing his feet onto the rope. When tired, he rests, hanging by his hands until finally his strength drains away, his grip loosens, and he drops.

"Don't worry," their D.I.s reassure them. "There aren't any piranhas, no water moccasins, no D.I.s with big fangs—just frogs, mosquitos and mud."

Also, an occasional alligator, until the pool was fenced in. Last year, a newly graduated Marine was showing his parents around the Confidence Course when an 8-foot, 120-pound al-ligator surfaced in the Slide for Life pool, and regarded them enigmatically. With admirable aplomb, the new Marine shrugged, "Oh, yeah—they keep him there to make sure re-cruits hang on tight. . . ."

The Slide for Life has its own protocol. If, for example,

something falls out of a recruit's pocket, left there despite his
D.I.'s instructions to empty them, he is ordered: "Go pick it
up."

The unhappy recruit is expected to release his grip at once,
and drop into the pool. In common with all those who take an
involuntary plunge, he is invited to salute his D.I. on the way
down. Furthermore, while struggling out of the muddy water,
he must clasp his hands behind his head and bellow the Marine Hymn at the top of his lungs, enroute back to the cargo
net and another attempt. Of the first twenty of Platoon 1036's
to try it, six made their solo singing debut, and both Garcia
and Santiago returned dripping for an encore.

The Hand Walk looks easy after the Slide for Life. Iron
parallel bars start about six feet off the ground then slant, first
upwards, then downwards, along their twenty-five-foot
length. The body hangs suspended between arms in compres-
sion and aching shoulder sockets for the length of what becomes a very long short journey.

The Arm Stretcher comes next, no doubt designed to coun-
teract the effect of the Hand Walk. It is simply a long metal
ladder, bent in several planes some distance off the ground.
The recruit starts at one end and swings, an apprentice Tarzan, rung by rung to the other end. Upon reaching it he does
a full pull-up, and drops to the ground. If he fails in the pull-
up, he gets to do the exercise all over again.

The last event on the circuit is the Sky Scraper, a three-
story house without stairs or walls. Working in pairs, each
recruit must grasp the edge of the floor above, and swing his
body up and onto it. Getting to the first level, with the
sawdust-strewn ground comfortably near, is no problem.
Reaching the second level requires strength and dexterity.
Strength, dexterity *and* strong nerves are needed to swing to
the third floor, from which descent is made at last to solid
earth by means of a cargo net.

Rare is the recruit who does not fear the Confidence
Course for the first time, when his D.I. blithely demonstrates
how easy it is to negotiate it. "I can never do *that*," he says
to himself.

But he can. Spurred on by his D.I.s, anxious not to lose face before his shipmates, he conquers each obstacle in turn. The confidence each small victory generates gives him the moral strength needed to take on and conquer the next. Climbing down the net from the Skyscraper, he looks back over the course with a surge of pride. "I actually *did* it!" he says to himself, lost in wonder.

Not only does he do it—he does it three times during Boot Camp, and the initial terrors of heights and falls melt away with repetition. The most agile performer in the series may be Velezar Petrović, who shinnied down the Slide for Life and negotiated the other obstacles with the verve of a veteran aerialist. He's all smiles: he's finally found something he can do better than anyone else.

> . . . Like pugil sticks, the Confidence Course is a great morale builder. Funny thing, muscle-men like Garcia sometimes got soaked during the Slide for Life while beanpoles like Musser sailed across. In the Confidence Course, muscle is not enough. You also must have balance, agility and strong nerves. . . .

TD-45 is a break in a week otherwise filled with physical exertion. Morning and afternoon sessions are devoted to close-order drill, in preparation for the final competition on TD-51, the most significant of six intra-series contests during boot camp. There is also a discussion of Security of Classified Information.

It is widely believed that only high-ranking officers have access to top secret information. In fact, many lower ranks—typists, communications personnel, couriers, guards and drivers—routinely handle classified materials on which national security depends. Clearance categories for access to classified documents are three: confidential, secret and top secret.

Servicemen, like civilians, must undergo security in-

vestigations and be declared loyal and trustworthy before
being allowed access to materials in these categories. Even
then, those with clearances must be vigilant to protect the
nation's secrets by following strict procedures for the protection, storage and destruction of classified information. Above
all, they must observe the strictest self-discipline by discuss-
ing such information only in the line of duty. The World War
II warning that "A slip of the lip can sink a ship" is even
more pertinent today, when the loss of nuclear secrets, for
example, could sink the ship of state.

The challenges of Week Nine resume the next day with
rappelling, which requires few muscles, moderate daring,
and a lot of confidence in rope. Rappelling is a relatively
new art, but of vital importance as Marine assaults are increasingly carried out through "vertical insertion" of troops
from hovering helicopters into dense jungles and mountainous
terrain.

In the intimidating shadow of the forty-five-foot, five-story
steel rappelling tower, the recruit is taught to fashion a
twelve-foot sling rope (tensile strength: 3840 pounds) into a
seat harness. To this is attached a steel snaplink (tensile
strength: 2000 pounds). He then takes heavy leather engineer
gloves in hand and mounts the six flights of steps to the top
of the tower. Looking down, he sees the tops of tall pines
and far below, ranks of recruits awaiting their turn, looking up.

The recruit, swallowing hard, inches toward two red
footprints painted on the deck, and plants trembling boots
upon them. The tower's edge is just twelve inches away. The
recruit tries not to look down.

The seven-sixteenths-inch rope with which the recruit
will rappell is one hundred twenty feet long, made of three-
strand nylon, and has a snap-strength of 5,800 pounds. It is
tied to an anchor point on the tower, looped over a high projecting steel beam, and bent around the snaplink on the recruit's harness by the D.I. rope-master. The recruit holds the
rope's free end in his right hand. If he holds his right arm

straight out to the side, there will be no tension on the snaplink, and he will free-fall. To brake, he brings the line smartly to the small of his back, and tension on the snaplink stops him instantly. If he freezes or forgets what to do, a "belay man" on the ground, holding the other end of the rope, merely hauls on the line and the rappeller is stopped forthwith.

Now, the heart thuds against the ribs, the throat tightens, and the ground looks far, far away. On instructions from the rope master, the recruit takes one step to the very edge. He keeps his eyes on the horizon. His right hand presses the rope against his sweat-soaked spine. With as much nonchalance as he can muster, he sings out: "Recruit Drymouth, on rappel!" And he leaps into space.

But not very far. The drop is limited to the amount of slack the instructor left between the beam and the snap link, usually seven or eight feet. When it pays out, in a fraction of a second, the harness bites into the rappeller's thighs, and he jerks to a stop. With a shout of *"Marine Corps!"* he flings his right arm straight out and free-falls to within five or six feet of the ground. As the ground rushes up, he snaps his hand to the small of his back, then milks the line the last few feet to the ground. On landing, the recruit places his hands over the twin lines running through the snaplink and double-times backward until they fall free. He does one side-straddle hop, and announces: "Recruit Cool, off rappel!" He walks off the tower's tanbark skirting, feeling exhilarated and very pleased with himself.

Every recruit must make, not one, but two descents. The first simulates rappelling from a hovering helicopter. The second rappel requires the descent of a vertical wall, practice for rappelling down a mountain face.

Mounting the tower and repeating the hook-up procedure, the recruit this time walks *backward* to the brink, and carefully hooks the heels of his combat boots over the edge. He milks the line held in the small of his back. His body bends into an "L" shape as he eases back, his torso upright, his legs parallel to the ground. Still slacking off on the line, he walks backward one-third of the way down the wall. At that point he pauses, flexes his legs, and thrusts himself away from the wall. This he does three times, and on the third bound, swings his right arm straight out and free-falls, braking five feet from fracture.

As the instructor says, "Rappelling is just another means of getting at the enemy. It *looks* hard, and has a very large fear factor, but is actually easy and safe."* The recruit, looking down from the top, has his doubts about the safety; looking up, after he's done it, he's a believer. The rappelling tower, in fact, is a confidence course telescoped into the four to six seconds it takes to make the forty-five-foot drop.

Rappelling is done in the tranquil hours of the morning of TD-46. In the afternoon, the recruits come down to earth in another manner—with their final academic examination. The First and Third Phase Academic examinations, the Rifle Range and the Final Inspection are the four requisites every recruit must complete successfully in order to graduate. Failure in any one of the four *may* be waiverable at the series commander's discretion, but failure in two results in his automatic drop to a following platoon or even ELS.

The final examination leads off with a practical section devoted to identification and problem-solving. In this test, the recruit must: identify four types of hand grenades, and the parts of a fighting hole; identify various ranks and grades of officers and NCOs; field strip the M-16-A1 in two minutes and name the principal parts; react correctly to a sudden overhead flare at night; probe for a buried land mine; don a gas mask and perform a serviceability test; defend himself against simulated aerosol attack with blood,

---

* Since rappelling became a part of training, male recruits have made 104,000 descents with two accidents, female recruits 24,000 descents with one accident. None were fatal or disabling.

nerve and choking agents (twenty-second time limit); identify various badges of rank and place them correctly on a uniform; and demonstrate treatment for burn and shock victims.

The written test covers a considerably wider range of subject matter than First Phase Testing, and the question are tougher, too. The eleven categories include sixty questions, of which the following are representative:

M-16-A1: Which of the following is not a part of the magazine for the M-16-A1 rifle? (a) follower (b) case (c) propellant (d) base.

History: Who awarded Lt. Presley O'Bannon the Mameluke Sword, and where? (a) Prince Hamet, Mexico (b) the Commandant, Marine Corps (c) Barbary pirates, Tripoli (d) Prince Hamet, Tripoli.

First Aid: Which of the following is not one of the four life-saving steps? (a) treat for shock (b) restore the breathing (c) protect the wound (d) start the bleeding.

Customs and Courtesies: Which is the appropriate way to address an officer? (a) "Have a good day, sir." (b) "How are you, sir?" (c) "Good morning, sir." (d) "What's happening, sir?"

Code of Conduct: Which of the following best answer this article: "I will never surrender of my own free will. If in command, I will never surrender my men while they still have the means to resist"? (a) I am a U.S. Marine. I am proud to protect my freedom and my country. (b) I am the senior member and maintain morale and unity in the camp. (c) Surrendering will occur only as a last resort when there is no other choice. (d) I will not accept the offering of drink, cigarettes or medical aid in return for agreeing not to escape.

UCMJ: What offense has been committed under Article 86? (a) drunk on duty (b) larceny and wrong appropriation (c) absent without leave (d) burglary.

Interior Guard: If you were walking post and smelled smoke, what General Order would govern your action? (a) 5 (b) 7 (c) 8 (d) 1.

Uniform and Grooming: When must you replace a uniform item? (a) when they are two years old (b) when they look old (c) whenever unserviceable (d) every four years.

Law of Land Warfare: Name the illegal target: (a) parachutist (b) paratrooper (c) enemy infantry (d) all of the above.

Individual Tactical Measures: Who is the assistant fire-team leader? (a) automatic rifleman (b) grenadier rifleman (c) rifleman (d) assault rifleman.

NBC: What is the antidote for a blood agent? (a) atropine (b) amyl nitrate capsules (c) M13 kit (d) there is no antidote.

The recruits of 1036 Series went into the examination room with a full ALICE pack of alibis, if needed: their heavy post-ICT schedule, practice for the regimental field meet, a change-of-command ceremony, and field days for battalion and regimental inspections gave them little time for study (although nobody told them they couldn't review their Green Monsters during their daily free hour). In the event, Platoon 1036 needed all the excuses it could get, for fifteen out of its sixty recruits failed.

As on the first academic test, the failing recruits got the reprieve of a second test. On this test, all sixteen made passing grades but Recruit Kenneth Michaelson.

Unfortunately, Michaelson had also failed to qualify on the Rifle Range. The failure in Third Phase Academic Testing therefore automatically disqualified him from graduating with Platoon 1036. An otherwise sincere, highly motivated recruit, he is dropped back the same night to another platoon, to repeat the last phase of instruction. The chances are good that, with additional study time, he will succeed.

Recruit Aubrey Shields won't. He had refused to jump off the eight-foot platform during water-survival training. He refused to jump off the rappelling tower. His failure to practice an exercise on which his comrades' lives and his own may depend is fatal to his career as a Marine: only two weeks short of graduation, Shields is recommended for immediate discharge.

The Marine Corps, like life itself, is predicated on the survival of the fittest.

Unlike Shields, Petrović has twice proved himself a survivor—in escaping from his barbed-wire-ringed native land, and in conquering a new language, an alien environment, and the toughest boot camp in the armed forces. He's the kind of rock on which the U.S. Marine Corps is built.

Double-Time

Growing up in Romania, Velezar Petrović had at least one advantage over American youth—simple food, and just enough of it to survive. Too many of his Platoon 1036 shipmates were not so lucky, bloated from childhood on fast food, candy, sugar-rich pastries and coke. Since today's "Marine" rhymes with "lean," such fat bodies have but one choice: shape up or ship out.

One short, spherical, would-be Marine shed one hundred pounds of excess weight before he reported to Parris Island for boot training. Even so, he was still too fat and flabby to pass the Initial Strength Test, and he was sent to the Special Training Division for further conditioning. After more than two months of diet and intensive training, during which he lost an additional sixty-three pounds, he remained unable to meet minimum physical fitness standards, and was returned to civilian life, a sadder, wiser, and definitely leaner, man.

Few Marines experience such a deflating fate. Most pass the IST, requiring only 2 pull-ups, 35 sit-ups in 2 minutes, and a 1.5 mile run in 13.5 minutes. Even those who fail, like Recruit Guerra, may be retained by the platoon on the recommendation of its Senior Drill Instructor, if he feels the recruit has the ability and determination to meet the fitness goals of the next test, three weeks hence.

Of the roughly twenty-five thousand recruits who come to

Parris Island each year, some 7 percent, or about eighteen hundred, typically fail the IST, and are assigned to the Special Training Division to get in shape. The STD, whose PCP, MTP and MRP sound more like hallucinogens or motor-oil additives than the special-purpose remedial platoons they are, is quartered on the Rifle Range.

There the recruits in PCP (Physical Conditioning Platoon) strive to become less than they are, for virtually all owe their poor physical condition to excess fat (underweight recruits are a rarity). At PCP, they will lose weight—not infrequently in excess of thirty pounds each, develop their endurance and upper-body strength, add muscle, and improve their reflexes and coordination.

Egregiously overweight recruits, some 60 percent of the total, will be put on a weight-reduction diet of 3,000 calories per day, so that with the average expenditure of 4,200 calories daily in drill and vigorous exercise, recruits register weight loss of from two to five pounds a week.

In PCP, no man is an island—though in some the resemblance is uncanny—for each new arrival is assigned a veteran in PCP to help him get through the twenty-one days or more he will be in training. The pair of recruits are then interviewed by the STD commanding officer and told what to expect: all the help and encouragement possible for the motivated, a quick ticket home via Casual Company for malingerers, malcontents and poor performers.

For the next three weeks, their days will begin in darkness, with Reveille at 0430, two hours for breakfast and morning clean-up, then three hours of strenuous physical drill. High-intensity work-out days alternate with days of low-intensity work outs. Both begin with two sets of pull-ups, then a full 25 minutes of stretching exercises to warm up and prevent muscle injuries. Next come exercises designed to strengthen specific muscle groups. The three-hour session is topped off with a run whose duration depends on the recruit's time in PCP. If he has been here less than seven days, he wears a white shirt and runs 1.5 miles, with a time of 13 minutes or less as his goal. The next week he wears a gray shirt and runs 2 miles in 17:30, increasing to 2.5 miles in 21:30. By the end of the third and usually final week, he will wear a yellow shirt and run 3 miles in under 23:30.

An aid truck with a corpsman is always standing by at the circular dirt track to transport to the sick bay any recruit having heat problems or muscle injuries. Stragglers from the pack, meanwhile, are accompanied at all times by drill instructors monitoring their condition while dispensing words of encouragement. Recruits who fake exhaustion—rolling their eyes, groaning, panting or staggering—are easily separated from the genuinely fatigued (a pulse rate below 150 per minute is the giveaway), and just as quickly separated from the service.

On high-intensity days, in addition to regular physical drill, recruits in PCP work out on Nautilus and Universal weights, covering 12 stations in 36 minutes with progressively heavier weights and numbers of repetitions. Each buddy puts his partner through his paces, and if the partner shirks or cheats, the buddy pays by having to attend remedial sessions, missing classes, and sometimes being sent back to a more recently formed platoon. Close supervision of recruits at all times—a drill instructor is always among them—forestalls "dumpster diving," when ravenous but dieting recruits scavenge food discarded by the mess hall.

After showers and lunch, recruits face three hours of regular academic instruction and an hour of close-order drill, mirroring the progress of the platoon they left behind. With luck and application, they will be able to rejoin their platoon after their three-week stint at PCP. Their instructors are PCP D.I.s, whose competence is reflected in the 98 percent pass rate achieved by PCP recruits on First Phase Academic Testing, which takes place at STD on TD-16.

Though the vast majority of PCP recruits join the special

platoon on TD-1 and stay the minimum twenty-one days, recruits also report here after failing the Inventory PFT on TD-16, or even the Final PFT the week before graduation. Training battalion commanders may also assign especially awkward recruits to PCP, as well as those who persistently perform poorly on the Obstacle and Circuit courses. The twenty-one-day minimum can also be extended to a total of forty-five days in exceptional cases, when the recruit's efforts and progress warrant the extra stay.

PCP is tough. In a typical year, 440 of the 1,800 PCP recruits are discharged for failure to achieve minimum standards, insubordination or insufficient effort. Of the 1,300-odd returned to the Recruit Training Regiment, another 100 will be dropped before graduation, for an overall attrition rate of 30 percent. Regardless of the cause of assignment to STD, recruits must do a minimum of 5 pull-ups, 50 sit-ups in 2 minutes, and run 3 miles in less than 24:30 minutes, in order to be sent back to training. Those who fail at least won't have to walk home: they get a free bus ticket.

The rigors of boot training often traumatize soft civilian bodies. It is the responsibility of the Medical Rehabilitation Platoon (MRP) to make those bodies whole again, and to return them to recruit training where they will undergo more of the physical punishment which brought them to MRP, with a significant difference: now they will be able to take it in stride.

The most common serious recruit ailment, in some 70 percent of the total, is stress fracture, mainly to the tibia or fibula, which need six to ten weeks to heal. Recruits entertaining second thoughts about becoming Marines often complain of stress fractures, in the hope they'll be sent home; revealed by x-ray as being deficient in backbone, they usually get their wish.

While PCP recruits sweat at physical training each morning, MRP recruits attend therapy sessions at the depot sick bay. On Mondays, Wednesdays and Fridays those with injuries to the lower extremities work out on the Universal and Nautilus machines to build upper-body strength. Twice a week they go to the swimming pool for physiotherapy. And each Wednesday they are bussed to the sick bay for examination, evaluation and prognosis. Otherwise, they pursue the same Basic Daily Routine as other recruits at STD, attending academic lectures and drilling under arms if sufficiently fit.

The 64 percent attrition rate of MRP is more than double that of PCP. Of the 900-odd recruits who come to MRP in a typical year, 280 will be discharged by medical boards for pre-enlistment medical conditions (more rigorous recruiting standards could have excluded nearly all these, at a savings of several thousand dollars each to the Government). Another 200, mostly malingerers—and already documented as such by their original D.I.s—will be sent to Casual Company for ELS. Of the 400 returned to training, about 80 will be discharged for a variety of reasons before graduation.

The average stay in MRP is twenty days, with a ceiling of thirty-five days in unusual circumstances, for experience has shown that unless there is dramatic improvement in a recruit's performance within thirty days, he is unlikely ever to attain the degree of fitness required for recruit training. That degree of fitness must correspond to that of PCP recruits returning to training, confirmed by performance in the STD test for pull-ups, sit-ups and running.

Though of much briefer duration, the Marksmanship Training Platoon (MTP) has by far the biggest turnover of STD's special units. It also has the highest success rate.

On the Rifle Range, Thursday is pre-qualification day, and the results are a fairly accurate forecast of Qualification Day scores on Friday, when recruits fire for record. The "unks"—unqualified shooters—of Thursday are given the privilege of an extra chance by being placed in the first two relays firing Friday morning. If they qualify, they then take their turn in the butts in the afternoon. If they have failed to qualify, however, they are permitted to fire the KD course in the afternoon. Those who fail this last chance pack their gear and move down the road to the MTP barracks, like those of PCP and MRP, across Wake Boulevard from the Rifle Range.

Saturday afternoon sees the unks on the grass, snapping-in, as their MTP coaches pay special attention to the shooter's deficiencies listed by the firing-line coach in the recruit's rifle data book. On Monday morning, the recruit fires the KD course; if he qualifies, he returns immediately to his platoon, now on Mess and Maintenance. Should he score below 190, he is allowed one final try on Tuesday morning. If the magic Marksman's score still eludes him, he rejoins his platoon Wednesday unqualified. On the other hand, whatever *qualifying* score he makes at MTP is recorded at the Marksman's minimum of 190.

Of the three-thousand-odd recruits who pass through MTP annually, an average of 87 percent qualify as Marksmen.

As a rescue operation for young men who would otherwise be unable to complete training, STD is a resounding success, saving roughly two thousand recruits from a fate veteran Marines consider worse than death—becoming a civilian the hard way.

Young:
One of
the Few

In its perennial search for "a few good men," the Marine Corps accepts only promising candidates, then subjects them to a rigorous boot camp designed to separate the men from the boys. During their eleven weeks at Parris Island, the recruits of Platoon 1036 see, one by one, a quarter of their number fall by the wayside. The also-rans' shortcomings include physical incapacity, mental instability, or failure to measure up to Marine standards of marksmanship, intellectual achievement or discipline. Among the survivors is Recruit Thomas E. Young, the occasion for no surprise to his D.I.s, who were sure from the first that Young would make it to become one of the Marine Corps' "few good men."

Young had a sound background for the Marine Corps. In the Catholic high school in suburban Washington, D.C., which he attended on scholarship, he excelled in science and mathematics. He was also, despite his modest stature, a fervid basketball player. Hungry for an alternative to the certitudes of college and career, Young decided the Marine Corps was most likely to provide the spice and adventure civilian life lacked. At the age of eighteen, he signed up for six years as a regular, despite parental reservations which, fortunately, mellowed as he conquered each of boot camp's challenges in turn.

"Extremely motivated," and "adjusting smoothly to the military atmosphere," was the early verdict of his S.D.I., S/Sgt. Dawson, who consistently rated Young in the top 10 percent of the platoon. On the Rifle Range he qualified as Marksman, in swimming survival was rated S-3, and was a high First Class in his Final Physical Fitness Test, with a score of 270 of a possible 300.

In the personal relations that are crucial to a recruit's adjustment, Young encountered no problems besides being one of the many victims of mass punishment for the derelictions of the platoon's habitual offenders. His proudest boast is that "nobody has had to pay for me in all the time I've been here." As for those whose poor performance made *him* pay, Young has a ready prescription: "If the D.I.s had been allowed to drop the goldbricks and sea lawyers, they'd have cut the platoon in half, and those who remained would have got more training and been better Marines."

The physical aspect of that training over the past ten weeks is tested in the cool, early morning hours of the eleventh, on TD-48. The daily PT, the Circuit, Obstacle and Confidence courses have exercised every muscle group, but the Final PFT emphasizes only the most important. Pull-ups are a measure of upper-body strength, sit-ups of abdominals, and running of strength and endurance of the legs.

The scoring system awards 5 points for each pull-up to a maximum of 100 points; 1 point for each sit-up during a two-minute interval (2 points for all above 60), to a maximum of 100; and 100 points for a three-mile run in under eighteen minutes, with a one-point penalty for each ten seconds over that figure. In the entire 1036 Series of 240 men, only one, Recruit Alan B. Secrest of Platoon 1037, achieves the maximum score of 300 points.

Platoon 1036 does very well, overall, with every recruit raising his individual score dramatically. All the recruits run the three miles, for instance, in the range 18 to 23:55 minutes, averaging a swift 20:55. Sit-ups range from 46 to 80, averaging 70 within the allotted 120 seconds. Pull-ups range from 4 to 20, averaging almost 14.

In Platoon 1036, the low PFT score is 162, well above the "unsatisfactory" figure of 134 and below. The high is claimed by Recruit Sean Atkins. Of 3rd Class qualifiers, scoring between 135 and 174, 1036 has but two; 20 score between 175 and 225 to achieve 2nd Class; and 37 range upward from 226 to gratify the requirements for 1st Class. Had the Platoon average of 231 been reached by every individual, all would have been 1st Class.

Boot camp is not the end but the beginning of physical fitness, which will be pursued on a scheduled daily basis in the Fleet. Officers as well as enlisted men are expected to maintain a trim, athletic physique, and the day of the big-bellied Gunnery Sergeant is long past.

So is the day when new-hatched privates were paid $21 a month. With an average pay check in excess of $600 monthly, and numerous personal and family benefits, today's Marine private has financial responsibilities that most are facing for the first time.

A series of lectures, the last in boot camp, during Week Ten prepares the recruit to manage his personal and professional affairs, including finance, with forethought and care. The burden of the young married Marine is lightened by free medical care for himself and his dependents, commissary and post exchange privileges, a $35,000 life insurance policy, and competent advice on budgets, banks, credit, savings and debt.

The recruit's long-term financial health often depends on intelligent selection of a Military Occupational Specialty (MOS), to best exploit his natural talents, and accelerate promotion and pay raises. While the MOS 0300, Infantryman, is still the common denominator of all Marine Corps battle planning, the interlocking complexities of the combined land, sea and air operations which Marines have polished to a fine art demand a legion of specialists as well.

The main MOS classifications include the ho-hum categories of 0100 Administration, 0400 Logistics, 1100 Utilities (water, electric supply, etc.), 3000 Supply Administration and Operations, 3300 Food Service, 3400 Auditing, Finance and Accounting, and 4000 Data Systems.

But the young man with an itch for adventure who is left cold by 4100 Marine Corps Exchange or 4600 Audiovisual still has a wide range of challenges in 1800 Tank and Amphibious Tractor, 0200 Intelligence, 5700 Nuclear, Biological and Chemical Defense, 7000 Aviation Operations—which include firefighting and rescue, 7300 Air Traffic Controller and Enlisted Flight Crew. Those who seek even closer contact with things that go *bang!* can opt for 0300 Infantryman or Grunt, as he proudly calls himself, or 0800 Field Artillery or even 2300 Ammunition and Explosive Ordnance Disposal. The thirty-eight main MOS classifications have, literally, scores of sub-specialties, such as 6541 Aviation Ordnance Repair and 7212 FAAD gunner. (The first two numbers indicate the occupational field, the last two the sub-specialty normally acquired through advanced study.)

> . . . One of my buddies is going into Auditing, Finance and Accounting, and another into Audiovisual. And me—I'm tapped for Communications. That's three Marines right there who won't be shooting at the enemy. In fact, only one out of five Marines are what civilians consider real Marines. Grunts, that is. In modern war, I guess all these specialties are necessary. But when shooting time comes, I wonder if those 40,000 grunts won't be so busy defending us 160,000 specialists that they won't have time to kill the enemy. . . .

Whatever their specialty or rank, all Marines receive exactly the same leave, which accrues at the rate of two and a half days for every thirty days of duty. Annual leave is granted subject to a unit's operational commitments, but seven other types of leave afford additional time off duty in exceptional circumstances. Convalescent leave, rest and recuperation leave and environmental/morale leave—granted in areas of high stress— are not deducted from the Marines annual thirty days.

In addition to leave, Marines not in the field have liberty—in effect, overnight or weekend leave. At many bases, liberty extends from 1730 daily until 0600 Reveille the following morning, and from 1630 Fridays until Reveille the following Monday.

Marines are counseled to preserve that inspection-uniform look at all times when off base, to spend their money wisely, stay sober and avoid brawls. Marines are trained to be—and *must* be—tough and aggressive. "But remember," their instructor cautions, "your close combat skills could qualify you for the hospital. There are a lot of combat veterans out there who are tougher than you are. Anyway, you can't whip the whole world, so don't try. Mind your manners and your own business, and you'll last longer."

The transition from boot camp to the FMF (Fleet Marine Force) or other new duty will be somewhat traumatic for the soon-to-be Marine. At Parris Island, virtually every move the recruit makes is dictated by his D.I. To prosper, he merely must do as he's told. In the Fleet, for the first time, he will be expected to accept considerably more responsibility and initiative. He must understand his place in the military hierarchy, and seek to improve it through study and efficient performance in his MOS. In addition to his specialty, he will be called upon for such diverse tasks as working parties, mess duty, guard duty, rifle range details, inspections, parades and ceremonies.

The compensations for this very full life are not to be found in a fat pay check. The rewards of service have always been intangibles: service to one's country, pride in an elite profession, the constant challenge of the difficult—and the glow of pride and power in achieving the impossible, and the warm and lasting friendships of men forged by stress and hardship.

A military environment is not a breeding ground of saints, and Marines are spiritually closer to cannons than to can-

onization. This is especially true of the brawling, beer guz-
zling individualists who, out of pride or concern for
reputation or the plain hell of it, fall on hapless civilians in
peace as readily as they do on hand grenades in war. Such
free spirits are indispensable when war clouds darken the
horizon. But such men are regarded by officers with a frosty
eye and, indeed, statistics show that 80 percent of disciplinary problems are directly related to alcohol abuse. It is one of
many ironies that newly spawned Marines, who in boot camp
lectures are inspired by the wartime exploits of hell-raisers-
turned-heroes, are advised to give them wide berth in peacetime.

TD-50 moves recruits one step closer to such choices when
they are issued orders for their first posts, and given the Navy
Department ID cards which allow them to travel as U.S. Marines. Even at this stage, however, it is by no means certain
that all will graduate. Some of Platoon 1036 have failed to
qualify on the Rifle Range, and failure of the final inspection
by these recruits will result in their being dropped. Separate
inspections by Series Commander First Lieutenant D.S.
Greenburg and the new Bravo Company Commander, Captain J.C. Olsen, are designed to detect and correct deficiencies in uniform, rifle drill and maintenance, hygiene and
"knowledge" before the final inspection by the First Recruit
Training Battalion commander, Lieutenant-Colonel J.P. Farrell.

The series commander's inspection, already behind them
on TD-47, has been a preview of the manner in which inspection will be held during the rest of the recruit's career as a
Marine. Knowing now what to expect, recruits spend several
hours in the afternoon of TD-50 in preparations for the second inspection, in the full green Alpha uniform, under arms.
Uniforms have been sent to the depot dry cleaners for pressing, thus allowing recruits additional precious minutes to
spend on their manual of arms, rifle cleaning, cramming
"knowledge" from their Green Monsters, snipping Irish pen-
nants, buffing their brass and spit-shining their shoes. Web

belts are cut back to remove frayed ends and fit waists slim-
med by physical training. So that no fingerprints mar their
gleaming surfaces, burnished brass buckles are fastened on
web belts with hands gloved in wool socks. The D.I.s measure with a ruler the one-eighth-inch interval between the top
of the left pocket of the green blouse and the rifle badge,
correcting deviations of even a single millimeter.

Sgt. Montgomery shows recruits how to tie the military
four-in-hand, attach collar stays, affix brass belt tips to web
belts, stand on a foot locker in order to don trousers without
breaking the crease (bunkmates tie each other's shoelaces),
slip on tie clasps at the prescribed distance from the knot.

Long before the bleak morning hour of 0700, when the
Company Commander is due to appear, recruits have been
getting dressed by the numbers, as called by Sgt. Montgomery. They have laid out all clothing on their racks. Dressed in
shirt, trousers and shoes, they form a line to the quarterdeck,
where Sgt. Montgomery sternly oversees recruits as they
scrub their hands and nails with soapy water and Chlorox,
and gargle with Listerine. The recruits then put on neckties,
collar stays and tie clasps, followed by green jackets and
green belts. The go-to-hell hats are centered on the head,
with precisely the width of two fingers between the forward
peak and the eyebrows.

Seconds remain before the Company Commander is due to
appear as a sweating Sgt. Montgomery makes a fast final inspection of his platoon, man by man, as they form up in four
ranks. There is nothing, of course, for him to worry about.
Everything has been foreseen, everything explained, every
move rehearsed, everything done in unison and by the numbers. But Sgt. Montgomery is an experienced drill instructor.
From the recesses of memory comes that old D.I.'s refrain:

"If you put a recruit in a padded cell with two steel ball
bearings, in five minutes he'll lose one and break the other."

To his dismay, though not to his surprise, he detects two
glaring discrepancies: one recruit has a button missing from

his tunic, another has somehow managed to put on his tie inside out, with pleats outward. Sgt. Montgomery has time to deal only with the tie when, at precisely 0830, he hears the shout announcing Capt. Olsen's approach:

"Attention on deck!"

The inspecting party is heavy with brass: three captains and two first lieutenants, plus the first sergeant, a gunnery sergeant, and half a dozen staff sergeants to inspect weapons. Company Commander Olsen starts his inspection with the first man in the first rank, the guide. As the captain halts before him and does a left face, the guide snaps from Parade Rest to Attention, and executes Inspection Arms.

Capt. Olsen snatches the rifle from the Guide's grasp with a *pop!* of the handguard, and subjects it to a minute inspection, looking for tell-tale signs of inadequate rifle hygiene—carbon dust, oil and grit. Thrusting it back, he observes the Guide bring his weapon to Order Arms, then inspects the fit of the recruit's uniform. He uses a small ruler to measure the interval between rifle badge and pocket, the lengths from buckle to tip of the web and green jacket belts.

The recruit's hands and fingernails, face and neck, are examined for cleanliness, his neck and cheeks for stray whiskers. His knowledge is tested with from five to ten questions covering everything he should have learned since TD-1. Observations on the recruit's rifle manual, rifle maintenance, uniform, hygiene and "knowledge" are each characterized as "unsatisfactory," "average," or "above average," and corresponding notations made in the recruit's boot camp record.

While the Company Commander is inspecting the first squad, the other officers are proceeding slowly down the other ranks. As each recruit is inspected, he falls out and reports to an NCO, who deftly strips his rifle and with a Q-tip probes recesses the recruit never suspected exist. He then brandishes before the crestfallen recruit a cotton swab blackened with carbon and oil. Bunched in a tight bouquet, the Q-tips will substantiate the inspector's invariable claim that the platoon's rifles are unspeakably foul, and will require hours if not days of work before the depot armory will accept them from the recruits.

> . . . Some things that go on here are downright silly. Keeping clean is good, sure, but gargling with Listerine so the CO doesn't smell your bad breath? Military appearance is good, too, but wearing garters between socks and shirt tails (officers and D.I.s do) to keep the shirt taut? They say that in wartime they'll drop this stuff, but if we're training for war, then why waste time on these things in the first place? Unless they're ashore on liberty, why shouldn't Marines sweat and stink? Proves they're doing their job. . . .

At 1301, having learned that they have passed the Company Commander's inspection despite a few reservations—neckties tied too long, dry rifles, too many unsats in "knowledge," and a tunic button missing—the recruits of Platoon 1036 march onto the parade deck for their Final Drill Evaluation. Last night during free time, Recruit Michael E. Knight, the platoon's sole college graduate, who a few weeks ago superseded Santiago as Guide, drilled the platoon in the manual of arms until lights out. The platoon feels itself ready, and marches confidently onto the field under the command of S/Sgt. Dawson.

As during initial drill, four judges closely monitor each evolution during the twenty-minute routine, which includes nearly every movement they have learned. In the reviewing stand, meanwhile, the assembled D.I.s observe recruits with a critical eye, quick to remark any deviation from procedure, any irregularity in the absolute uniformity of the ranks. In this drill, it is assumed that the recruits have mastered the fundamentals of the thirty movements they are to perform. Here the emphasis will be on details: cover, alignment, rifle carriage, rifle manual, thumbs, pop and snap.

When the fourth platoon finishes its turn, second-guessers in the stands are divided as to the winners, but unanimous that it will be a close decision. It isn't. Platoon 1038 wins with 352 points, while 1036 and 1037 tie for third at 330, one point behind 1039. Dark are the countenances of the losers, intense if muted their complaints and recriminations. The judges defend their ratings, pointing out that Platoon 1036, for instance, was guilty of "snaking in 'open ranks,'" failed to get alignment on "Fall In," marched at too fast a cadence, carried knees too high on "Half Step," and executed "Order Arms" incorrectly. Compensating for the kick in the teeth with a pat on the back, Sergeant Major D.L. Wildenhaus reminds the smoldering D.I.s that the usual score on final drill averages only 300, and all four platoons did considerably better than that. As the platoons form ranks to witness S/Sgt. D.J. Pass receive the trophy on behalf of Platoon 1038, they take small comfort from the Sergeant Major's rationalization. In fact, there's not a man among them who's not fighting mad.

The next day men and D.I.s get some of the bile out of their systems with the early morning five-mile endurance run on a circuitous course around the Recruit Depot. In their present excellent physical condition, there is no question that all will complete the circuit, and each recruit runs only against the clock. At the same hour the next day, TD-53, the five-mile run is repeated, but this time as a Motivation Run, in which the entire series runs as a unit, in formation. Repeating D.I.'s chants as they go, the recruits jog along easily at a nine-minute-mile pace, reveling in the knowledge that this is the last physical test they'll experience in boot camp.

But not the last exercise. During the last two days of the week they receive their introduction to hand-to-hand combat, a skill they will perfect in the Fleet.

In a huge square sawdust arena, the series assembles to watch the ICT instructor, Sgt. Martin, demonstrate just how vulnerable are the bodies they mistakenly believed they've forged to the toughness of steel.

"The human skull is as fragile as a robin's egg," Sgt.
Martin says with a disarming smile. "It'll crush easy. Or, if
you don't like crushing sounds, you can snatch out your enemy's eyeballs and stomp them on the deck. Or you can
sneak up and pop his ear drums, and watch his brains leak
out his ears. If you prefer seeing him strangle in his own
blood, you can chop at his Adam's apple with the side of
your hand. Then there's the collarbone—you can snap it like
a toothpick. . . ."

In giving a brief overview of calculated violence, and the
mortal injury that can be visited on practically every part of
the human anatomy by the well-trained Marine, Sgt. Martin
does not neglect the stomach, kidneys, spine, groin, knees,
elbows, fingers and toes.

"Devildogs are surgeons," he says, but they don't need a
medical degree to operate on the enemy with the bayonet or
other "weapons of opportunity" such as the steel helmet (to
crush skulls), entrenching tool (to cleave), tent pegs (to im-
pale), sand and dirt (to blind), and web belt or shoestrings (to
garrotte).

"In hand-to-hand, anything goes. Hit him in the solar
plexus and make him drown in his own vomit, or suck his
eyeballs out through his toes. Remember, you're the doctor."

Among the therapies Dr. Martin prescribes for those mis-
guided enough to take on a Marine are the hip and shoulder
throws, followed up by an assortment of kicks, stomps, elbow thumps and arm bars. He demonstrates a variety of
strangles, useful in neutralizing sentries without noise, as
well as the uppercut punch and front kick. He advises on the
best way to use a knife in attack ("work fast, with short,
quick slashes and thrusts"), and how to avoid it, though as a
Marine he eschews mention of that layman's favorite: Run!

The killing blows Marines learn, he emphasizes, are to be
used only in self-defense or in close combat against the enemy, not in barroom slugfests. "Cultivate your skills and use
them wisely. Remember, our enemies are learning the same
techniques. . . ."

. . . When I make Commandant of the Marine Corps, there'll be more training in hand-to-hand combat, and less time in nitpicking inspections, than we've had here at P.I. By the time he leaves boot camp, every Marine will be so tough and well-trained in the martial arts that when bad guys see a Marine coming, they'll cross the street. That's what every guy who joins the Marines secretly hopes will happen. I wish it was so. . . .

Hand-to-hand combat is a fitting finale to the recruit's training program, marshalling those elements indispensable to fighting men: the ability to think fast, act decisively, and pursue their overriding objective—the destruction of the enemy. With their initiation into the arcane arts of self-defense, the recruits have become fledgling members of the Mean Green Machine.

Mean—and lean, too. In ten weeks, while 17 of 1036's recruits have added an average ten pounds of sinew and muscle (and another 14 merely converted flab to muscle), 29 recruits have shed an average of 13 pounds of fat. Guide Knight and Recruit Guerra lost more than 30 pounds each, with the end still very much in sight.

For some, the fight against flab will be an uphill battle, as they discovered during their first liberty on Sunday, 12 May. While some visited the depot museum, went bowling, or called Suzie or home to wish Mom a Happy Mother's Day, many more made the pilgrimage to the depot restaurant, a fast-food emporium, there to indulge the nearly forgotten delights of french fries, thick milk shakes and cholesterol-crammed hamburgers. Not Recruit Thomas Young's bunkmate Antonio Garcia, though. He made a beeline for the depot Health and Fitness Center, there to spend a blissful Sunday afternoon adding weight to barbells, instead of his waistline.

Women Marines

Women fighters have a long and illustrious lineage that goes back as far as the Amazons of Scythia in Greek mythology, and extends into the present day with the M-16-firing female fighters of Mount Lebanon. Women Marines are heirs of that bellicose tradition, with one important difference: they are not allowed to fight.

Still, having successfully invaded so many of man's once-exclusive domains, women Marines may one day be permitted by law to test their skills not merely against male Marines, but the nation's enemies in the heat of battle. Indeed, recent changes in their training program point unmistakably in that direction.

Fewer women than men seem to join the Marine Corps for a job, being motivated more by an appetite for travel, adventure and education. In order to enlist, a woman must have a high school diploma or twelve years of regular schooling, which is reflected in the average female recruit GT score of 105, slightly higher than that of males. All women, whose median age is twenty years, train at Parris Island under female officers, NCOs and drill instructors, and live in strictly quarantined quarters.

Women recruits do not have to meet any minimum fitness standards, but their Inventory Physical Fitness Test requires a run of three quarters of a mile in 7.5 minutes, a bent-arm hang of 12 seconds, and 19 sit-ups in 1 minute. Those who fail are sent to a Physical Conditioning Platoon, along with those more than eight pounds overweight. Ten to 15 percent of women recruits arrive overweight; they lose five pounds, on the average, during training. Of the two platoons in a women's series, between 110 and 120 young women, from 10 to 20 percent will pass through PCP.

Until mid-1985, women recruits had three days of Processing, three days of Forming, and forty-eight training days. Since then, the training program has been expanded until it is virtually indistinguishable from that of the men. All academic subjects have long been the same, and under the new order field training has been expanded from three days and two nights to the full seven days and nights. On the march, they carry the same load as the men, including ALICE pack, rifle, helmet, and two full canteens. The former brief familiarization course with the M16A1 has been replaced by a full week on the grass, followed by another firing the M16A2 on the KD course for qualification.

Women can usually fire as well as men and often, because they are more highly motivated and amenable to instruction, better. On 15 November 1985, Pvt. Anita Lobo proved it. Shooting with the first series of women recruits to qualify with the service rifle, the eighteen-year-old Texan scored 246 out of a possible 250 on the KD course, breaking the longstanding course record of 245.

Certain features of women's training are less strenuous than that of the men, however. Instead of five-mile runs, women are never required to run more than three miles. They do not have the upper-body strength to complete the Confidence Course, and their Obstacle and Circuit courses are modified to conform with their physical capabilities.

As a group, women perform better on tests and drill than men, and usually as well in marksmanship, where meticulous observance of instructions is crucial. Women leap off the rappelling tower with the same mixture of trepidation and determination as men, and are just as elated when they prove to themselves that they can conquer fear. Swimming qualification is the same as that for men, but for reasons not yet clear black women, like black men, have difficulty in passing the test.

Women recruits eat the same food as the men, sleep in double-decked racks in squad bays identical to those of male recruits, and wear clothing designed for male recruits, except for underclothing which they themselves provide. Their barracks and grounds are not patrolled by sentries, but they are under close supervision to prevent a mingling of the sexes.

Of all the problems women recruits face, those of the feet are the most severe. Finding a fit for their smaller and narrower feet in boots designed for men is a problem few overcome, and the small number of women Marines does not make the design of a special boot commercially attractive for contractors. The same is true of women's uniforms, where choice of sizes is more limited than for men.

Though female Marine drill instructors insist that their recruits are more tractable, less aggressive, and easier to train than men, difficulties with performance, attitude and discipline do arise. In such cases, their D.I.s have resort to the ultimate tool, Incentive Physical Training, usually meted out to a group in order to apply peer pressure on the miscreant.

One distinct contrast with male recruit training is the Professional Development Package, a six-hour course under a special instructor and the representative of a cosmetics manufacturer, during which recruits are taught how to apply make-up effectively. After physical training and the shower that follows, recruits apply only lipstick and eye liner. At all other times they may wear full make-up, including blush. Nail polish is not worn—not due to esthetic considerations, but simply because its application is too time-demanding. Recruits' hair is trimmed to reach, but not cover, the uniform collar, at least twice during boot camp. The one strict cosmetic prohibition is against perfume: it attracts sand fleas.

When they graduate from boot camp, women Marines take their place alongside men at most of the posts and in all the specialties except those which might involve them in combat.

They are thus ineligible for sea duty, combat-capable air crews, infantry, artillery, and tank/amphibious vehicle crews.

The corps of 700 female officers and 8,500 enlisted Marines now serving are being progressively expanded toward a goal of 10,000, but this objective remains elusive because of the high discharge rate. Despite a boot camp attrition rate of 15 percent, the same as for men, 2,400 women a year graduate. Yet, only half will finish their first enlistment, and half of those will be separated because of pregnancy.

The main reason women get out of the Corps, according to women Marine veterans, is a lack of job satisfaction, or the attraction of a better paying job on the outside for which the Marine Corps has trained the woman Marine, usually at great expense. Avionics is a case in point. Women may get up to eighteen months training in one of many specialties which, in the civilian world, pay a gross salary of up to five times what the woman Marine makes. In the past, a woman determined to leave for a civilian job did so by the pleasurable expedient of becoming pregnant, which assured an early discharge. Marine Corps policy now provides that pregnancy is no bar to retention, for a woman either married or single.

No one seriously believes the new policy will work. In these permissive times, Marines who want out, *get* out. The all-volunteer service has become a revolving door, easy to enter, easy to leave.

WEEK ELEVEN

Bail:
The Berth
of the Blues

The Blues have finally arrived at home port, and the recruit who will proudly wear them is Dennis Bail, twenty-two, of Springfield, Ohio.

The award of the prestigious Dress Blue uniform, with its high-necked navy-blue jacket with red piping and brass buttons and sky blue trousers, is assuredly the high point of any recruit's career. Only the recruit judged best among his sixty-odd shipmates, in the opinion of his S.D.I., receives the honor, although other Marines may purchase it at a later date.

According to S/Sgt. Dawson, "Recruit Bail was selected honorman for outstanding leadership qualities and overall performance. Bail has demonstrated conspicuous motivation. He has experienced few problems in adjusting to military life, and quickly grasps what is taught."

In addition to kind words from his D.I., Bail has compiled some kind numbers, too. From a physical fitness level of 201, in ten weeks he has raised his score to 286, only 14 points short of the maximum 300 mark. He qualified as an S-3 swimmer on his first try. On the rifle range, he tied the series record with a score of 231. His only statistic that doesn't require large numbers is his marital status: he is single.

Recruit Bail is one of the few Platoon 1036 recruits of American parentage with extended residence and schooling abroad. After a year in Athens—Ohio—at Ohio University, he went to South Africa where his father was project manager building a factory. During his two years there, Bail studied at the South African Engineering School in Durban, and received a certificate in Mechanical/Electrical Engineering from that institution.

On returning to America, he worked two years at Wright-Patterson Air Force Base in Dayton on drafting and design of the F-16-B. Seeing how the Air Force lived and worked decided him on a military career—in the U.S. Marine Corps. Though the decision came "out of the blue," as he recalls it, the seed had been sown in his early youth, when he saw John Wayne in *The Sands of Iwo Jima*.

Those school years in his home town, Springfield, Ohio, were not spent at the movies, however. He was also a four-year letterman and all-Central Buckeye Conference defensive end in football, played baseball, and was an all-Ohio wrestler. In addition he was a bugler in the local drum and bugle corps, and played the trumpet and flugelhorn in his own jazz-and-blues band.

Bail intends to be a career Marine, and will apply for officer training at his next post, where he will study electronics to become a Communications Center Operator. At some future date, he hopes to complete requirements for a doctorate in engineering during night school or service-related study.

Besides Recruit Dennis Bail, who received a meritorious promotion to Pfc, S.D.I. S/Sgt. Dawson was pleased also to recommend Recruits Barker, Atkins, Cyr, Young and Gillen to the same rank. All six qualified with the M-16-A1, passed their swimming and academic tests—several with a perfect score—and were well above the minimum level for 1st Class in their Final PFT.

Though he received no official honors, Recruit Francisco Guerra won the respect of his shipmates and his D.I.s by the constancy of his efforts to keep up with the platoon's pace. Decidedly overweight on TD-1, so deficient in upper-body strength that on the Inventory PFT he was unable to do a single pull-up, with foot trouble which prescribed orthotics failed to alleviate, Guerra never gave up. He ran all the runs, finished all the marches, passed his Final PFT—having

flunked the first, and dieted from 206 to 175 pounds. In
S/Sgt. Dawson's opinion, he was easily the outstanding recruit in terms of personal and professional improvement.

The fate of the others turned on that bland all-purpose Marine Corps alibi, "the needs of the service," used to justify
anything from prohibiting the wearing of beards to ordering
troops to carry unloaded weapons in war zones such as
Beirut.

Recruit Calvin Hall, warmed by the hell-fire breath of
S.D.I. Dawson on the back on his neck, finally got religion.
Gone was the studied air of boredom, the languid pace, the
aura that he was doing everybody a favor just by being there.
He'll never have the motivation of a Guerra, the dogged determination of a Petrović or the versatility of a Bail, but his
progress with Platoon 1036 has been sufficient to be recognized with selection for Electronics School—and the right to
be called a U.S. Marine.

The invisible men—Grant, Keane and Townshend—finish
boot camp very much in character, blending into the background rather than standing out from it. Grant is slated for
avionics training, Townshend for Supply and Administration,
Keane for Motor Transport, specialties seemingly tailor-made
for anonymity, but without which the vast and intricate Marine Corps machine would grind to a halt.

Harris Slaney is long gone, near-forgotten, unmourned.

The glint of golden bars on his collar tabs still dazzles the
imagination of Albin Charneski, but it will be some time before he will be eligible for the university program whose successful completion will allow him to pin them on.
Meanwhile, the Marine Corps will put his expertise in pho-
tography and art to use by making him an Audio-Visual
Training Equipment Specialist.

Bitter disappointment has been the lot of Edward Santiago.
After a promising beginning as platoon guide, he was edged
out of that coveted billet by Recruit Michael E. Knight halfway through the boot camp schedule. Now, upon graduation,
he learns that, instead of his anticipated assignment to com-

puter technology training, he is destined to serve as a grunt with the Fleet Marine Force. He'll have a hard fight to get back on the computer track.

Tony Garcia, too, will become a grunt, a felicitous example of the round peg—almost literally, considering his bulging muscles—for the round hole. He's equipped with physical strength and endurance, a temperament that rolls with the punches, and the ability to scrounge which is the mark of the successful infantryman. If anybody can be happy campaigning in the boondocks—and a surprising number of grunts would have no other life—it will be Tony Garcia.

Darrell E. Johnson would have gladly joined him. He found life in the field as exhilarating as the classwork was dull, and let it be known that he was amenable to cancellation of his pre-enlistment guarantee of a billet as Operations and Communications Specialist to 03 Infantryman. The Marine Corps, in its wisdom, agreed to void the pre-enlistment guarantee: it assigned Johnson to Motor Transport.

Another square peg in a round hole is Velezar Petrović, putative descendent of the Roman legionnaires who survived 26 campaigns or 26 years of service to be paid off with a plot of land in the wilds of Dacia, present-day Romania. He vindicated his heritage by demonstrating enterprise, hardihood, flexibility and the capacity for swift and silent movement that characterizes the infantryman. The Marine Corps, in its continuing wisdom, assigns Petrović to . . . Motor Transport.

Thomas E. Young, the "extremely motivated" recruit who showed talent in high school for science and mathematics, will have the opportunity to build on that foundation as an aviation ordnance specialist. That he smiles at the news of his selection is not surprising: he's the kind of recruit who is happy wherever he's sent, just so long as it's the Marine Corps.

With graduation nearly upon them, Platoon 1036 has but two more bridges to cross: rifle turn-in and the battalion commander's inspection.

The rifles are a devilment and a vexation, although these

are not precisely the terms recruits use to describe them.
After firing on the range, it takes anywhere from six to
twelve hours by an expert to remove all the carbon deposits,
and one D.I. estimates that at ICT, "one blank cartridge deposits as much carbon as fifteen live rounds." Since ICT, the
recruits have spent every spare minute scrubbing
their rifles with metal and nylon brushes, and soaking them
with CLP. Their D.I.s have washed the rifles with hot water
under pressure five times, and still the rifles bleed carbon like
dye from a Bulgarian T-shirt. On TD-55, having done their
best, Platoon 1036 turns in their rifles at the armory where,
somewhat to their surprise, all are accepted as being clean
and serviceable.

By contrast with the rifle turn-in, the battalion commander's inspection is almost anti-climactic. It is axiomatic
that the higher the rank of the inspecting officer, the easier
the inspection. Battalion Commander Lt. Col. J.P. Farrell's
bears this out: though far from perfunctory, the colonel's inspection is less traumatic than either of the others, or perhaps
the recruits are merely getting used to them. With a sigh of
relief, the platoon learns that every man has passed. The last
bridge has been crossed.

But where do they go from here?

Over the past ten weeks fifteen of their number have already gone, seven of them straight through the main gate
back to civilian life. Their places have been filled with pick-
ups, drops from earlier platoons requiring further training.
Approximately half the remaining total—29, including the
six meritorious Pfcs—are graduating with one stripe on their
sleeves, the other 23 having been guaranteed that rank in pre-
enlistment contracts. Two, including Recruit Young, will become lance corporals. The racial mix is virtually unchanged:
45 whites, 14 blacks, 1 Asian. Thirty-seven are Regulars on
four-year enlistments, 11 have enlisted for six, and 12 are
reservists. All six married men have survived.

After boot camp, and leave from 16 to 28 May, it is
highly unlikely that they'll ever be all together again. The

wide range of duty stations and MOSs practically assures it. The greatest number of them—twelve—will be 03 Infantrymen. Seven, including Guerra, who will finally get a chance to sit down and rest his feet, go to 3500 Motor Transport, five to 2500 Operational Communications, three each to 6000 Aviation Machinist's Mate and 6300 Avionics, and the other 27 to 22 varied specialties. The MOS assignments occasion few surprises: 51 of the 60 recruits were guaranteed an MOS on enlistment.

On the eve of their graduation, reflecting on their experiences in boot camp, the attitudes and conclusions of the recruits in most respects are surprisingly uniform.

Not one of the sixty feels boot camp was too demanding, and one-third feel it was far too easy.

By unanimous agreement, the recruits believe that the absolute prohibition against D.I.s swearing is hypocritical and puerile. After all, D.I.s and recruits alike swear like gunners among themselves. Not one recruit says he would take offense at the D.I.'s swearing at him, and most admitted they expected and frequently deserved such treatment.

Fifty of the sixty recruits favored the re-institution of the Motivation Platoon for undisciplined recruits. (At the Motivation Platoon, abandoned due to congressional pressure in 1975, recruits were subjected to hard and nasty labor, a preview of combat conditions, but shorn of terror and mortal danger. One day at the Motivation Platoon usually cured all but the most refractory recruits.)

Nearly all recruits feel the D.I.s should have the authority to ELS—without limit stated or implied—foot-dragging, insolent recruits. The general opinion of the platoon is that those who really wanted to be Marines, and hadn't enlisted for three-squares-a-day, would have had consistently better training, and more of it, had the D.I.s had the authority to drop for cause anywhere from fifteen to thirty of their graduating shipmates.

Only two of the sixty recruits would resent the use of mild physical abuse—a kick in the slats, e.g., or grabbing a handful of cami jacket—to steer the lazy and recalcitrant into the paths of righteousness, in preference to peer pressure as the result of IPT inflicted on the entire platoon, at present the only weapon the D.I.s have to combat laziness, laxness and insolence. Recruits and D.I.s are alike mightily frustrated that the system allows inferior men to become Marines simply because the D.I.s lack means of coercion or the right to dismiss foul balls. Gresham's law—bad coin driving out good—is demonstrated in Parris Island with the smoldering discontent of committed long-service D.I.s, leading with disconcerting frequency to their transfer or even departure to civilian life, because they are compelled to graduate recruits who don't belong in the Marine Corps. Despite the D.I.s' prestige, extra pay and substantial perquisites, and the fierce desire of the vast majority to train fighting men, last year fewer than 10 percent requested extensions of D.I. duty at Parris Island, and only 13 percent at the San Diego Recruit Depot.

Among recruits there is considerable disagreement about drill. Some feel that it is indispensable in creating group solidarity, discipline and an appreciation of the importance of detail. One recruit, representing the contrary opinion, says: "Less learning how to drill, more learning how to kill."

Of their classwork, the consensus is that Marine history, Individual Combat Training, first aid and UCMJ are valuable, whereas lectures on family planning, MOS, pay and benefits and male anatomy are a bore and a waste of time.

One recruit had come into the Marine Corps apparently with mistaken expectations: "I thought—and hoped—it was going to be a lot tougher, demand more sacrifice. I thought I'd be part of a gung-ho, fire-breathing, ass-kicking elite. It hasn't been that way at all. All I've had to do was what I was told and keep my mouth shut. Frankly, I'm disappointed. I'm going to pull my time and get out." This recruit admits that his fifty-seven days have not been entirely wasted, however: "I've seen changes in my attitude for the better. I deal with people and situations in a more mature manner. It's been good for me." Having it to do over again, would he join the

Marine Corps? He hesitates, thinks it over, and says, a little sheepishly, "Well, yes, I guess I would, at that. After all, it's the only wheel in town."

> . . . Well, Mom, tomorrow is the big day, and I've got a lot of preparations before lights out. Tell you one thing—these eighty-eight days have gone by in a Green Marine Blur. And another thing: I've changed quite a little. I've learned a lot of things, made some good buddies, lost nineteen and a half pounds, got used to all kinds of discomfort, and managed to control my temper when things weren't going my way. You'll know from my letters that some of the people and policies here are stupid and petty, but I guess that's true anywhere. Even so, I've had the best basic military training the United States offers, and in less than three months. The self-discipline and ability to take punishment will put me ahead of other guys when I get out. It'll take me a long time to decide what was really good, and what only *looked* good, about boot camp, but I can tell you this, it made me,

> Your loving son,
>
> Scott, a Marine.

TD-57: Graduation Day.

The only training today has been an hour of graduation rehearsal and another of parade preparation, to make sure that recruits don't misunderstand commands and start marching into each other.

S.D.I. S/Sgt. Dawson, mustering his recruits for the last time in front of the barracks, tells them: "I've aged fifty years since you people got off the boat. Listen, do me a favor—if out in the Fleet anyone asks you who your S.D.I. was, tell them Cpl. Smith."

Recruits are not permitted to laugh except on command.
S/Sgt. Dawson doesn't give that command, but a few of the
more daring laugh anyway. In a quiet, controlled manner, to
be sure, because they aren't quite sure he doesn't really mean
it.

"Right, face!" he orders. "Forward, march!"

Platoon 1036 moves out toward the reviewing stand on the
far side of the parade deck. The time is 0830. The weather is
sunny and fine, as it has been, blessedly, for the platoon
nearly all the time it has been at Parris Island. As they march
onto the asphalt the sand fleas, faithful to the discipline of
their own disagreeable species, begin biting for the fifty-sev-
enth consecutive day. In front of the distant reviewing stand a
truck moves slowly along, spewing an insecticide fog against
their kamikaze attack. The recruits grin wryly. Forget it, they
think: these are *Parris Island* sand fleas, the old breed.

S.D.I. S/Sgt. Dawson, relief in sight, breaks into another
of his apparently inexhaustible store of chants as they march
toward a side road to form up with the band, the Colors, and
the other platoons for the march on. For once, every man
sounds off.

At 0900 precisely, the band strikes up a martial air by a
late fellow Marine, Major John Philip Sousa, and Platoons
1036 and 1037, followed by the national and service colors
and Platoons 1038 and 1039, march onto the parade deck.
They aren't Marines yet, but their military bearing and precision cadence are scarcely distinguishable from those of veteran leathernecks. The bleachers and reviewing stand are
filled with relatives and friends—most recruits expect three or
more guests each, and nearly all are recording this climactic
event on film.

The actual graduation ceremony is impressive but brief.
The four platoons, each in two sections six ranks deep, come
to a halt and face the reviewing stand, where the Commanding General and his party sit. The chaplain reads a prayer.
The First Recruit Training Battalion CO makes a brief address. The recipients of awards—the four platoons honor

men, the four winners of the Marine magazine *Leatherneck*'s Marksmanship Award, and the recipient of the Physical Excellence Award—come forward.

The National Anthem is played, as the recruits snap to attention and the visitors rise.

In quick succession, Lt. Col. Farrell presents the winners with their awards, the recruits pass in review, and their guidons are retired until next year. The band plays the Marine's Hymn, and the series commander dismisses the troops, to the cheers of the multitude and their own back-slapping mutual congratulations. From this moment, they cease to be recruits.

They're Marines, and proud of it.

So are their parents and friends. Sgt. Montgomery is surrounded by recruits eager to introduce him to their parents. Then the Third Hat comes in to shake hands, to smile an unaccustomed smile, their hearts to gladden. A mother embraces and kisses her son, whose appearance and bearing have changed almost beyond recognition, then seeks out S.D.I. Dawson and takes him aside. "I don't know what you did, but whatever it was," she says, fervently, "*thank you*. He was such a *punk*."

Marching to their first parade an hour earlier, S/Sgt. Dawson's chantey at last seems eminently appropriate.

> You can keep your Army khaki,
>   You can keep your Navy blue.
>   I have the world's best fighting man,
> To introduce to you.
>
> His uniform his different,
>   The best you've ever seen.
>   The Germans call him "Devil Dog,"
> His real name is "Marine."
>
> He was born on Parris Island,
>   The place where God forgot.

The sand is eighteen inches deep,
The sun is blazing hot.

He gets up every morning,
   Before the rising sun.
   He'll run a hundred miles and more,
Before the day is done.

He's deadly with a rifle,
   A bayonet made of steel.
   He took the warrior's calling card,
He's mastered how to kill.

And when he gets to heaven,
   St. Peter he will tell,
   One more Marine reporting, sir,
I've served my time in Hell.

So listen, all you young girls,
   To what I have to say:
   Go find yourself a young Marine,
To love you every day.

He'll hug you and he'll kiss you,
   And treat you like a queen.
   There is no better Fighting Man:
The *United States Marine!*

Elites

A recruit in the French Foreign Legion runs 4.5 miles in his first *week* of training. By the end of four months, he will be running 13 miles regularly, and required to complete a night run of 15.5 miles over rough, unfamiliar terrain, carrying rifle, helmet, canteen and thirty-three-pound pack, in under 3 hours.

British Royal Marine recruits complete 30-mile cross-country speed marches in 7.5 hours, carrying rifle, 30-pound pack and other gear.

The Soviet Union's Naval Infantry, Russia's closest approach to a marine corps, pour out of their barracks winter and summer at 0605, chests bare and clad only in boots and trousers, for thirty-five minutes of rigorous physical training followed by a long run in the open, even in the teeth of a minus forty degree blizzard.

By the standards of many foreign military leaders, American recruit training—even that of U.S. Marines—is soft. To these leaders it is axiomatic that if their troops become inured to maximum mental stress, physical discomfort and privation in training, then in the field—where brutal conditions are the norm—they will be able to concentrate on the battle, rather than be distracted from their mission by cold, heat, rain, insects, hunger, thirst, fatigue, sleeplessness and terror. As Thucydides, Athenian general and historian of the Peloponnesian War, remarked: "We must remember that one man is much the same as another, and that he is best who is trained in the severest school.''

British Royal Marines sweat from the day they arrive until their basic training is finished, thirty-six weeks later. At Lympstone Commando, their recruit training center, they combine the Marine boot camp function with the four-month infantry training U.S. Marines receive after becoming grunts. Where the U.S. Marines emphasize upper-body strength, the British stress endurance and leg strength. In addition to their forced marches cross-country, they run a mile-long "Tarzan" obstacle course, in under thirteen minutes. Their swimming test involves, among other things, leaping off a ten-foot board with rifle and full combat gear.

British Marines, who number only seven thousand in all, enlist for three and a half years, or can sign on for twenty-two years with the option of discharge on 18 month's notice. Despite very slow promotion—it usually takes six to eight years to make lance corporal—so esteemed is the service that prospective Royal Marines face a six-to-twelve-month waiting period before being called. After twelve weeks of training, the recruit is offered the choice of discharge or serving out his enlistment. Standards are so high, and training so rigorous, that attrition is 75 percent over the nine months. Approximately 25 percent of those who make the grade become career Marines.

Royal Marine chow is less varied, nutritious and plentiful, their living conditions more spartan, their occupational specialties more restricted, and their tours overseas longer, than those of U.S. Marines. Yet, pride of service is more intense in the Royal Marines—unlike many U.S. Marines on liberty, e.g., the British customarily wear their uniforms ashore. British Marines believe their high morale is the result of the commando's test by ordeal, which only the superior 25 percent survive, and the intimacy of a service most of whose members are known to one another, either personally or by reputation.

The recruit, or *engage volontaire*, in the French Foreign

Legion, does not, as he once did, sign up one day and start on his way to Algerian exile in Sidi-Bel-Abbes the next. The Foreign Legion is, like the U.S. Marines, seeking "a few good men," with sound educational qualifications and skills with military potential. Applicants must spend three weeks undergoing mental and physical tests, as well as a thorough security clearance, before being permitted to enlist for five years. Once cleared, they may adopt any name that suits them, and their civilian past is forgotten.

The *volontaires* are kitted out with a *paquetage* of about $1,000 worth of combat gear, mess gear and clothing including the blue waist sash and the white kepi, and shipped off to the Legion's training regiment at Castelnaudary in southern France. For nearly four months the small group—only 350 recruits are in training at any one time—will be subjected to intensive and exhausting training by 35 officers and 120 NCOs. For all recruits it is an agonizing, and for some a terrifying, experience.

The recruit shaves from his mess tin, learns Legion marching songs, stands 192 hours of guard duty—two hours on and four off—has his hair cut to one quarter-inch (but no shorter), and receives 8,816 francs—approximately $1,000 a year—in pay.

"We get very hard men," says a *caporal* drill instructor, "and hard men expect hard treatment. Discipline: that's why they join. The Foreign Legion's a very exclusive club. You have to do it off your own bat—get your balls kicked around your ears, carry your sack, sweat, and when you've got that white *kepi* on your head, you know that no amount of money can buy it. I've found my home. It's the Legion."

A similar pride may animate the Soviet Naval Infantry, but if so, it is not advertised. Currently numbering only twelve thousand men, since its formation by Peter the Great in 1705 it has been repeatedly disbanded in time of peace and reactivated in war. Significantly, today the Naval Infantry is operating at full strength. To fulfill its mission of seizing beachheads, supporting sea flanks of ground troops, and staging reconnaissance and sabotage raids behind enemy lines, the Soviet Naval Infantry has specialists in many fields: each two thousand-man regiment, in addition to three infantry battalions, has headquarters, tank, rocket artillery, antitank, antiaircraft, chemical defense, reconnaissance, signal and rear service units.

Recruitment is very selective and training rigorous, with all boots learning basic military skills, vehicle driving and swimming before branching off into such specialties as communications, electronics, medicine, cooking, and maintenance. Some get training as parachutists or frogmen, and all participate in sports promoting endurance and physical fitness. The qualities sought in naval infantry are decision, initiative, ease in water, and the ability to surprise the enemy.

These traits do not distinguish the average Soviet soldier, whose greatest military virtues are extreme hardihood and absolute obedience to orders. These are instilled from the very first day after induction at age eighteen, when recruits are chased out of their beds eighteen or twenty times a night to teach them to get into uniform quickly, clean out lavatories with their toothbrushes, and conduct nonstop 16-hour field exercises in the extremes of Russian weather.

For the Soviet army recruit, reveille is at 0600, followed by thirty-five minutes of physical training and breakfast consisting of two slices of black bread, one of white, a sliver of butter, a bowl of gruel and a mug of tea with a single lump of sugar. At 0800 recruits parade, to listen to orders and army-wide punishments, which may be for five to ten year's imprisonment, occasionally death. Close-order drill until 0900 precedes three two-hour periods in tactics, technical training, weapons, drill, physical training and political indoctrination. Ninety-five percent of this training is held outdoors in all weather, and in all but political indoctrination physical activity is intense. Every move is on the double and every evolution, given a time goal, is endlessly repeated until that goal is met.

At 1500, exhausted and dripping sweat, recruits return to

barracks, clean up, go to chow that, as a former soldier recalls, is "disgusting, thin soup; semi-rotten potatoes with over-salted fish; and three slices of bread." From 1600 to 1800 the recruits clean weapons and barracks and police the area. For the next two hours comes "self-tuition" in tasks involving exhausting physical activity and stress, such as running three kilometers while wearing gas masks. Supper from 2000 to 2030 is of *kasha* or potatoes, two slices of bread, tea and a lump of sugar. Thirty minutes of free time is followed by roll call—and the reading of more punishments—at 2100. The last scheduled event is the "evening stroll," thirty minutes of drill to the beat of drums. The recruit washes up at 2145, cleans and polishes his gear for the morrow, and hits the sack at 2200 unless, as is frequently the case, he must attend scheduled night exercises.

This taxing regime is administered six days a week for six months with calculated brutality by drill sergeants, upon which recruits completing their two-year hitches depart, a new influx of recruits arrive, and the entire process is repeated—three times. This is the Soviet Army, Mr. Ivanovitch.

Naval Infantry training is, as befits elite troops, more rigorous. Soviet marines are trained to swim under combat conditions in full uniform and battle gear, negotiating underwater obstacles and mine fields, and landing on beaches under live fire. Their physical training includes the usual physical drill, mass sports, gymnastics, obstacle courses, forced marches, cross-country running, mountaineering and unarmed combat. They study the enemy and his organization, equipment, weapons and tactics. They train constantly in defense against air attack, in assault landing tactics and shore battles and firing from moving platforms, with emphasis on surprise, rapid and decisive action, and developing and maintaining momentum of attack.

Comparisons between the training of these foreign elites and that of Marine recruits reveal sharp differences. Without exception, discipline is tighter, physical drill tougher, and exposure to extremes of weather more severe for these foreign troops than our own, who enjoy barracks heated in the winter and air conditioned in the summer. Foreign drill sergeants are incredulous (until they see with their own eyes) upon being told that U.S. Marine drill sergeants cannot swear in the presence of their troops—let alone *at* them—kick them in the butt for doing something stupid which might imperil the entire unit, or administer a salubrious, muscle-tautening "incentive" physical drill for more than two and a half minutes at a time and never more than five minutes per hour. Do America's enemies, they must wonder, shoot back but five minutes an hour?

Are these distinctions important? Will they make a difference in war?

Marine drill instructors think so, and because they feel thwarted by a system which is under constant, distrustful scrutiny by Washington bureaucrats—and fearful officers who must heed congressional strictures or see their budgets cut or even the Marine Corps itself disbanded, as certain congressmen continually threaten—these drill instructors are leaving the Marine Corps in disgust, and in disturbing numbers. With a few exceptions, speedily removed from duty when detected, these drill instructors are not sadists, but competent, patriotic, humane and conscientious veterans of five to fifteen years exemplary service who wish they could echo Josephus when, two thousand years ago, he said:

> The Romans are sure of victory . . . for their exercises are battles without bloodshed, and their battles bloody exercises.

THE MAN

A Marine

He sits straight in his seat, legs out-thrust, so as not to break the sharp creases he was at such pains to put in his trousers the evening before. His shoes are spit-shined, his necktie two-blocked, his shirt military pressed with two creases fore, three aft. His hair is one-quarter of an inch long, and from now on it is going to stay that way: Marines have better things to do than spend their time on razor cuts and hair dryers.

The bus pauses at the main gate kiosk, turns left at the traffic light, and heads toward Charleston. He almost looks back, but knows there is nothing to see but a big stretch of estuarine marsh, with the road cleaving it down the middle, and in the distance the nondescript, utilitarian buildings of the Recruit Depot. If he never sees it again, he'll remember it all—forever.

From its refuge in his left sock he extracts the pack of cigarettes he bought just before boarding the bus. He inhales the almost forgotten aroma of fresh tobacco, forbidden to him for the past eighty-eight days, during the first week of which he learned new dimensions of desire. Now, a full-fledged Marine, he can smoke again. He regards the package for some time, turning it over and over in his hand, listening to the crinkle of cellophane. Then he opens the window and tosses it into the ditch by the side of the road.

He leans back against the headrest and falls instantly asleep. For the rest of his days he will be able to sleep like this, at any time, in any position. He missed so much shuteye over the past weeks, what with standing fire watch and walking post and skulking around the boondocks on night patrols, that the word insomnia will completely disappear from his vocabulary. If he slept for three years straight, he'd never catch up.

When he awakes, they are halfway to Charleston. It's time to take stock of the jumble of impressions and experiences he has undergone the past eleven weeks. Until now, there has not been a single minute for reflection, and at his next duty station he will probably be even busier. What has it all meant?

Well, there are the obvious things: he has mastered the rudiments of close order drill, for what that is worth, probably not much except to be able to act in precise coordination with other men in this increasingly complex military machine that is the U.S. Marine Corps. He has shed flab and put on muscle in all the right places, quit smoking, vastly improved his endurance, become an expert rifle shot and absorbed lessons in weapons and tactics that may save his life if he's ever called upon to fight, sharpened his dress and appearance, made half a dozen lasting friendships, and discovered that life has fewer terrors and limitations than he imagined. The Marine Corps has convinced him that he can accomplish darned near—*damned* near—anything, provided he sets mind and will to the task, and applies the self-discipline which is the most important habit he's acquired from boot training.

He has confidence. He has self-respect. He is determined that, peace or war, he will bring honor to himself and his country.

Is he a Marine?

No, not quite yet. Ahead lie forty-six months of slogging in the boondocks, spit-and-polish inspections, chewing out by sergeants, specialized schooling, stretches of boredom broken by riotous liberties, tests to evaluate his emerging professionalism, bull sessions, the slow, painstaking initiation into the world's premier fighting fraternity. At some point along that stony road, he'll become aware that he's become a different breed. He'll be a man. He'll be a Marine.

Glossary

Marine jargon has more in common with Navy than Army lingo, since Marines have traditionally served aboard ship, and used ships as the springboard for the amphibious landings in which they specialize. Like other aspects of the Marine Corps, its vocabulary is changing fast, as it incorporates vapid acronyms into its speech at the expense of salt-soaked terms such as "blivet," "snafu," "bear a hand," "show a leg," "stanchion," and "gizmo," all of which, the World War II veteran will note with sorrow, have gone AWOL.

Listed below are terms a recruit will encounter during his stay at Parris Island.

aboard	on base; on ship
AFQT	Armed Forces Qualification Test
alibi	round fired to compensate for stoppage or misfire
ALICE	standard field pack, acronym for All-purpose Lightweight Individual Carrying Equipment
all hands	everybody
ashore	off the base
ASC	Assistant Series Commander
ASVAB	Armed Services Vocational Aptitude Testing Battery, a measure of IQ

As you were!	Resume what you were doing!
Aye, aye, sir!	acknowledgement of a superior officer's command
barracks	communal living quarters
BCD	Bad Conduct Discharge (also known as "Big Chicken Dinner")
BDR	Basic Daily Routine
BDU	Battle Dress Uniform (see also *cami*)
berm	earthen rampart protecting butts
BFA	Blank Firing Apparatus—small metal box screwed on a rifle flash suppressor to avoid accidental burns while shooting blanks
Big Dad	Senior Drill Instructor
billet	job; assignment
bivouac	campground
black	in the black; in the bull's-eye
black belt	Senior Drill Instructor (from black patent leather belt he wears)
blanket party	admonitory punishment of misfit by shipmates, who beat victim wrapped in blanket so he can't identify them
blister bandits	recruits whose blisters exempt them from heavy duties
blouse	uniform jacket
blousing garters	elastic retaining bands for trouser cuffs
Blues	Dress Blue formal uniform
boondocks, boonies	wilderness
boot	recruit
boss	Senior Drill Instructor

brass	officers, as a class; brass fittings, such as belt buckles, door knobs
brig	jail
brightwork	brass or other lustrous metal
bug juice	government-issue insecticide, notoriously ineffective
bulkhead	wall
bunk	rack, bed
burnout	D.I. battle fatigue, the toll of fighting piffling bureaucratic regulation
butts	sheltered area behind and below Rifle Range targets
BZO	Battlesight Zero, basically three-hundred-yard *dope*: "Where you aim, you hit."
cadence	rhythmic chant to keep unit in step
cami	camouflage; camis: short for camouflage utility uniform, worn in field.
carry on	continue as before
Casual Company	catchall company for men awaiting reassignment or discharge
catch a hit	get dressed down, chewed out, told off
CG	Commanding General
chit	a paper authorization or receipt; the smallest pebble in the bureaucratic rock pile
chow	food
chow down	the meal is ready
chrome dome	aluminum-painted fibre helmet, worn during HOT/SOP to ward off sun's rays

circuit course	series of timed exercises to promote development of specific muscle groups and endurance
CLP	Break-Free oil ("cleans, lubricates, penetrates") used to clean rifles
cleaning rack	outside concrete washstand where recruits clean rifles after firing
CMC	Commandant, Marine Corps
CO	commanding officer
Cold Standard Operating Procedure, COLD/SOP	period from 15 October to 15 April, when heat precautions do not apply
colors	national flag; ceremony at which the flag is raised or lowered
commander's time	unscheduled time which officer or NCO uses to correct platoon's deficiencies
com rats	commuted rations: subsistence payment for those not eating in the mess hall
congrint	congressional interest—letter or call from congressman, usually on behalf of needlessly panicked mother
corpsman	Navy enlisted medic; those serving with Marines are considered Marines
cover	hat
cover ass	provide for anticipated disaster by shifting responsibility to the blameless
CPR	cardio-pulmonary resuscitation
cruise	enlistment period; shipboard deployment
dark-green	black (as in "He's a dark-green Marine.")

data book	written record of recruit's marksmanship and range conditions
deck	floor
deuce gear	782 gear—ALICE pack, web belt, and other impedimenta carried by Marine in the field
D.I.	drill instructor
D.I. shack	D.I.s' quarters off squad bay, provided with desk and bunk for duty D.I.
ditty bag	issue zip bag for athletic gear
dog	girlfriend (other than speaker's)
dog and pony show	guided tour of base for visiting dignitaries
dope	adjustment of rifle sights for various ranges and wind conditions
double-time	run thirty-six-inch-steps at the rate of one hundred eighty a minute
down-range	between shooters and target
drill	military evolution; correct method
dry fire	rifle practice without ammunition
dry run	practice
dumpster diving	scavenging food discarded from the mess hall
ECWCS	Extreme Cold Weather Clothing System
ELS	Entry Level Separation; recruit discharge
esprit de corps	along with rigorous training, the main distinguishing feature of Marines, SEALS, Rangers, and other elite troops
EST	Essential Subjects Test, annual academic exam for sergeants and below

eye relief	spatial relationship between shooter's eye and rear sight
FAAD	Forward Anti-Aircraft Defense
F/A	first aid
fall in	assume military formation
FEBA	Forward Edge of Battle Area
field	training or battle area
field day	barracks clean-up
field fire	marksmanship practice in simulated battle environment
flag officer	admiral; equivalent to general officer in Army
flat-top	crew-cut hair, but shorter
fleet	short for FMF (Fleet Marine Force)
flight pay	(in boot camp) "loans" solicited by D.I.s from recruits—strictly forbidden
float	sea deployment by Marine unit
FMF	Fleet Marine Force, the basic infantry fighting force
foxtail	short-handled brush to push sweepings into dust pan
FPFT	Final Physical Fitness Test, given in tenth training week
FST	Field Skills Training
FTU	Field Training Unit
galley	kitchen
gangway	gangplank
Gangway!	Make way!
gear	equipment

gear locker	room for brooms, swabs, other cleaning
GED-GCT	General Equivalency Diploma-General Composite Test
GI	government issue materials (never denotes *soldier*, whom Marines term *dogface*)
GI can	(government issue) garbage can
go-fasters	running shoes
go-to-hell hat	cloth overseas cap; also called *fore-and-aft cap*
Grass Week	week devoted to dry fire, before firing for qualification
green belt	assistant drill instructor
Green Marine Blur	movement slightly slower than the speed of light; also *Green Amphibious Blur*
grinder	the parade deck
grins and [hand]shakes	visitor's tour
grunt	Marine infantryman, member of FMF
GT	standard intelligence test
guide	bearer of guidon, usually best recruit
guidon	small, rectangular flag with platoon number in black, borne on staff by guide at head of platoon
gung ho	Chinese for "work together"; motivated
hat	drill instructor
hatch	door
head	toilet or bathroom
head call	trip to the bathroom
heartburn	objection, resentment

Heavy A	assistant D.I., in charge of instruction
heavy barrel	to cheat
high and tight	shaven head, except for about one-quarter inch of hair on very top
hog board	bulletin board on quarterdeck on which are posted photos of family and Suzies
holiday	gap in painting, or in swabbing deck
hootch	two-man field tent
HOT/SOP	Hot Standard Operating Procedure, period 15 April to 15 October, when precautions are in force to avoid heat-related illnesses
ICT	Individual Combat Training
IG	Inspector General
infiltration course	advance through obstacles under simulated fire
IPFT	Inventory Physical Fitness Test, usually administered on TD-16
IST	Initial Strength Test, on TD-1
Irish pennant	dangling thread or strap, personal affront to D.I. detecting it on recruit's uniform
junk-on-the-bunk	equipment laid out on bed for inspection
KD	known-distance (rifle course)
Kentucky windage	adjusting (rifle) aiming point by intuition
klick	kilometer
knowledge	facts and principles recruits must master
ladder	stairway
leave	authorized extended absence from duty
liberty	absence from duty not exceeding seventy-two hours

light-green	white; Caucasian (as in "She's a light-green Marine.")
LP	listening post
LTI	inspection of weapon function by armorer
Lurps	(Army) Long Distance Reconnaissance Patrols
LVT	Landing Vehicle, Tank
LVTP	Landing Vehicle Track, Personnel
Maggie's drawers	red disk (formerly red flag) drawn across rifle target, denoting clear miss
mainside	main base
MEPS	Military Enlistment Processing Station
mess cook	mess hall waiter and cook's helper
mess hall	military dining quarters
MOH	Medal of Honor
Molly Marine Award	prize bestowed by peers on female recruit best exemplifying *esprit de corps* and other military virtues
Moment of Truth	last opportunity to admit fraudulent statements before training begins
momgram	postcard sent home to announce safe arrival at Parris Island
moon beam	flashlight
MOS	Military Occupation Specialty
motivation table	table on quarterdeck for display of trophies won in competition with other platoons in same series
MRE	Meal-Ready-to-Eat (if you're *really* hungry)

MRP	Medical Rehabilitation Platoon; also called "fat squad"
MTP	Marksmanship Training Platoon
M16A1	standard infantry rifle since Vietnam days, replaced in 1985 by M16A2
mustang	officer commissioned from the ranks
MZ	Mechanical Zero, dope to put shooter on target, after which fine adjustments are made to put shots in black
NBC	Nuclear, Biological, Chemical
NCO	non-commissioned officer
NCOIC	non-commissioned officer-in-charge
NJP	non-judicial punishment, punishment less than that awarded by courts martial
office hours	company commander's court to determine guilt and mete out punishment
on quota	assignment of D.I. to collateral training duties—as close combat or swimming instructor, etc.—usually once in two-year tour, to relieve stress
on the street	working actively as a drill instructor
outpost	assignment to duty station
overhead	ceiling
over the hump	more than halfway through a long period, especially an enlistment
parade deck	drill field, parade ground
passageway	corridor
pay off	to discharge (from the service); get even
PCP	Physical Conditioning Platoon
peepsight	rifle's rear sight

pencil whip	write up fictitious occurrences for the record; see *cover ass*
Pfc	Private First Class
PFT	Physical Fitness Training
phase	one of three stages of recruit training
pick-up	starting point of platoon's training
piece	rifle
pitch liberty	go ashore
pits	dirt-covered area between barracks where IPT is inflicted; also, *butts*
PMI	Primary Marksmanship Instructor
POI	Program of Instruction
POL	petroleum, oil and lubricants
police	to clean, make orderly
police sergeant	NCO in charge of cleaning details and materials
polyjohn	portable head, such as used at construction sites; today's effete substitute for slit trench
poolee	recruit with delayed (up to one year) entry
pot shack	chamber near galley where pots are washed
PPD	Purified Protein Derivative (vaccine against tuberculosis)
pugil stick	padded hickory staff used as bludgeon, to inculcate fighting spirit through individual combat (pronounced as in "pugilism")
PT	Physical Training

PX	Post Exchange, the base department store, off limits to recruits
px issue	basic clothing and supply issue
quarterdeck	*n.* sacrosanct area outside D.I. shack *vb.* administer IPT in this area
quartermaster	NCO in charge of supplies; lacquer applied to brass to prevent tarnish, which must be removed to achieve high polish
quarters	living space
QEP	Quality Enlistment Program
RAC	Recruit Administration Center
rappel	descend from helicopter or precipitous slope by rope
rack out	go to bed
RAM	Recruit Accessions Management System—endless enlistment paperwork
range flag	platoon pennant designed and executed by recruits, emblazoned with D.I.'s names
range tower	lofty wheeled platform from which range procedures are dictated and supervised
ready box	wooden ammunition box
recall	appointment, visit (as in dental recall)
reconn	reconnaissance
recycle	cause to repeat training
reefer	galley's walk-in refrigerator
reps	repetitions, as in weight exercises
Reveille	wake-up time
RIS	Recruit Information System, formerly called informing, or ratting

road guards	recruits assigned to stop traffic while platoon crosses roadway
round	bullet or artillery shell
RTLO	Recruit Training Liaison Office
sack in; sack out	rack out
SC	Series Commander
scuttlebutt	gossip; water fountain
scuz rag	rag for wiping floor and other chores
S.C.D.I.	Series Chief Drill Instructor
schedule	the minute-by-minute routine of boot training
scribe	recruit detailed to assist D.I.s with otiose paperwork
S.D.I.	Senior Drill Instructor
seabag	sausage-shaped canvas bag, big enough to contain recruit's gear
SEALS	Sea-Air-Land Forces (U.S. Navy commandos)
Second Hat	assistant drill instructor in charge of instruction
secure	stop; lock; put away
series	four platoons undergoing identical stages of training at same time
shelter half	half of two-man tent, carried by each Marine in the field
short	near an end, as in "getting short"— nearing the end of an enlistment
sick bay	base hospital
sick bay commando	recruit with a talent for falling sick upon the approach of work

sick call	formation for the sick and ailing
SIR	Serious Incident Report, sent to Headquarters, Marine Corps, in cases of nonroutine occurrences
six, six, and a kick	six months confinement, six months loss of pay, and bad-conduct discharge
skivvies	underwear: skivvy shirts, skivvy shorts
sling palsy	tremor, weakness or numbness of arm due to excessively tight rifle sling
smoking lamp	permission to smoke; allowed when "smoking lamp is lit," denied when "smoking lamp is out"
snap in	to practice firing position and operation of rifle
SNR	Subject-Named Recruit, time-wasting circumlocution for "he"
SOP	Standard Operating Procedure; the "Bible" for training recruits
sound off	shout; complain
spotter	cardboard disc used to mark bullet hit on target
square away	put in order
squared away	in order; neat; savvy
SRB	Service Record Book, a file containing Marine's personal history and records
782 gear	equipment carried by Marine in field, so named from obsolete supply form
spit shine	mirrorlike sheen put on leather by means of spit, polish and infinite labor
S.S.D.I.	Series Senior Drill Instructor
STD	Special Training Detachment

stock weld	conjunction of cheek and rifle stock so eye relief is, ideally, invariable
stoppage	failure of weapon to fire
survey	turn in worn or unserviceable equipment for new
Suzie	short for Suzie Robincrotch; generic term for the girl left behind
swab	*n.* floor mop; *vb.* mop
swoop the platoon	investigate recruit's allegation by seeking corroborative or contradictory evidence from his mates
Taps	bugle call played at lights out
T-block	plastic plug inserted into rifle breech to prevent accidental discharge
TD	training day (but never on Sunday)
temp fire	safety violator on rifle range, sent temporarily to another series to make up deficiency
things-on-the-springs	junk-on-the-bunk; equipment inspection
Third Hat	assistant drill instructor in charge of discipline
thunder	the crash of boot heel on pavement *a la Wehrmacht*
TMO	Traffic Management Office—the Marine's own travel agency
T/O	table of organization
topside	upstairs
tri-fire	triangulization fire
turn to	begin work; get going
Twelfth General Order	"Don't get caught."

UA	unauthorized absence, AWOL
unk	unqualified
unsat	unsatisfactory
void	to relieve a drill instructor from duty and of his D.I. MOS 8511
wagon wheel	large cool-down circle in which recruits walk after PT
war belt	wide web belt on which Marines in field hang canteens, ammunition pouches, etc.
WBGTI	Wet Bulb Globe Temperature Index

G. GORDON LIDDY

Patriot. Adventurer. Insider. Man of unshakable principle. And writer of some of the most provocative fiction—and nonfiction—you'll ever encounter.

WILL

Liddy's autobiography—an amazing account of an amazing life—now with an explosive new update on recent Watergate revelations.

_____ 92412-7 $6.99 U.S./$8.99 Can.

THE MONKEY HANDLERS

A national bestselling novel. Michael Stone kept the tools of his former trade closed up in a trunk. Now he must open his SEAL war chest—to strike at the heart of international terrorism . . .

_____ 92613-8 $5.99 U.S./$6.99 Can.

OUT OF CONTROL

Richard Rand, CIA rogue, is called back into The Company for one last incredible mission. But someone in Washington wants the CIA to lose this one—and wants Rand dead . . .

_____ 92428-3 $5.99 U.S./$6.99 Can.

IT WAS A WAR WITHIN A WAR—AND IT
TOOK NO PRISONERS . . .

COVERT OPS
THE CIA'S SECRET WAR IN LAOS

James E. Parker, Jr.

For the first time, veteran James Parker, codename
"Mule," reveals the story of the covert war in Laos—a
bloody battle that raged behind the face of the Vietnam
War. As Parker takes you inside the hell and devasta-
tion of war, he provides a first-person account of the
people who courageously fought until the bitter end.

(Previously published in hardcover as *Codename Mule*)

**AVAILABLE WHEREVER BOOKS ARE SOLD
FROM ST. MARTIN'S PRESS**

They go where no one else will go.
They do what no one else will do.
And they're proud to be called . . .

TWILIGHT WARRIORS

INSIDE THE WORLD'S SPECIAL FORCES

MARTIN C. AROSTEGUI

From deadly Scud hunts in the Gulf War to daring hostage rescue missions at London's Iranian Embassy, Special Forces go where no other army would dare—fighting for their countries and their lives on the world's most dangerous missions. Now, journalist and counter-terrorism expert Martin C. Arostegui tells their story—a fascinating true account of bravery, daring, and the ultimate risk.

UNARMED, UNDERWATER, UNDER FIRE— THEY WENT TO WAR, AND BEGAN THE LEGEND OF THE NAVY SEALS.

Facing a fanatical, dug-in enemy in Europe and in the Pacific, U.S. planners turned to a new kind of warrior: daring swimmers who could knock out mines, map out enemy beaches, and pave the way for Allied naval assaults. With a few extraordinary and brave men, the U.S. Navy's Underwater Demolition Teams went to war.

Now, a founder and legendary commander of UDT-1 takes you into the world of the underwater soldiers. This is the inside story of a unique breed of warrior—and the bloody battles they helped win.

NAKED WARRIORS

Cdr. Francis Douglas Fane, USNR (Ret.) and Don Moore

For four years at Annapolis he prepared for this, pledging his youth, his ambition, and even his life. But when junior officer Dan Lenson finally gets his commission, it's aboard the U.S.S. *Ryan*, an aging World War II destroyer. Now, with a mix of pride and fear, he heads into the world's most dangerous seas.

As the *Ryan* plunges into the dark waters of the Arctic Circle at the height of storm season, Lenson and the crew pursue a mysterious and menacing enemy. But he soon discovers a foe even more dangerous within the *Ryan*, advancing a shocking agenda that drives the ship closer and closer to disaster—testing Lenson's life and loyalty to their very limit.

THE
CIRCLE
DAVID POYER

"POYER KNOWS WHAT HE IS WRITING ABOUT WHEN IT COMES
TO ANYTHING ON, ABOVE, OR BELOW THE WATER."
— *The New York Times Book Review*

AVAILABLE WHEREVER BOOKS ARE SOLD
FROM ST. MARTIN'S PAPERBACKS